Penguin Education

Law and Society

General Editors: O. Kahn-Freund and K. W. Wedderburn

Family Security and Family Breakdown

John Eekelaar

# Family Security and Family Breakdown

John Eekelaar

Penguin Books

Penguin Books Ltd, Harmondsworth,
Middlesex, England
Penguin Books Inc, 7110 Ambassador Road,
Baltimore, Md 21207, USA
Penguin Books, Australia Ltd,
Ringwood, Victoria, Australia

First published 1971
Copyright © John Eekelaar, 1971

Made and printed in Great Britain by
Richard Clay (The Chaucer Press) Ltd, Bungay, Suffolk
Set in Monotype Times

# Contents

Editorial Foreword 7
Preface 9
Introduction 11

Part One
**Family Security** 49
1  Before Marriage 51
2  During Marriage: The Matrimonial Home and other Assets 75
3  During Marriage: Financial Security and Assistance 108
4  During Marriage: Protection of Children 143
5  During Marriage: Emotional Security 173

Part Two
**Family Breakdown** 189
6  Illegitimate Children 191
7  Provision on Death 216
8  Separation 227
9  Divorce 230
10  Remarriage 268

Part Three
**The Administration of Family Law** 273
11  Court Structure 275
Conclusion 281

References 289
Table of Cases 294
Table of Statutes 296
Index 301

# Editorial Foreword

This is the first volume in our series to deal with legal problems of the family. It was only a few years ago that the educational possibilities of family law were 'discovered' by Law Faculties. Those who teach and those who study this subject quickly realize that it cannot be understood as a self-contained legal discipline. Here, if anywhere, the law must be seen as the outcome of social forces and as a force which in turn impinges on people in society, on their habits and their convictions.

It is for this reason that Mr John Eekelaar's book is of special importance. He examines the relation between family law and its social environment in both directions. He shows both how society helps to shape the law – his sociological and comparative introduction is most welcome – and also what law seeks to do and what it does, or fails to do, in preventing family breakdown and in coping with its consequences.

All legal principles affecting family life, marriage and divorce, family property, all legal principles governing the relation between parents and children, can be seen as directed to pathological situations, to 'family breakdown'. This function of the law is more prominent and more obvious in this context than anywhere else. The normal behaviour of directors of a company towards their shareholders, or of the officials of a local authority towards the councillors, is regulated by law, and must be. The normal behaviour of husband and wife or parents and children towards each other is beyond the law – as long as the family is 'healthy'. The law comes in when things go wrong. More than that, the mere hint by anyone concerned that the law may come in is the surest sign that things are or will soon be going wrong.

Nevertheless, Eekelaar is, we believe, the first author to have allowed this insight to fashion his presentation of the whole subject. He writes about family law in terms of family breakdown, and he shows how all the rules are geared towards this event, from the rules about the age of marriage to family property and to guardianship of children. He also shows, however – and this is vital – that to prevent family breakdown, and to mitigate its consequences, the law needs to step in before the marriage has collapsed, and even where no collapse is yet in sight; and with good reason he refers to the 'inherent disadvantage in the policy of English law in intervening only when a crisis situation has arisen'. If one wants to pursue a functional method in presenting this subject, it cannot be presented in any terms, this book convinces us, other than those of pathology. This is not a unique feature of family law. That subject shares it with the criminal law and with the law of tort. But we cannot think of any other subject centred around an institution rather than around events or conduct which can and, as Eekelaar seems to demonstrate, must be presented in this way.

This book will open the eyes of many law students to the social significance of what they are learning, and it will stimulate their thinking and ease their understanding of the law itself. It will also help the empirical social scientist to grasp the role of the law as a social force in the matters of most intimate concern to him; and it may help the theoretical sociologist to gain a better informed and deeper insight into the function of law as a formative influence in the shaping of attitudes and of behaviour.

O.K-F.

K.W.W.

# Preface

On 1 January 1971 the Divorce Reform Act 1969 came into operation amid much publicity. But on the same date a number of other reforms of importance for family law and policy also took effect. The powers of the courts to make orders for financial provisions during marriage and on divorce were considerably widened. The first section of the Children and Young Persons Act 1969 became effective. Various social services with special importance for the family were unified both at central and at local government level. These reforms are significant not so much in their extent, but in their nature. They reflect the acceptance of the view that many individual problems are the symptoms of a malfunctioning family unit. They direct the legal and administrative response to them towards trying to sustain family life and to salvaging as much of it as possible when a crisis situation occurs. The philosophy might be expressed, crudely, in these terms: look after the family and this will take care of the individuals.

This policy has not appeared in 1971 for the first time. It has been gradually emerging during this century, most of all after the last war. A cluster of important reforms took place in the years immediately preceding 1971. Many more may now be expected to follow. So, on 1 January 1971 family law faced in two directions. Many of its doctrines were survivals from the era of individualism. But more were directed towards new paths. I have placed special emphasis on the law as it stood at that date because a revolution can be better appreciated when it is still possible to see the old system from which the new has emerged.

This upheaval in family law is not simply the result of exceptional energy on the part of our legislators. It is part of a profound change in social attitudes to the family and the role it is expected to play in modern society. I have therefore attempted to set the account of the legal provisions against this background. In doing so I hope this may assist students of the law in understanding the impact of these rules on family life in general. But I have endeavoured to keep the exposition of the law as simple as possible so that non-lawyers will be able to understand how and why it operates as it does. I regret that the invaluable study of the matrimonial work of magistrates' courts by O. R. McGregor, L. Blom-Cooper and C. Gibson (*Separated Spouses*, Duckworth) appeared too late for reference to it to appear in the text. Their findings do not detract from anything I have said, but do provide massive further evidence on the unsatisfactory working of that system.

I must record my gratitude to Professor Otto Kahn-Freund, whose encouragement and wisdom have been an unfailing stimulus.

# Introduction

## Definition and functions of the family

The breakdown of a marriage involves more than the cessation of a relationship between two individuals, for it signifies the ultimate collapse of what is the most important social group in the community. This at once justifies the use by the community of social control through its laws over situations leading up to and resulting from that disturbance. But the law has not created the family. The family is a social organism which arises to fulfil certain needs of society and of individuals and which is subject to natural processes of decay and ultimate dissolution. Society cannot eradicate these processes, yet it can, by social pressure and by law, so channel them as to lessen the risk of family disruption. To this end it employs the purely legal concept of marriage to confer special recognition upon certain family groups in order to enable them better to perform some of the functions required of them in society.

Although these functions have varied from culture to culture and from age to age and many might, in theory, be fulfilled by agencies other than the family, no convincing alternative has yet been discovered. The universality of the family has often been remarked upon by sociologists and anthropologists. Differences have arisen over the correct classification of the types of family group evident in diverse societies. The group to which we are accustomed in the West is the so-called *nuclear* family which consists solely of a married man and woman and their offspring. But there is also to be found the *polygamous* family, where there will be a plural marriage by a spouse with two or more of the opposite sex and the *extended* family which includes, in addition to the married parents and the children, the spouses of those children. Murdock (1949) regarded the last two as being simply special combinations of the nuclear family which, he says, ' is a universal human social grouping. Either as a sole prevailing form of family or as the basic unit from which more complex familial forms are compounded, it exists as a distinct and strongly functional group in every known society.' This view has not passed unchallenged. Fox (1967) prefers to describe the nuclear family as the *conjugal* family, in which the basic unit is that of mother and child, the 'conjugal' link between parents displaying varying degrees of permanence and stability in different cultures.

It is unnecessary to enter into controversies of definition. But it is important to notice from the evidence of anthropologists that some form of institutionalized cohabitation between individuals of opposite sexes on a more or less permanent basis and at least for the period necessary for the rearing of children is to be found practically everywhere. This is necessarily true in those societies where conjugal residence is *patrilocal*, i.e., where wives are brought from outside to live with their husbands within a community. It is also true in societies like our own where spouses usually live apart from the kindred group of either of them in what is sometimes called *neolocal* residence. More difficulty is caused by those comparatively rare societies which follow matrilineal rules of descent. There, the offspring of a marriage belong to the kin group of the mother and it is her brothers who have rights over the children and to whom duties are owed. But even in these societies, residence is often patrilocal, the wives living in their husband's community, where the children are reared up to a certain age upon which they are sent to their uncles. Where, however, the residence is *matrilocal*, i.e. the couples live amongst the wives' kindred, special tensions arise. The intruding husband may come into conflict with his wife's brothers, while his own interests, which are at home with his sisters, may suffer. In Malawi, the Yao, a matrilocal people, commonly mitigate this problem by allowing an exception to the matrilocal residence rule in the case of the eldest male of the community, who is permitted to remain with his own sisters and to bring his wife into his community. There is in any case conjugal cohabitation. Only among the Nayar of Kerala did husbands and wives live apart. This was a society where descent was determined matrilineally. Daughters were married ritually before puberty to a man of appropriate caste, but he did not live with his wife, nor necessarily have sexual relations with her. After the marriage the women were allowed to receive a large number of 'visiting' husbands from the same or higher sub-caste, who simply stayed overnight. Yet, as Gough (1959) points out, this was not a promiscuous community without any idea of legitimacy, and a woman might suffer death or expulsion if a child she bore was not recognized by one of her visiting husbands, though he need not be its biological father. Even so, it is true that these people were 'highly unusual' for 'they had a kinship system in which the elementary family of father, mother and children was not institutionalized as a legal, productive, distributive and residential unit'. But that state of affairs was already in decay in the nineteenth century. Adams (1960) discusses other unusual cases of loose conjugal relationships to be found in Guyana and parts of Latin America. Yet even here the men play an important economic role in the households with which they are connected. Their long sojourns away from the household and frequent failure to return demonstrate only an unusually weak conjugal tie, not its total absence.

## Alliances and descent

The universal prevalence of incest taboos has been the subject of exhaustive comment by anthropologists and psychologists. Whatever its cause, this phenomenon has led to the practice of exogamy, whereby persons marry outside their own family or kin group. The concept of the 'romantic' marriage, although comparatively recent, has so permeated Western culture that the use of the institution of marriage for the formation of alliances between family and kin groups is now frequently regarded as immoral. Yet our own history books and literature testify to the widespread use of this form of alliance for both political and social reasons. Its use in the early middle ages to terminate or prevent blood feud appears, from the literature, to have met at first with limited success (Rosenthal, 1966), but in later times alliances by marriage became more important, at the cost probably of a decline in the independence of women. The marriage between Henry VII and Elizabeth of York cemented the peace between York and Lancaster, and political unions of this kind have continued to be of importance down to the present day.

The use of marriage as alliance coupled with the rules of inheritance has been a valuable means by which certain classes of family have perpetuated their social and economic superiority. This adds a new dimension to the alliance and brings to the forefront the important function of the family in the establishment of a lineage. The legitimate method of procreation through marriage enabled property and wealth to be retained in a recognized group devolving in a predetermined way upon lawful successors. This should not surprise us in England. The great landed families, having benefited from their share in the monastic properties seized in the sixteenth century, used the combination of marriage alliance and rules of inheritance not only to maintain that wealth in their own hands, but also to add to it. They were assisted by rules of law which not only rigidly excluded illegitimate persons from the family wealth, but in addition provided machinery for the successive settlement of family property upon the legitimate successors. The strict settlement was the classical device produced by the real property lawyers to this end. It has been estimated by Habakkuk (1950) that, in the middle of the eighteenth century, about half the land in England was held on strict settlement. Settlements of this kind would be made before a marriage was entered and so constructed as to ensure, generally, that the property would pass intact to the eldest son of the marriage. Security would also be provided for his wife by imposing a rentcharge in her favour upon the property when her husband died (a jointure) and provision would be made for younger sons by requiring capital sums to be paid to them (portions). The capital required for payment of these portions might not readily be available, so it was often raised by borrowing on security of the estate. It then became desirable to offset the heavy encumbrances with which settled land began to be burdened by receipt of monies (also called portions) from the wife's family. In many cases the sums involved in portions of this kind were large enough to enable yet more land to be acquired for the family estate and in the eighteenth century the size of portions which fathers had to pay to enable their daughters to enter into a good marriage with an eldest son (thus establishing their eldest grandson in the landed aristocracy) increased considerably. If the daughter happened to be an heiress and would inherit her own family's estate this was greatly to her advantage for her marriage to an eldest son would concentrate property in still fewer hands. Among the peerage it has been estimated that, in the early seventeenth century, one in every three marriages was with an heiress. One Francis Osborne, advising his son in 1656, said that 'by the greatness of a Wive's portion may much of the future conjugal Happinesse be calculated'. This mercenary attitude was by no means uncommon and, according to Stone (1961), marriages between parties who were practically strangers on their wedding day were frequent and led to much marital unhappiness.

It is not surprising to discover in such a society strong sociological and legal forces supporting the concept of legitimacy. Blackstone, in his *Commentaries on the Laws of England* (1765) defends the rule then prevailing in England which prevented an illegitimate child being legitimated by the subsequent marriage of his parents on the ground that, to allow such legitimation (as the Roman law and European systems based on it did) would be 'plainly a great discouragement to the matrimonial state; to which one main inducement is usually not only the desire of having *children*, but also the desire of procreating lawful *heirs*'. The institution of marriage therefore assumes great legal importance for it is the source of legitimate birth, and children born during wedlock are presumed to be legitimate, a presumption particularly difficult to displace. Wills and instruments referring to 'children' will be presumed to refer only to legitimate children. Any legal or social rights and duties between a father and his illegitimate children will be kept at a minimum. The illegitimate child is seen as a threat to the established system of patrilineal descent. Davis (1939) doubted whether illegitimate persons could ever be given complete legal equality with the legitimate without eliminating marriage. This is too pessimistic. The rise of individualism, democracy and estate duty has relegated the function of marriage as a means of family linkage and a channel for legitimate descent to an incidental advantage, important only to the few, but remote from the contemplation of society at large. This decline has, as will be seen, led to remarkable modifications in the law of illegitimacy without in any way diminishing the importance of marriage as a framework for determining the rights and duties between spouses.

## The extended family

Mention has already been made of the extended family in which the married children of the spouses remain with their parents, assimilating the new married partners into the original nuclear family. It is important to observe how widely the extended family is to be found, so that it is apparent that marriage can involve relationships extending far beyond that between the spouses. Although Murdock (1949) considered that the neolocal residence common in Western countries was inconsistent with extended family organization, more recent research has shown that this is not necessarily true. Goode (1963), after a survey of the major societies in the modern world, concludes that the majority of the population in *most* societies have in fact *lived* in nuclear family units for some time, whatever the 'ideal' family residence may have been. Even in societies like India, where the 'joint family unit' of parents with their sons and their sons' spouses has been the ideal residential unit, this is no longer the norm. This information has been supported by data on Egypt acquired by Petersen (1968). But it does not follow that relationships with members of the extended family have broken down. Even in Western countries, contacts between nuclear family members and the extended family are so frequent that Goode surmises that there has probably been no reduction in social participation with the extended family over the last hundred years, despite increased mobility. Studies in Britain and the United States, notably those by Young and Willmott (1957) and by Winch (1968), have confirmed a high frequency of contact with the extended family, although this has come under strain when young couples move away from their original communities to new housing estates.

The role of the extended family is still, therefore, an important one even though its members may not all live under one roof. It is particularly valuable in transmitting economic and emotional security from one generation to the other, especially in times of need. When a child gets married, the newly wed couple will not only receive financial assistance from their parents but, in the event of a housing shortage, may often spend their first few years of married life in the home of one of the sets of parents. In England where there is a distinct tendency to matrilocal residence, it is usually that of the wife's mother. This enables the mother, who is very much the centre of the working-class extended family, to assist the young wife in advice and services in the first few years of marriage, and this may continue after the couple have moved to a home of their own. And it may be that relatives have been instrumental in the procurement of that home or of employment for the husband. The importance of the extended family can be seen in another way. Comparing those families which, during the wife's confinement, entrusted their children into the care of the local authority with those which made alternative home arrangements, Schaffer and Schaffer (1968) found that neither group resorted to any appreciable degree to the help of neighbours, but that among, the former in contrast to the latter, there were either strained relationships with their immediate relatives, or they had lost contact with them altogether. And when the backgrounds of 129 problem families in contact with Family Service Units between 1952 and 1958 were analysed, Philp (1963) reports that, though most of the men and women concerned came from large families, more than half of them had virtually no contact with their brothers or sisters and it was clear that the extended family hardly operated in these cases. More will be said of problem families later and of the serious difficulties they pose for the maintenance of family structure, but it is worth noting at this point that the failure of individuals in these families to integrate properly with their wider kindred often throws upon the community at large the difficult task of helping them to sustain their immediate family relationships.

This wider aspect of family organization follows from the initial conjugal union and is generally dependent on it. If the marriage dissolves, contact with the extended family of the opposite spouse usually ceases. In England, legal provisions are generally confined to the relationship between the spouses and their children and in so far as they tend to stabilize that unit, they serve to keep alive the extended family. But despite their social importance, relations with the extended family itself are left outside the legal framework. This need not necessarily have been the case, and it is not uncommon for other legal systems to make legal provision covering the rights and duties amongst the extended family. Some aspects of this will be considered where appropriate, but the attitude of English law to the matter prevents the subject from being considered as anything more than peripheral to the central relationship, which is that between the married pair.

### The residual functions
The decline of the use of the family for alliance and descent and a supposed weakening of the influence of the extended family have led

some to conclude that the twentieth century has seen the disintegration of marriage and the family system. That this is a gross exaggeration, indeed, distortion, has been demonstrated by McGregor (1957) and by Fletcher (1966). It is true, however, that some of the functions hitherto performed by the wider family and the nuclear family itself are now performed by other agencies, throwing into sharper relief the conjugal relationship between the spouses. Ogburn (1938) listed as having been the main functions of the family its economic, status giving, educational, religious, recreational, protective and affectional roles, but considered that only the last four remained vigorous. Parsons (1955) reduced its role to two spheres. On the one hand, it was the 'primary agent of socialization of the child', while on the other, the 'primary basis of security for the normal adult'. In the same way MacIver and Page (1950) characterized as the 'essential' functions of the family the inter-relationship between satisfaction of the sex need, production and rearing of children and the provision of a home.

The fact that extra-familial agencies may now perform some tasks hitherto performed by the family unit does not mean that those functions are no longer carried out by families. The agencies may simply provide supplemental services. They may even try to encourage families themselves to perform these tasks as far as they are able. Nevertheless those functions of the family now designated as 'non-essential' can conceivably be performed entirely by external groups. The statement that certain other functions are 'essential' could mean that they are those to which, at this stage, the family has been reduced, that further reduction is possible, but that if that were to happen we would no longer have a unit we could properly call the family. But it might also imply that no further reduction is possible because no other social unit could successfully perform those functions. To take such a dogmatic stand would be unhelpful. Nevertheless, for a better appreciation of the needs fulfilled by the family, it is useful to consider attempts which have been made to institute community systems where functions thought to be 'essential' to the family have been assigned to other social groups.

The early communists, following Engels (1884), saw the family as it existed in contemporary bourgeois society as a product of class oppression and private property. In communist society, unions between the sexes were to be based on love alone, and the woman would be freed from the 'slavery of the kitchen' by state provision for the rearing and education of children. A Soviet Decree of 1920 legalized free abortion, and the Soviet Code of Marriage, Divorce, Family and Guardianship of November 1926 provided that the fact of cohabitation alone was sufficient to constitute a *de facto* marriage. Marriage could, then, be entered informally, but it could be abandoned equally informally since dissolution could be obtained simply by registration of that fact by either of the parties. Despite the apparent liberality of these measures, it is of interest to observe that the proposers of its draft argued that the recognition of *de facto* unions would discourage promiscuous relationships because such recognition resulted in the imposition of a community of property system for goods acquired during the cohabitation and of a limited alimentary obligation towards a husband or a wife in need who was unable to work which lasted for one year after the union was dissolved.

Furthermore, the Code created reciprocal maintenance obligations, not only between the parties, but also between parent and child, between grandparent and grandchild and between siblings. Indeed, the criteria which were to help courts to decide whether a *de facto* union existed included the fact of cohabitation, whether there was a common household, and whether outsiders regarded the couple as spouses. All this shows that even at this stage Soviet law was obliged to recognize the fact of family organization, although its virtual withdrawal of supervision over the inception and dissolution of family units was calculated to weaken it.

It would appear that the new system succeeded to some extent in its objective, but far from pursuing it, the Soviet state subsequently reversed this policy. In 1936, in the face of impending war, a Decree was passed which prohibited abortion except in special circumstances. It also increased state aid to mothers, the penalties for avoiding family maintenance obligations and the fees for the registration of divorce. Under the pressure of war, extreme steps were taken to encourage motherhood and the family. Co-education was abolished in 1943 and the consequent emphasis on domestic training for girls stands in strong contrast to earlier denunciations of uxorial slavery. The Family Law of 8 July 1944 restored state supervision over the contracting of marriages, which now had to be registered, and put formidable obstacles in the way of divorce. The reasons for this reversal appear to have been two-fold. The first, and overwhelmingly dominant one, was that officials were alarmed at the figures yielded by the population census of 1936. The nature and extent of the population trends this revealed, and how far they were attributable to the attitudes to child rearing which followed on the revolutionary family laws of the 1920s can only be guessed because the census has never been published. Concern about population increase also characterizes the legislation of the 1940s which not only saw the imposition of a 'birth stimulation' income tax on the childless but also relieved fathers of any obligation whatsoever towards their illegitimate children and the mothers of those children. This encouragement of illegitimate parenthood met with some success. There were an estimated six million illegitimate children in the USSR by 1962. The injustice to women implicit in this policy led to criticism and, as described by Stone (1969), eventually to substantial modification in June 1968.

The second probable cause for the abandonment of the revolutionary family code was its failure on the individual level. The partial recognition of the family and the persistence of conjugal unions led to expectations which the state was failing to underwrite. The extreme informality surrounding marriage encouraged frivolous attitudes much criticized by *Isvestia* in 1935, which complained that some 20 per cent of marriages were being entered after acquaintance of no more than a month, to be followed, for the most part, by rapid divorce. In 1959 the feelings of (primarily) Soviet women were rewarded by the opening of a 'marriage palace' in Leningrad, and the 1968 Family Code now requires marriages to be registered in a ceremonial atmosphere. But an even more disturbing failure was the inability of the state to make adequate alternative provision for children. Geiger (1968) recounts the anxiety caused by reports that, even amongst those children for whom state supervision was made, serious retardation, especially in speech ability, had been discovered. This is an aspect of institutional child care to which we will return and on which far more is now known than could have been understood at the time of the Soviet experiment. Nevertheless, it remains that with respect both to the relationship between spouses and the successful socialization of the children, the Soviet attack on the family encountered considerable obstacles and lasted no more than a single generation.

Another, and very different, type of experiment at the abolition of the family also lasted no more than a generation. This was the Oneida community which flourished in New York state from 1848 until 1880 under the religious leadership of John Humphrey Noyes. The community, which at one stage reached about three hundred strong, lived in an ascetic atmosphere devoted to sober living and hard work. Private property was eliminated and all wealth shared. Family units were abolished and all adults had access to others of the opposite sex. Birth was strictly controlled, however, and the few children born to the community were brought up separate from their parents after reaching the age of fifteen months. The reasons for the collapse of the community are obscure owing to lack of adequate documentation, though it may have been due to a considerable degree to pressures from a disapproving society around it. It is therefore inadvisable to draw any conclusions from its experience of non-family living. However, societies of a similar nature do exist today which warrant serious consideration in a study of family life. These are the Israeli *kibbutzim*. These vary in size and in tradition so that generalization about them must be guarded. But as a rule it may be said that in these communities a conscious attempt has been made to replace the nuclear family by the collective as the unit of production and education. Property is communally owned, economic effort is joint and its rewards paid into a common pool. Residence and dining are communal and the children are reared in communal nurseries. But there is nothing approaching the 'complex marriage' which characterized the Oneidan community. Promiscuity is strongly disapproved but, in the early days of the communities at any rate, marriage was also discouraged, so that couples who established sexual relationships would not be married, would not set up common home together and were not expected to sit together at mealtimes. However it has not proved possible to maintain these requirements of *kibbutz* doctrine without considerable modification. Emotional relationships between the sexes now assume an appearance similar to those in our own society. The room in which the couple would formerly only sleep together is looking increasingly like a 'family home' and the pair will often sit together during the communal meal. Marriage ceremonies are becoming common (Leslie, 1967). The children are still regarded primarily as children of the community, and they see themselves in that light. Although from an early age they are reared communally and will seldom be permitted to sleep in the room of their parents, nevertheless it is mainly with the child's physical requirements that the community concerns itself. His emotional needs are still largely provided by the parents. Mothers will usually breast feed their infants, and thereafter visits are paid daily, often four or five times. Periods spent together by parents and children are treated with considerable solemnity. In spite of this parental attention and the high quality of nursery care which they generally receive, a marked degree of thumb sucking, enuresis and nocturnal fear among these children has been observed. Bettelheim (1969) has commented that this does not lead to a lesser degree of adjustment on the part of *kibbutz* children when they reach adulthood than in the case of normal family-reared children, but he also stresses that the high degree of cohesion in a *kibbutz* community and close association between members of peer groups itself demands uniformity, leaving less room for dissatisfaction and dropouts.

At this stage it may be possible to formulate some conclusion as to the kind of needs which the family unit satisfies in our society. It might be useful to categorize those functions as those which are *internal*, that is, which relate to the requirements of the individuals who constitute the family, and those which are *external*, which concern its impact on society as a whole. Considering the internal functions first, one range of these appears to comprise the fulfilment of emotional needs of the spouses. That this is not confined to the provision of a sexual outlet is clear from the existence of societies where extra-marital sexual activity not only before but also during marriage is tolerated. Murdock (1949) found this to be the case in 65 of the 250 societies he considered. Spiro (1954) concludes from his examination of emotional relationships in *kibbutzim* that 'in addition to the physical intimacy of sex, the union also provides a psychological intimacy that may be expressed by notions such as comradeship, security, dependency, succorance etc. And it is this psychological intimacy, primarily, that distinguishes couples (in permanent union) from lovers.' This appears to have been recognized in the People's Republic of China. There the commune is the effective economic unit which also assumes responsibility for the tending and education of children. The conjugal unit is, however, encouraged, not only because provision of state facilities for child rearing on such a vast scale is not practicable, but because, as Goode (1963) puts it, 'people in all sections apparently feel a psychological need to have a small, emotionally cohesive unit within which they can, in effect, take off their shoes and feel comfortable and protected from the outside'.

The strength of this psychological drive might vary in different societies. It is, however, high in our own society. Slater and Woodside (1951), examining the reasons for marrying given by a wide selection of British soldiers in hospital from 1943 to 1946, found that the emphasis on sex was a negative one and that desire for a home was the most common reason for marrying. This has received support from psychologists. Fairbairn (1952) saw marriage as the striving of the personality for an object of support, a view which contrasts with the Freudian explanation in terms of impersonal neuro-physiological or hormonal activity. Building upon Fairbairn's work, Dicks (1967) examines the interaction between the personalities of married persons and defines the 'psychological core' of marital life as the 'unconscious forces which flow between the parties' which binds the persons into a 'dyad, an integrate different from the mere sum of parts'. A striking instance of the fulfilment of emotional needs in the partners appears from a case discussed by Dicks where an unmarried couple continually resumed cohabitation despite extreme conflict which certainly, had the cohabitation been legal, would have given grounds for separation.

A second range of the internal purposes of the family concern the rearing of children, and for some this is the most important role it performs. What the family achieves in this direction can be appreciated by consideration of the research undertaken into the effects upon children who are deprived of a family life. The Russian experience of this has already been noted, and in recent years research into this field has been so extensive that it is not possible to review all of it here. Attention in this country was directed to the problem by the publications of Burlingham and Freud (1942 and 1944) who drew on their experiences in residential nurseries during the war. Then in 1951, Bowlby published his report for the World Health Organization. This alleged grave and far-reaching effects on children deprived of maternal care, in particular during the first three or four years of life. In 1962 further evidence was collected by the WHO. In her contribution to it, Ainsworth (1965) distinguishes between cases of maternal deprivation due to absence of a mother figure (or infrequent contact with it) and deprivation due to unsatisfactory or distorted interaction with the mother figure. She also considers the question of continuity of the interaction. The evidence emphasized the effect that deprivation had in retarding intellectual development, especially in regard to language and abstraction. However, even more damaging was the effect on the ability to develop affectional relations. Further evidence strongly suggested (although not conclusively) that this was a causative factor in delinquency and subsequent inability to form stable marital relations. Not all deprived children, however, suffer from these effects and the extent to which those who do can respond to treatment is a matter for further investigation. In 1967, Dinnage and Kellmer Pringle, under the auspices of the National Bureau for Co-operation in Child Care reviewed research into the subject in the United States, West Europe, Great Britain and Israel. They reported that the early studies following on Bowlby's work 'are unanimous in finding retardation (especially in speech), either gross or considerable, according to the standard of care provided, and some indication, even at (an) early stage, of atypical emotional development such as lack of curiosity, restlessness and, later, indiscriminate, shallow friendliness to adults'. More recent research had not seriously shaken the results of this earlier work.

The implications of these findings on psychoanalytical theory have been developed by Bowlby (1969). Drawing heavily on data provided by investigations into animal behaviour, he advances the view that an infant's need for attachment to a mother-figure is an instinctive mechanism originally acquired in order to protect itself against danger from predators. The development of this process of attachment to the mother figure gives the young child confidence in exploring external objects and, eventually, in developing other relationships. The impact of this explanation of attachment behaviour and its implications on the theory of personality development is as yet unclear. However, its importance for any understanding of the family process is evident. Not only does it suggest reasons why the family unit is so universally and 'naturally' used as the primary means of rearing children, but it also provides an insight into the causes of marital conflict and breakdown. For inadequate personalities produced by malfunctioning family units (or by institutions) will themselves be likely to establish insecure families, thus setting up a perpetual cycle of failure. Consideration of these factors is of vital importance in framing social and legal policies towards family breakdown, not only in a general approach to rehabilitation but also in respect to particular problems, as, for example, that of adoption.

Of the external functions of the family, little need be said in the context of this book. Clearly it is of service to the community in providing for the replacement of the population in a recognized and relatively stable manner. In so far as it provides for the basic needs of the individuals within a community, it contributes to the welfare of the society as a whole. Whether the conjugal family contributes to the economic prosperity of our industrial society, and the part played by it in the development of industrialization are complex matters that cannot be discussed here.

## Family disintegration

A family has to be complete before it can properly be said to suffer a process of decline. But many families are incomplete. These are the families of unmarried mothers. Other families succeed in completing their formation, publicly attested by the marriage of the partners, but fail in varying degrees to fulfil their social role. This may take place even though the partners are cohabiting and to a certain extent satisfying their own personal needs. The children may be so neglected that the family, far from acting as a unit catering for their physical and emotional needs, becomes a positive danger to them. In this category are to be found mainly that class of family described as the 'problem' family. A further step towards disintegration, though one not necessarily related to problem families, is that of separation between the spouses, which often, but not always, ends in the final dissolution by divorce. And finally there is by far the largest cause of dissolution, and that is the death of one or both of the partners to the marriage. It would be useful at this point to examine further these forms of handicapped family, to assess their extent and to consider possible causes.

## Unmarried mothers

In our society the unmarried mother and her child is so different a unit from the legitimate nuclear family that it requires special attention both from the law and social policy. The unmarried mother faces difficulties of a complex nature peculiar to her position. She has no husband to sustain her economically and emotionally during pregnancy, confinement and child rearing. She attempts to combine the dual role of mother and breadwinner. She, and often the child, may be faced with the reactions of a hostile society. Myerscough (1967) describes the risks to which illegitimate children are exposed. Although mortality of illegitimate compared to legitimate infants had by then fallen to an excess of only 17 per cent, that figure covers only deaths from the age of four weeks to one year. But for the period of the first four weeks, the death rate of the illegitimate child remains about 50 per cent greater than for the legitimate, while the still birth rate is 35 per cent greater. These figures are not explicable by reference to the age of the mothers but to more obscure factors, amongst which the social and emotional problems of the unmarried mother are probably dominant. One obvious example is lack of care taken by many unmarried mothers during their pregnancy. The probability that the surviving illegitimate child will suffer from some form of maternal deprivation is extremely high and, while the effects of the absence of a father figure have not yet become fully known, these too will be a contributory factor to the inadequate socialization of these children.

In view of those considerations it is disturbing to discover that the incidence of illegitimacy in England and Wales increased during the 1960s by probably an unprecedented degree. Figure 1 expresses the numbers of illegitimate births as a percentage of the total number of live births registered. The increase since 1960 is remarkable, and Table 1 examines the position in the years 1956, 1964 and 1967 in more detail. In Table 1 figures are given for maternities rather than live births and therefore includes still births but ignores multiple births. Column (a) in each year group expresses the number of illegitimate maternities in each age group as a percentage of the total number of maternities, both legitimate and illegitimate, for the same age group for that year. It will be seen that between 1956 and

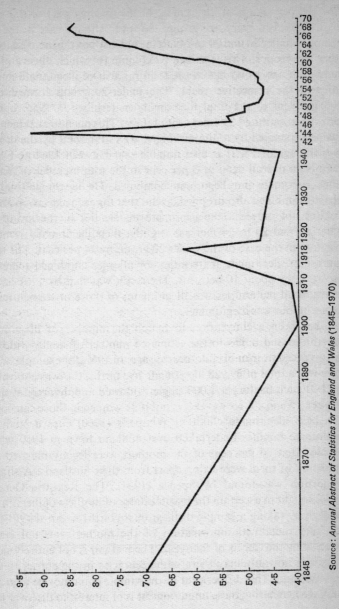

Source: *Annual Abstract of Statistics for England and Wales (1845–1970)*

Figure 1   Percentage of all births registered as illegitimate (selected years)

1967 the percentage of illegitimate births forming part of the total has increased in every age group. However, the increase in the age groups of under 20 and 20 to 24 has far outstripped the increase in the other age groups. This is shown by column (b) which illustrates the share each age group has in the total number of illegitimate maternities in the respective years. The under-20 group formed only 18·8 per cent of the total illegitimate maternities in 1956, but by 1967 it had captured 31·1 per cent of them. This phenomenal increase was accompanied by a diminishing share in the total by the groups over the age of 25. It is also notable that between 1964 and 1967 there is an overall drop of 5 per cent in the total number of maternities, legitimate and illegitimate combined. The legitimate total for all ages combined also dropped, as did that for each age group above 25. But not only did the legitimate maternities in the groups of under 20 and 20 to 24 increase slightly, their illegitimate numbers rose too, in the case of the under 20 group by 24 per cent. The total number of illegitimate maternities for all ages combined therefore also rose, by about 10 per cent. The result was that by 1967 one in twelve of all maternities was illegitimate; of those of women under 20 one in four was illegitimate.

It has been a convention to match the number of illegitimate maternities and births to the estimated number of single, widowed and divorced women of child-bearing age. In 1967, for example, when there was a total of 69,928 illegitimate live births, this was equivalent to 21·01 such births per 1,000 single, widowed and divorced women between 15 and 49. However it is not only women in those categories who bear illegitimate children. Wimperis (1960) cites a study of illegitimate families undertaken in a midland town in 1950 which revealed that 26 per cent of the mothers were legally married but almost all of them were living apart from their husbands. A similar proportion was found by Spence (1954). The Registrar-General (1964) sought to ascertain the marital status of mothers of illegitimate children by taking a sample of illegitimate births in April 1961 and matching them with information of the mother's marital status acquired by the census of that year. The method is not entirely satisfactory as not only may there be inaccuracies in the entries, but it was also found that 17 per cent of the sample could not be matched at all. Remembering these limitations, it is of interest to discover that

# Table 1 Maternities

| Age of mother at maternity | 1956 Total | Legitimate | Illegitimate | (a) | (b) | 1964 Total | Legitimate | Illegitimate | (a) | (b) | 1967 Total | Legitimate | Illegitimate | (a) | (b) |
|---|---|---|---|---|---|---|---|---|---|---|---|---|---|---|---|
| All ages | 707,921 | 673,808 | 34,113 | 4·8 | 100 | 880,173 | 816,248 | 63,925 | 7·3 | 100 | 835,433 | 764,977 | 70,456 | 8·4 | 100 |
| Under 20 | 38,493 | 32,066 | 6,427 | 16·7 | 18·8 | 77,418 | 59,809 | 17,609 | 22·7 | 27·5 | 85,221 | 63,341 | 21,880 | 25·8 | 31·1 |
| 20–24 | 205,838 | 195,570 | 10,268 | 5·0 | 30·0 | 277,168 | 256,532 | 20,636 | 7·4 | 32·3 | 292,766 | 268,720 | 24,046 | 8·2 | 34·1 |
| 25–29 | 224,553 | 217,494 | 7,059 | 3·1 | 20·7 | 271,494 | 259,286 | 12,211 | 4·5 | 19·1 | 244,225 | 232,318 | 11,907 | 4·9 | 16·9 |
| 30–34 | 144,258 | 138,827 | 5,431 | 3·8 | 15·9 | 153,949 | 146,623 | 7,326 | 4·8 | 11·5 | 130,422 | 123,542 | 6,880 | 5·3 | 9·8 |
| 35–39 | 72,167 | 68,637 | 3,530 | 4·8 | 10·3 | 76,037 | 71,697 | 4,340 | 5·7 | 6·9 | 63,584 | 59,459 | 4,125 | 6·5 | 5·9 |

Figures for ages above 40 are omitted
(a) Percentage of illegitimate maternities in total number maternities (legitimate and illegitimate) in each age group.
(b) Percentage of illegitimate maternities by age group in total number illegitimate maternities, all ages, for the year.
Adapted from *Statistical Review of England and Wales* (1956, 1964, 1967).

it was found that 29 per cent of the births were found to be to women described as 'married' on the census form, and in two-thirds of these cases a man acknowledged paternity. It is therefore misleading to match illegitimate births to the single, widowed and divorced female population as about one-third of illegitimate children are probably born to married women, of whom most are living apart from their husbands in some form of stable cohabitation. To this proportion of illegitimate births into stable illicit unions must be added those to unmarried women living with married men who have not been divorced from their wives. So in all it is probable that about 40 per cent of illegitimate children are born into relatively stable unions. This was the percentage found by Wimperis (1960) in her midland survey, and it corresponds to the percentage of illegitimate children registered in the joint names of mother and father in the 1961 Census. It may be, then, that not more than around 60 per cent of illegitimate children are born into a 'one parent family'. However it also appears from the Registrar-General's breakdown of the figures into age groups that mothers who are under 20 are the least likely to be married or to be living in a stable relationship, and it is in that age group that the illegitimacy rate has increased most steeply. Unmarried parenthood is still a serious social problem.

Attempts to uncover the causes of illegitimacy have met with little success. The case of the married woman, however, is relatively simple, for hers will usually be an example of a marriage that has broken down. But two-thirds of the mothers are unmarried. Many explanations for unmarried parenthood have been suggested, some attributing it to personality, others to environment, in particular that of childhood, but none has been conclusive. In particular it has been difficult to account for the rise in the rate during the 1960s. The Legitimacy Act 1959 might have had some influence. This allowed a child to be legitimated by the subsequent marriage of his parents even though he had been born while either or both his parents were married to another at the time of his birth. A mother giving birth to an adulterine child before her divorce would have less motive for concealing the fact of its illegitimacy on registration of the birth as she could legitimate it by subsequently marrying the father. But this cannot account for the size of the increase and is in any case irrelevant to the largest area of the increase, that among unmarried mothers. It may.

however be relevant that it was in about 1960 that children born during the Second World War entered in the 15–20 age group. The wartime period was itself one of increased illegitimacy and unsettled home conditions, and accordingly this might suggest a causative factor. But the strength of this argument is weakened by the observation that no similar increase in illegitimacy was seen at the corresponding period (commencing in 1934) from the date of the First World War. However environmental factors and social norms are very different now from those prevailing in the 1930s, and an explanation may be found in the prevalent publicity given to sexual behaviour. While more widespread indulgence in pre-marital sexual experience may be relatively harmless for many, it exposes to greater risks those vulnerable to unmarried pregnancy and the suffering this can cause.

*Problem families*

In 1946 the case histories of selected families to which Pacifist Service Units were giving assistance in some of Britain's major cities were published (Stephens, 1946). These revealed the existence of some families in conditions of indescribable squalor which could not be attributed simply to poverty but seems to result from inherent personality weaknesses in one or both of the married partners. A thorough study of these families is reported by Philp (1963). These were not cases of families which had broken up by separation. In 79 per cent of them the parties were cohabiting and were legally married, and in 7 per cent they were cohabiting in a *de facto* union. These relationships had suffered from a considerable degree of disruption and often temporary separation had occurred. Yet only in a very small number of cases had the parties remained apart.

Philp examines the characteristics of the spouses in families of this kind. The physical health record was very poor and that of mental health even worse. In only about 5 per cent of the families were one or both of the parents symptom-free from emotional instability, and it is of interest, when considering causative factors, that Philp records that 'at least two-thirds of both men and women had had a disturbed childhood and, leaving aside our Not Known category, there were no families where both husband and wife were unaffected'. These people appeared to undergo difficulty in forming stable relationships, not only with each other, but also with their own neighbours and extended families. In particular, their inability to provide adequate physical and emotional security for their children is very marked. At the time of the study reported by Philp, 12 per cent of the children were in care and about one-quarter of those under one year and nearly one-half of those between the ages of one and three years had experienced deprivation of normal home life. One-quarter of the children at the age of 'risk' for juvenile court proceedings had committed some kind of offence: a delinquency rate of over twice that of normal children.

It is extremely difficult to estimate the extent of problem families. Packman and Power provided the Seebohm Committee (1968) with an estimate that, omitting for lack of data cases of adverse family relationships, children who were at risk of requiring assistance from the social services due to their (intact) family being in poverty amounted to one in seventeen in the population, a total of 695,000 under the age of sixteen. Of course, not all these children come from families classed in this category, which form only a very small minority even amongst families suffering from poverty. Nor do all the children in need of social service assistance or protection come from problem families. Nevertheless, the existence of these families demands special attention on the part of those who frame legal and social policy towards families.

### Separation and divorce

Packman and Power put the number of children whose families were broken by divorce or separation at 5 per cent (about 575,000) of all the children under sixteen in 1968. Four years earlier Wynn (1964) had made a conservative estimate of the number of dependent children of families made fatherless by divorce or separation at 455,000, and these she estimated accounted for 58 per cent of all fatherless children. Bereavement, in her estimate, accounted for 33 per cent and children of unmarried mothers made up the remaining 9 per cent. These estimates are rather rough. Attempts have been made to ascertain the extent of family breakdown by reference to the divorce rate, but these are misguided. This is because divorce is a legal process, the incidence of which can depend upon variable factors such as the grounds allowed for divorce, the cost of proceedings and extent of legal aid: matters which bear no relation to factual marriage breakdown. This has been convincingly demonstrated by Rowntree and Carrier (1957–8) and becomes immediately clear on consideration of Figure 2.

Between 1901 and 1905, when the annual average of divorce decrees made absolute was 546, the sole legal ground for divorce was adultery, and unless the adultery was in the nature of rape or an unnatural offence, even that was not sufficient against a husband. Some other matrimonial offence had to be added to the charge of adultery. This double standard was abolished only in 1923.[1] The divorce figure clearly does not reflect the true breakdown rate over that period, of which a better picture is obtained by referring to the annual average of matrimonial orders made in favour of wives in the magistrates' courts. That figure is 7,595. One may surmise that in most cases where a wife seeks such an order, usually for mainten-ance, the spouses are living apart. But even the result of combining that figure with the number of divorces omits an incalculable number of cases where wives did not, or could not, obtain orders against their husbands and cases where wives had deserted their husbands, for maintenance orders could not be made in favour of deserted husbands.

The increase of nearly 50 per cent in the number of divorces granted from 1936 to 1939 does not, therefore, reflect a rise in the number of marital breakdowns, but is the result of the passing of the Matri-monial Causes Act 1937 which added as grounds for divorce the offences of cruelty, desertion and the supervening insanity of the other spouse. The increase in 1947 does, however, reflect a vastly disturbed situation as a result of wartime and all other European countries (except, ironically, Germany) show a similar reaction. Thereafter the figure drops until a sharp rise in 1952. This was due, however, to a flood of petitions filed the previous year after the coming into operation in October 1950 of the Legal Aid and Advice Act 1949. Thereafter the figure begins to drop again, but this again is no reflec-tion on the true breakdown rate, but is related to a falling off in the granting of legal aid under a scheme not properly adjusted to meet inflation. In 1959 and 1960 steps were taken to remedy this, resulting

1. Matrimonial Causes Act 1923, s. 1.

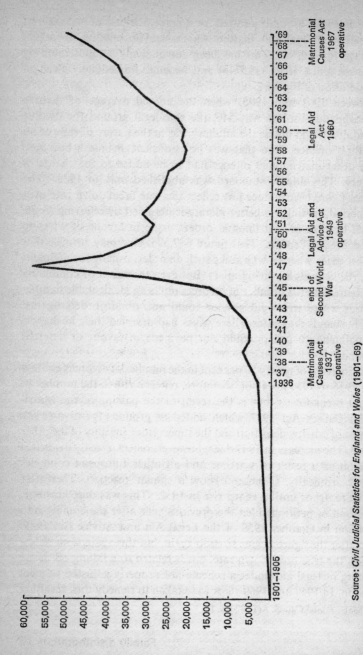

Source: *Civil Judicial Statistics for England and Wales* (1901–69)

Figure 2 Divorce decrees absolute 1901–69

in the enactment of the Legal Aid Act 1960. Shortly thereafter we again see a steep rise in the number of divorces. In 1959 only about one-third of divorce cases were legally aided. By 1968 the number had increased to two-thirds. A further rise could be expected after April 1968, from which time undefended cases could be heard in the County Court instead of having to be heard by a High Court Judge or Special Commissioner.[2] It may be that, with the greater ease with which divorce could be obtained in the 1960s, the figures during this period are a closer approximation to the actual numbers of marriages which broke down than they were formerly, but divorce statistics are totally unreliable as any indication of the rate of marriage breakdown before this period.

At the present time, however, the evidence discloses the following situation. In 1969, 60,134 petitions for divorce were filed. There were also 26,753 applications in the magistrates' courts for mainten-ance orders, and, although only 17,424 were granted, the very application is an indication of marital estrangement. It is estimated that only about half of these applicants eventually seek divorce. Nevertheless, a large global number of cases where spouses have sought legal proceedings with respect to their marriage is revealed. Without minimizing the seriousness of the extent of marital break-down in modern society, it is necessary, nevertheless, to see the situa-tion in perspective. The marriage rate (that is, the number of per-sons marrying per thousand of the total population) has, in England and Wales, remained almost constant since 1841 at about 16·0. Since the beginning of this century, the total population has increased by about 50 per cent and so too have the total number of marriages. Between 1901 and 1905 there was an annual average of 260,170 marriages. In 1967 there were 386,052 marriages. It is hardly sur-prising to find an increase in the number of breakdowns of marriage. It is more useful therefore to look at the divorce rate per thousand of the married population, and in 1967 this figure stood at 3·5. But for a truer picture of the extent of actual breakdown one would have to include separated but not divorced people, and the result of this might, at a very rough estimate, be double that figure.

What causes separation and divorce? To this question there can be no clear answer for the deeply personal nature of the relationship

2. Matrimonial Causes Act 1967.

involves areas of personality development and conflict about which generalization is dangerous. Moreover, examination of sociological material does not provide evidence of *causes* of marital breakdown. Sociologists and psychiatrists can do no more than to provide information about the kinds of factors which are commonly *associated with* separation and divorce. Since a consideration of these is relevant for family policy, some of them will be discussed here, and they are arranged into four groups – pre-marital behaviour, age at marriage, economic circumstances during marriage and 'other' factors.

*Pre-marital behaviour.* The most obvious area to examine in the calculation of factors associated with marital success is the length of time the parties were acquainted before marriage. There is general agreement that very short acquaintance is far more likely to lead to an unsuccessful marriage than longer acquaintance. This is convincingly demonstrated by Goode (1956) in his thorough and invaluable review of the personal histories of 425 divorced women conducted in Detroit in 1948. In his sample, he found that over 70 per cent of the divorcees had been engaged for six months or less. This gave some support to an earlier study by Locke (1951) in which 55 per cent of divorcees had been engaged for five months or less. Conversely, comparison of his percentages with random samples of happily married couples made by Burgess and Cottrell (1939) and Terman (1938) showed that a far lower percentage of the happily married had been engaged for periods of less than three months than of Goode's divorcee sample. Comparisons such as these cannot provide any clear cut 'optimum' period for which engagement should last for chances of a successful marriage to be at their highest, not least of all because the period of engagement is an unreliable indicator of length of acquaintance. Nevertheless, in so far as brief engagement might be associated with marriage undertaken under various kinds of pressure, and in particular a predominance of infatuation over rationality, it seems to indicate a relatively high degree of marriage risk.

There is another factor which might precipitate a hasty and brief engagement. This is the pregnancy of the woman. On this matter all who have investigated the problem of divorce proneness speak with one voice. Where a child is conceived before marriage the risk of divorce or separation is considerably higher than cases where the child is conceived in wedlock. In Britain, this has been demonstrated by Rowntree (1964). From a national sample of 3,000 men and women, she showed that of those couples whose first child had been conceived before marriage, 12·2 per cent had later parted and 6·8 per cent contemplated doing so. On the other hand, of the couples whose first child was conceived after the wedding, only 6·4 per cent actually separated, and only 3·1 per cent thought about it. The risk of breakdown in the case of 'shot-gun' marriages is, on these figures, about double that of other marriages, and this was particularly so when the bride married under the age of twenty. Findings of a similar nature have been made in the United States, where Christensen (1960) showed two further factors. First, that the risk was greater the longer the wedding was delayed after the discovery of pregnancy and second that the difference between the success rates of marriages with premaritally conceived children and those without them is less in a society which attaches less stigma to illegitimacy and pre-marital sexual behaviour. This is to be expected because in such a society there will be less pressure upon parties who are unsuited to each other to marry in order to throw the cloak of respectability over their pre-marital behaviour. But even in Denmark, where pre-marital sexual behaviour is tolerated to a comparatively high degree, the divorce rate of brides pregnant when married was found by Christensen to be about 50 per cent higher than of those who were not.

In so far as pre-marital sexual intercourse increases the risk of pre-marital pregnancy, and thereby puts pressure upon the parties to enter into marriage, such behaviour can be said to contribute to risks associated with marital unhappiness and disintegration. Whether pre-marital sex experience in itself has any bearing on the matter cannot be stated with any degree of certainty. There is some evidence, summarized by Burgess and Wallin (1953) that husbands and wives with no experience of pre-marital intercourse have the higher probability of marital success than those who had sexual relations with their future spouse or others before the marriage. Kinsey (1953), too, found that women who had pre-marital intercourse were more likely than others to have extra-marital intercourse once they were married. These findings, however, must be treated with extreme caution. In the first place, cases where there was pre-marital intercourse by the

Table 2 Marriages Dissolved or Annulled by Year of Marriage and Age of Bride

| Year of marriage | Number of marriages by age of bride | | Percentage of marriages dissolved or annulled in subsequent years | | | | | | | | Cumulative percentage |
|---|---|---|---|---|---|---|---|---|---|---|---|
| | Bride aged | Number | 1961 | 1962 | 1963 | 1964 | 1965 | 1966 | 1967 | 1968 | |
| 1957 | Under 20 | 73,937 | 0·73 | 1·11 | 1·29 | 1·37 | 1·32 | 1·23 | 1·21 | 1·20 | 9·46 |
| | 20–24 | 165,885 | 0·32 | 0·47 | 0·57 | 0·62 | 0·62 | 0·59 | 0·64 | 0·63 | 4·46 |
| | 25–29 | 46,120 | 0·25 | 0·39 | 0·38 | 0·46 | 0·45 | 0·48 | 0·41 | 0·40 | 3·22 |
| 1958 | Under 20 | 76,595 | 0·13 | 0·78 | 1·13 | 1·34 | 1·46 | 1·35 | 1·40 | 1·20 | 8·99 |
| | 20–24 | 162,908 | 0·06 | 0·41 | 0·56 | 0·63 | 0·69 | 0·67 | 0·68 | 0·63 | 4·33 |
| | 25–29 | 43,029 | 0·05 | 0·31 | 0·40 | 0·44 | 0·49 | 0·42 | 0·43 | 0·48 | 3·02 |
| 1959 | Under 20 | 77,320 | 0·04 | 0·13 | 0·91 | 1·31 | 1·53 | 1·49 | 1·46 | 1·40 | 8·27 |
| | 20–24 | 164,628 | 0·03 | 0·08 | 0·46 | 0·63 | 0·69 | 0·69 | 0·73 | 0·70 | 4·01 |
| | 25–29 | 41,070 | 0·05 | 0·05 | 0·31 | 0·43 | 0·49 | 0·50 | 0·50 | 0·45 | 2·78 |
| 1960 | Under 20 | 81,711 | 0·01 | 0·04 | 0·12 | 1·05 | 1·64 | 1·53 | 1·63 | 1·54 | 7·56 |
| | 20–24 | 164,802 | 0·01 | 0·03 | 0·07 | 0·46 | 0·69 | 0·70 | 0·74 | 0·73 | 3·43 |
| | 25–29 | 40,291 | 0·01 | 0·04 | 0·07 | 0·38 | 0·43 | 0·55 | 0·51 | 0·48 | 2·47 |
| 1961 | Under 20 | 89,528 | — | 0·01 | 0·05 | 0·15 | 1·07 | 1·60 | 1·7 | 1·64 | 7·22 |
| | 20–24 | 160,998 | — | 0·01 | 0·02 | 0·15 | 0·53 | 0·70 | 0·74 | 0·71 | 2·86 |
| | 25–29 | 39,835 | — | 0·02 | 0·03 | 0·08 | 0·30 | 0·52 | 0·56 | 0·50 | 2·01 |

Figures below dotted line represent marriages terminated within three years of wedding
Adapted from *Statistical Review of England and Wales 1957–61*

bride will include all those where she was pregnant when married, which is a disruptive factor in itself. Secondly, it may be that persons who, for other reasons, are unlikely to enter a stable marriage also tend to have pre-marital relations so that the fact of pre-marital intercourse may, in itself, be of no causative significance.

*Age at marriage.* Together with the pregnancy of the bride at marriage, the youthfulness of the parties can be stated with certainty as being strongly associated with marriage breakdown. This is illustrated by Table 2. The figures show the fate of marriages entered into in England and Wales from 1957 to 1961 by recording the percentage of those marriages which were terminated in subsequent years. The marriages of each of those years are further subdivided according to the age of the bride at marriage. It thus becomes possible to discover, for example, what percentage of the marriages contracted in 1957 where the bride was under twenty was terminated in 1967. It can be seen that where the bride was under twenty at marriage the percentage of those marriages terminated in subsequent years is substantially and consistently higher than that for other age groups. This is so irrespective, it seems, of the duration of the marriage. In 1961, for example, 0·73 per cent of brides under twenty who married in 1957 had their marriages dissolved or annulled; in 1967, ten years after the year of marriage, 1·21 per cent of those marriages were terminated. The corresponding percentages where the bride was between twenty and twenty-four at marriage are 0·32 and 0·64. Table 2 also shows that the termination rate is consistently higher for those marriages where the bride was between twenty and twenty-four at marriage than for those where she was between twenty-five and twenty-nine. Certain other points appear from the Table. The termination rate has been increasing year by year. Take the age group twenty to twenty-four. Of those married in 1957, 0·47 per cent had their marriages terminated in their fifth year of marriage. The equivalent percentage of terminations (that is, in the fifth year of marriage) of those married in 1958 is 0·56 per cent and for those married in 1961 it is 0·7 per cent. This may, however, reflect only an increasing tendency during the 1960s to resort to divorce when a marriage breaks down rather than an increase in breakdowns. On the other hand, it may provide some indication of the extent of breakdown. If so, it is of some interest that the figures confirm that there is a tendency for the termination rate to increase up to a period of six or seven years from the marriage, and thereafter to level out or drop away. While not conclusive, for divorce does not always coincide with time of breakdown, this would provide some evidence as to the period during a marriage when risk of breakdown is highest.

There are various reasons why these youthful marriages are so much at risk. The most obvious is that the personalities of the parties have yet fully to develop, and this development may throw unforeseen strains on the relationship. This may account for the fact that youthful marriages not only break down at a greater rate than those of older people within a short time of the marriage, but continue to do so even in the case of marriages of long duration. But there is another factor which may be present and this is that in youthful marriages the bride is more likely to be pregnant at the time of marriage than in the case of older brides. One in three of brides who marry under the age of twenty is pregnant at the time of the marriage. This is true of only one in six brides between twenty and twenty-four and about one in ten of brides between twenty-five and twenty-nine. The relationship between these figures clearly correlates with the breakdown rates of the marriages of these age groups. The alternatives of having to care for an illegitimate child or entering into a marriage with high breakdown potential are harsh but they obviously face an increasingly large number of women, especially those under twenty.

*Economic circumstances during marriage.* One circumstance that has been consistently found in studies in the United States to be relevant to divorce proneness has been the socio-economic status of the parties. The lower that status, the greater the prevalence of divorce. It is necessary, when considering research in that country, to make allowance for the fact that the divorce rate amongst the Negro population is rather higher than amongst the white population, and Negroes dominate the lower socio-economic groups, particularly in the cities. It may of course be simply because they dominate the lower groups that the Negro divorce rate is relatively high, rather than a reflection of different cultural norms. But in spite of the prevalence of divorce in the lower income groups, Goode (1956) warns that it is probably not the *amount* of income which is important, but its *stability*. So, in the lower income groups, families will be put under greater strain by unemployment and mobility of labour than the families of the professional, clerical and skilled classes. The tension in the families at risk lies in the failure of the husband to fulfil the social role of breadwinner assigned to him in the average family. It has, however, been questioned whether marriage failure can properly be attributed to social or economic causes. It is argued, for example, by Dicks (1967) that the fault is to be found in the personalities of the parties, in particular that of the failed husband. But economic strain can adversely affect personal relationships. Doubtless many cases of marital strain are a result of an interaction between personality and external difficulties. But where a relatively unstable personality is defeated by adverse economic conditions, the result for the wife and family can be assessed in concrete terms – lack of support. Thus it is significant that, of Goode's sample, non-support was the most common 'main cause' attributed by the divorcee herself to the breakdown of her marriage. An unusually large number of the divorced husbands (30 per cent) had failed to bring in a regular income. The adverse effects of financial hardship and insecurity upon marital relationships has been observed also in Australia by Goding (1969).

It is striking that, in Goode's sample, 40 per cent of the divorcees stated that there was no property of any value left for division at time of divorce. Levinger (1965), surveying American literature on factors associated with divorce, concludes that the research has shown that divorce is negatively associated with home ownership. So the possession of a home does seem to provide an additional element of stability into the relationship, and indeed this is not surprising if, as was suggested earlier, the desire for a 'home' is a strong motivation for marriage. The security provided by a home is particularly important for the wife, especially if she has children. So, even if her husband has provided a house, her very dependence on him for continuing occupation of it might place certain strains on the relationship if he is in financial difficulties, whether caused by misfortune or his own incompetence. The Married Women's Association, in giving its evidence to the Royal Commission on Marriage and Divorce (1956), stated that 'one of the basic and most insidious factors contributing to the stresses and strains of married life lies in the economic dependence of the wife on her husband. This, on the one hand, engenders in the wife a feeling of resentment and, on the other, gives the husband the power of ultimate decision conferred by economic domination.' This point is very difficult to substantiate by empirical evidence. But by and large it is probably safe to identify anxiety about economic security, in particular the provision of a home for the wife and children, as a factor contributing to strains which may eventually lead to marital disintegration.

*Other factors.* There are many other forces operating upon family life which work to weaken the relationships within it. A comparatively modern phenomenon is the increased life expectancy among married women. Improved medical services and techniques of limiting births have combined to subject women to fewer hazards and strains during the childbearing period, after which they can now look forward to a long period of active life. This has increased the period during which marriages are at risk. But, accompanying the emancipation of women and the growth of the 'romantic' conception of marriage has been a heightening of the expectations of each party, in particular the woman, as to the quality of the marriage. This is reflected in judicial sentiments expressed in matrimonial cases. A case is reported in the eighteenth century in which a wife alleged that her husband, who continually abused her, on one occasion entered the house with two other men and 'locked the parlour door . . . and said he would lie with her in the presence of the said men, and they said he was her husband and had a right to do so, and they would hold her for him to lie with her; whereupon she got out of the window, over a palisade, and over to the next house whither he and the said two men followed her, and he then pulled off her cap, and dragged her by the hair of her head, and attempted to drag her home, but was prevented; and that he afterwards declared that if he could get her in his power he would send her abroad, where nobody should see her, unless she would give him her money'. The judge said that she had not alleged sufficiently serious conduct to allow her to live apart from him, and he ordered her to return home.[3] In 1861 a judge dismissed a wife's charge of cruelty against her husband, saying: 'The violence consisted of one act only. No blow was given. The alterca-

3. *Holmes* v. *Holmes* [1755] 2 Lee 116.

tion arose out of the husband's suspicions, and then he took her by the throat, shook her and threw her down. It does not appear that any mark was left on the throat or that she was rendered ill by the transaction.'[4] In 1870, however, the leading judge in the divorce court was able to say that, although 'the subordination of the wife is doubtless in conformity with the established customs of mankind' yet, 'without disparaging the just and paramount authority of a husband, it may safely be asserted that a wife is not a domestic slave, to be driven at all costs, short of personal violence, into compliance with her husband's demands.'[5] As late as 1947 the Court of Appeal decided that the continual neglect of his wife by the husband as a result of his obsessive (though not, apparently, homosexual) preference for the company of a pig-man serving on his farm did not entitle his wife to leave him.[6] Lord Justice Asquith, referring, apparently approvingly, to some earlier cases, said: 'Habitual drunkenness (unless accompanied with a certain degree of violence or threats of violence), persistent nagging and insult, and even incest, forgiven but followed by an indecent assault on a girl of thirteen, to mention nothing else, have been held not to suffice.' It is very difficult to imagine many judges reaching the same conclusion today.

It is far more common nowadays, then, for complaints which relate to personality differences between the parties to lead to divorce than it used to be. The more that is expected out of the conjugal relationship, the greater and more frequent are the disappointments. Wallis and Booker (1958) record the major factors attributed by marriage guidance counsellors to the marital difficulties of clients attending the National Marriage Guidance Council. 'Personal defects' score the highest frequency of mention, with sexual difficulties and 'incompatibility' also high on the list. Personality differences also feature high on the reasons attributed by Goode's sample of divorcees for their divorces, together with excessive domination by the husband (including maltreatment) and drink problems. It can be asserted with some certainty, then, that the conjugal relationship is expected to be more finely balanced between the partners than was once the case and that the disturbance of the balance can be

4. *Smallwood* v. *Smallwood* (1861) 2 Sw. & Tr.398.
5. *Kelly* v. *Kelly* (1870) L.R.2 P. & D.31.
6. *Buchler* v. *Buchler* [1947] P.25.

caused by a variety of disparate factors which would take a considerable degree of investigation to identify but which can lead a spouse to seek to end the marriage.

One final possible factor causative of family breakdown should be mentioned. This is childlessness. In a sense, infertility is in itself a form of family breakdown. The unit is incomplete. It was at one time thought that childlessness was a strong reason for marriage breakdown, and indeed it is true that an unusually high number of divorces are granted to childless couples. But, as Dominian (1968) describes, many factors other than infertility might account for a couple remaining childless. If they include latent homosexuality, repugnance to childbearing or problems of accommodation; these may in themselves create a proneness to breakdown. And of course many marriages of childless couples may have been broken by separation well before the couple decided to have children. It is therefore extremely difficult to place much weight on childlessness in itself as a factor tending to marriage disintegration. Nevertheless, while many childless couples live extremely happy married lives, the fact of childlessness often adds to the strains imposed upon them, and their problems demand attention when family policy is reviewed as a whole.

### The role of the law

We have been considering the social forces from which the impetus to family living can be said to derive, and the countervailing forces which weaken the family, sometimes stunting its growth, sometimes undermining it so as to lead to its eventual dissolution. What is the role of the legal process in this interplay of forces? It is often alleged that the law has little influence on the social mores of a society; that 'true' law is to be found in the way people in fact behave and not in the examination of the written law. Indeed, it is said that, at best, the official law is simply a reflection of attitudes already adopted by society as a whole, and often a delayed one at that. For this view there is considerable evidence. Judges, after all, are drawn from their own contemporary society and will, by and large, express opinions consistent with those by which their society has moulded them during their formative years. The evolution of the judicial attitude to norms of marital conduct quoted earlier illustrates the reluctant adaptation of the law to changing social attitudes. And what is true for judges is true also of Parliamentary legislators so that statutory legislation, as Dicey (1914) so clearly described, is also a response to changes in community feeling. Therefore one is not surprised to find that in matters where common custom is most deeply ingrained, and this is so in the case of family relationships, attempts to impose vastly different patterns of behaviour by reforming legislation meet with little or no success. As an example, it is reported by Dror (1959) that while the introduction of Western law in Turkey did significantly influence certain aspects of life in Turkey, especially commercial activities, family life and marriage habits remained little affected despite legislative efforts to change them.

Yet such a pessimistic view of the utility of law as a means of social control is not justified. While it remains true that a law which deviates too drastically from communal opinion may fail (in the absence of a measure of coercion which would be considered unacceptable in a democratic society), toleration by the majority of reform coupled with its promotion by a few can have effective results. Thus the practice of 'baby-farming', by which strangers 'cared' for children for reward often in deplorable conditions, which was revealed on a scandalous scale at the end of the nineteenth century, has been largely eliminated by the enactment of child protection legislation. Legislation of this type requires a supervising agency to ensure its enforcement, but there are subtler ways by which legislation, or the absence of it, can affect population behaviour. The experience in the Soviet Union in this respect has already been mentioned. Legal provisions may deter people from seeking advice or reconciliation, or they may encourage them to do so. Facultative provisions may be enacted to meet the problems of special groups of people as, for example, in the case of the adoption law. The economic security of wives and children can be regulated. Family allowances and taxation benefits can provide incentives or disincentives for or against certain activities. In a cohesive and comparatively closely regulated society, legal pressures of this kind might have a measurable effect. More difficult to calculate is whether statements of principle by the legislature can influence community attitudes. It is often claimed that, if the legislature was to proclaim the principle of divorce by consent obtained by simple registration, this would lessen the respect with which marriage is held in the eyes of the community as a whole. It is probable that this is true, largely as a result of the overwhelming publicity given to matters of this kind in the press and other communication media. It is of interest to note that the Race Relations Board believes that the mere passing of the Race Relations Act 1968 has had an educative effect. 'We have argued,' its members say in the Report for 1968–69, 'that in a society that is basically law-abiding the mere passage of a law would produce positive results. Our experience before and since the Act came into force confirms us in our view. We have evidence of firms that have ceased to discriminate unlawfully as a result of the legislation.' It would be wrong, it seems, to underestimate the feedback from legislation into the customs and morals of a community.

It is not proposed to devote any discussion to what the basic objectives of family law in our community should be. This is largely because there is so little disagreement about them. Although the family as an institution has its critics, as for example, Leach (1968), the overwhelmingly dominant view is that social policy should support it, and when it functions inadequately, should devise measures to restore it rather than attempt to supplant it. Making this basic assumption, legal policy towards the family can simultaneously adopt two approaches. The first is to attempt to minimize the risk of family breakdown by seeking to prevent those situations arising where that risk is high and by promoting situations favourable to family cohesion. This 'preventive' role of the law therefore has both a negative and a positive side to it. The other approach is necessitated by recognition of the fact that the preventive function of the law in this area meets with limited success. Therefore it is necessary for legal provision to assume a remedial, therapeutic character. In all societies, no matter what the state of the law, there will always be children born outside marriage; there will always be breakdown of marriages. It becomes necessary, therefore, to devise the most effective means of re-adjustment by which the law may mitigate the harmful consequences of illegitimacy and marital breakdown and to provide some measure of compensation for the frustration of the expectations entertained by the parties concerned. There will naturally be some overlap in the operation of these two functions as some legal provisions may serve both purposes simultaneously. Nevertheless, policy is conceptually divisible into this dual role. Accordingly the legal and administrative provisions relating to the family will be examined by reference in Part One, to their efficacy as a means of prevention of family breakdown and in Part Two to their success in providing adequate remedies where these are called for.

# Part One
# Family Security

# Chapter 1
# Before Marriage

### Pre-marital pregnancy and illegitimacy

It may come as a surprise to British readers that in many states in the United States, fornication is a criminal offence. The extent to which these laws are enforced does not adequately appear from the statistics, and their influence upon behaviour is even less discernible. Other American state laws punish parties to whom an illegitimate child, or a certain number of illegitimate children, are born, thereby singling out for additional punishment those who for various reasons have not used contraceptives, or have used them unsuccessfully. English law knows no criminal sanction against extra-marital intercourse as such. However, it is a criminal offence for a man to have sexual intercourse with a girl below marriageable age, which is sixteen. He has a defence if he is himself under twenty-four, has not previously been charged with a like offence and can show that he had reasonable cause to believe, and did believe, that the girl was over sixteen.[1] It is also an offence to permit a girl under sixteen to use premises for the purposes of unlawful sexual intercourse and also to cause or encourage such acts by a girl under sixteen, or her prostitution.[2] These provisions are aimed against the exploitation and corruption of children rather than the prevention of illegitimacy as such. However, they are probably quite widely known and may have some degree of deterrent effect. But provisions also exist to prevent a girl becoming involved in a situation which may put her at risk. By the Children and Young Persons Act 1969 anyone who is under seventeen may be brought before a juvenile court by a local authority, or by the police or an officer of an association such as the National

1. Sexual Offences Act 1956, ss. 5 and 6; Criminal Law Act 1967, sch.2.
2. *ibid.*, ss. 25–8.

Society for the Prevention of Cruelty to Children where it is reasonably thought that he is 'exposed to moral danger' and is 'in need of care or control which he is unlikely to receive' unless he is brought under supervision.[3] If the court finds that this is the case it may, if necessary, remove the child or young person from his harmful surroundings, or it may arrange for him to be supervised by the local authority while remaining at home, or it may even bind his parents over to see he is better looked after. The local authority must also investigate any reports it hears that there may be grounds for bringing such proceedings in respect of a child or young person in its area, unless it is satisfied that this would be unnecessary.[4]

A supplementary, but little used, legal means of exercising supervision over young people is the wardship jurisdiction of the High Court. A person under eighteen becomes a ward of court automatically upon application by summons to the Family Division of the High Court but this will lapse unless the matter is dealt with within twenty-one days.[5] The court has wide powers to make orders controlling the activities of the ward and persons associating with him or (more usually) her. It may also, in exceptional circumstances, commit the child into the care of the local authority or place him under its supervision.[6] The evidence given to the Committee on the Age of Majority (Latey Committee) (1967) suggested that the intervention of the court in the case of teenagers nearing their twenties was not only seldom beneficial but might often cause positive harm. The relationship between the young people and the parents became increasingly embittered, and where the parents were refusing consent to a marriage, the girl might deliberately become pregnant. The Committee recommended that the wardship jurisdiction should end at the age of eighteen, and this was effected by the lowering of the age of majority to that age on 1 January 1970.[7] The value of the wardship jurisdiction over older children can be disregarded, except in very exceptional cases, and its usefulness in modern times is practically

3. C.Y.P.A. 1969 ss. 1(1) and (2). This does not apply to married people.
4. *ibid.*, s. 2(1).
5. Law Reform (Miscellaneous Provisions) Act 1949, s. 9; Administration of Justice Act 1970, s. 1. On the Family Division, see p. 278.
6. Family Law Reform Act 1969, s. 7.
7. *ibid.*, s. 1.

confined to it as a means of determining disputed custody cases with respect to very young children.

The wardship jurisdiction apart, once a person reaches the age of seventeen, concern for his 'moral welfare' suddenly ends. This is curious because the age of majority is attained a year later. Persons of seventeen live, therefore, in a strange half light between the night of minority and the dawn of adulthood. Yet even at seventeen they are protected against involvement in gambling[8] and may not buy or consume alcoholic liquor in a bar.[9] Few people would maintain that the law should attempt to regulate the sexual morality of adults. One residual area where it does attempt to do this is coming under increasing criticism. This is the law of obscenity. It is an offence, whether for gain or not, to *publish* an article which is obscene or to *have* such an article for publication for gain.[10] An article is obscene if its effect, taken as a whole, is 'such as to tend to deprave and corrupt persons who are likely, having regard to all relevant circumstances, to read, see or hear the matter contained or embodied in it'.[11] But if an accused person has examined the article and had no reason to believe that it is obscene he will have a defence if prosecuted, and he will also have a defence if he can show, by means of expert witnesses if he wishes, that the publication of an article, although obscene, is justified in the interests of science, literature, art or learning 'or of other objects of general concern'.[12] This defence betrays the confused and contradictory attitudes so often found in public pronouncements on sexual matters. Why should the interests of science, literature, art or learning justify depravity and corruption? It seems therefore that these words cannot be as strong as might be thought. The law has given no clear guidance as to their true meaning, but stimulation of an erotic kind is included. However, erotic stimulation permeates much of our cultural heritage from the past as well as modern contributions to it, as in the case with all societies. What appears to be a new development in our society is mass exploitation of sex motifs by commercial interests without

8. Betting, Gaming and Lotteries Act 1963, ss. 21 and 32(3).
9. Licensing Act 1964, s. 169.
10. Obscene Publications Act 1959, s. 2; Obscene Publications Act 1964, s. 1.
11. Obscene Publications Act 1959, s. 1(1).
12. *ibid.*, s. 4(1).

corresponding publicity to instruction in the responsible use of sex and the personal and social problems surrounding its misuse.

The 1960s saw a noticeable increase in the mass exploitation of sex, and as no other factor appears satisfactorily to correlate with the unprecedented increase in illegitimacy in that decade, one must assume some relationship between the two. It is explicable since the greater the emphasis on sex in mass circulated literature and entertainment, the greater the chance of its misuse by a vulnerable group. This group consists of adults with personality problems and young people. With respect to the problem of illegitimacy and pre-marital pregnancy, that group amongst adults is not large and would not justify controls over the sources of erotic stimulation in society except in cases of offensive displays or conduct in public. With respect to children and young people, greater supervision over their moral welfare and their protection against exploitation is justified in this area as well as in the more particular circumstances already mentioned. A limitation of the Obscene Publications Acts to publication or intent to publish to persons under eighteen is suggested by an analogy with the prohibition on the sale to them of alcoholic drinks and with the Children and Young Persons (Harmful Publications) Act 1955 which makes it an offence, broadly, to publish or keep for the purposes of publishing a work likely to fall into the hands of persons under seventeen which consists solely or mainly of stories told in pictures, portraying the commission of crimes or acts of violence or cruelty or incidents of a repulsive or horrible nature 'in such a way that the work as a whole would tend to corrupt' the child or young person.[13]

Theatre, cinema and television are subject to additional legal controls. Before 26 September 1968 scripts of plays written or translated after 1843 which were to be produced in Great Britain were subject to censorship by the Lord Chamberlain. However, the Theatres Act 1968 abolished this form of censorship. In its place the Act created a statutory offence of presenting or directing an obscene performance of a play. Once again the test of obscenity is whether the performance, taken as a whole, was such as to tend to 'deprave and corrupt persons who were likely, having regard to all relevant circumstances, to

13. Zellick (1970) makes a similar suggestion, but he would retain a measure of protection for adults generally.

attend it'. The Act applies to private as well as to public perform-ances, but not to a play 'given on a domestic occasion in a private dwelling'. The actual working of these provisions of the Act will depend to a large extent on the discretion of the Attorney-General of the day because his consent is necessary to any prosecution instituted under them. It is probable, therefore, that an erotic play stands in more danger of prosecution if children are likely to attend it than if it is confined to adults, but it is unfortunate that this distinction is not written into the law, for which the only criterion is whether any-one watching it would be 'corrupted'. Indeed, adults are more likely to be sexually moved than children, but the point is that they are likely to behave more responsibly in that event.

The cinema, on the other hand, remains subject to a form of censorship. This is exercised on a local basis, generally by Justices of the Peace to whom local authorities delegate their powers to issue licences for the exhibition of films. In practice the licensing authori-ties generally follow the classification of films made by the British Board of Film Censors which is an unofficial body established by the film trade itself to give guidance on the matter of censorship. The Cinematograph Act 1952 obliges licensing authorities to impose conditions in licences restricting or prohibiting the admission of children to films they consider unsuitable for them and in all cases to bear in mind what conditions or restrictions should be imposed on the admission of children. 'Children', for these purposes, are per-sons under the age of sixteen. The Board's classification is specifically related to the protection of children. On the one hand, no person below eighteen may be admitted to a film with an X certificate, while on the other, a U certificate film is open to everyone. There are two intermediary categories. A film with an A certificate may be attended by anyone, but parents are warned that it contains matter which they may consider unsuitable for children; films graded AA are open to everyone over the age of fourteen. However, local authorities are not bound by these classifications and some regional variation takes place. Films shown to members of clubs are not, however, subject to these licensing provisions, but they are covered by the Obscene Publications Acts. Control over broadcasting and television, on the other hand, is centralized. The British Broadcasting Corporation operates under a licence granted by the Postmaster

General, and is subject to directions from him. It is currently under an obligation to maintain standards of good taste and decency. There is, however, no express stipulation in the licence referring to the protection of children from unsuitable programmes and the matter is left to internal regulation. Independent television services broadcast under contract with the Independent Television Authority, which retains a considerable degree of supervision over their activities. The Television Act 1964 requires the ITA to satisfy itself, so far as possible, that programmes broadcast do not include matter which offends against good taste and decency, and is obliged to draw up a Code giving guidance to its contractors on standards to be observed, paying special regard to programmes broadcast 'when large numbers of children and young persons may be expected to be watching'. The Authority is obliged to secure that the provisions of the Code are observed. The legal framework for mitigating the impact upon children of commercial exploitation of sex by these media therefore exists, but the effectiveness of their operation depends upon the judgment of those operating them.

The combination of protection from an atmosphere of sexual permissiveness and promotion of knowledge about the risks of sexual irresponsibility and its prevention is often thought to create a dilemma. It is often resolved by perpetuating ignorance about the latter. Since, however, despite controls, children and young persons are always sexually at risk, or eventually become so, and adults are protected in no way at all, that solution is questionable. More widespread knowledge of contraception, one may assume, would have some effect upon the illegitimacy rate. Yet publicity about the subject is commonly regarded as improper. The ITA code on advertising, for example, until recently prohibited advertisement of contraceptives. It is clear that questions of taste are relevant here but it is very difficult to regard an advertisement for a contraceptive as being conducive to eroticism. The same ambivalence appears in controversies as to whether contraceptive advice should be given to the unmarried in family planning clinics. Some private clinics do this. Since the National Health Service (Family Planning) Act 1967 this advice may be provided by the National Health Service. Where unmarried people seek this advice, the argument that to give it encourages promiscuity seems weak as such people would appear already to have decided to experience sexual relations and it is unlikely that their decision would be altered if they did not receive this advice. Indeed, their very decision to seek advice would, in most cases, suggest that they wish to act responsibly and lessen the risk of illegitimate procreation. However, by October 1970 only one in twelve local authorities had established a free family planning service to persons irrespective of marital status.

Should pregnancy occur, there are three possibilities open. The parents might agree to marry; the girl might have the child without marrying; or she might seek abortion. The first and the last solutions obviate the problems of illegitimacy. The first, as we have seen, has risks. It will probably be considered the most desirable, but should not be considered an automatic way out. In many cases, in any event, it is not possible. The choice then lies between the last two alternatives. Abortion is morally objectionable to a large section of the population. However this is a matter of such moral complexity that no communal consensus can be assumed and it seems right that legal provision for abortion should be made, so this alternative exists for those to whom it is unobjectionable. Prior to 27 April 1968 abortion was an illegal operation unless its performance was necessary to prevent the woman becoming a physical or mental 'wreck'. The Abortion Act 1967, however, greatly widened from that date the circumstances in which a legal abortion could be performed. It retained the old law that any one registered medical practitioner may terminate a pregnancy if he genuinely believes that this is immediately necessary to save the woman's life or prevent grave physical or mental injury to her. But it adds that pregnancy may be terminated by a registered medical practitioner if *two* such practitioners certify that continuance of the pregnancy 'would involve risk to the life of the pregnant woman, or of injury to the physical or mental health of the pregnant woman or any existing children of her family *greater than if the pregnancy were terminated*.' It is expressly stated that in deciding this the practitioners may take into account the woman's 'actual or reasonably foreseeable environment'. Abortion is also permitted if the practitioners certify that the child, if born, would suffer from such physical or mental abnormalities 'as to be seriously handicapped'. Persons with conscientious objection to the operation are under no duty to participate in it, and the operation may be performed only in a National Health Service hospital or in a private clinic expressly approved for this purpose by the Minister. Finally, once the foetus becomes viable, and, unless the contrary is shown, this is presumed to happen when the woman has been pregnant twenty-eight weeks, destruction of the child remains an offence.[14]

It might be argued that, as a convincing case could be made that abortion, if legally carried out within a short time of pregnancy, has a lower statistical risk for the mother than actual childbirth, in all such cases the continuance of the pregnancy would involve a risk to the woman greater than if it were terminated. However the creation of abortion 'on demand' was not the intention of the legislature and the Act must be interpreted as referring to the risk *to the woman involved* and it must be assumed that, for her, normal childbirth in itself presents no more risks than would abortion. However, if other factors are present, the Act does not require that the risk of continuing the pregnancy should be substantially greater than those of abortion; it is enough if they are simply 'greater'. This is of importance if an unmarried mother seeks abortion, for it will not usually be difficult for her to demonstrate that the strains of bringing up a child alone in her 'reasonably foreseeable environment' would impose on her physical or mental health dangers of injury greater, at least to some extent, than if she were to be aborted. Of the 22,256 women aborted during the first eight months after the Act came into operation 47 per cent were single. The same period saw a slight decrease in the illegitimacy rate and, although it is as yet too early to confirm that the wider availability of abortion has checked or lessened the incidence of illegitimacy, it is probable that this will happen, though it remains to be seen whether the effect will be more than marginal. The number of abortions performed has risen, and the Secretary of State for Social Security stated that, in 1969, the first full year of the operation of the Act, there were 33,150 terminations and 12 deaths in National Health Service hospitals and 20,863 terminations and three deaths in approved clinics.[15] To many abortion may not warrant high priority in the allocation of medical resources, nevertheless, if the child is born, public expense is frequently incurred not only

14. Infant Life (Preservation) Act 1929; Abortion Act 1967, s. 5(1).
15. H. C. Deb., vol. 794, Written Answers, col. 159.

during the mother's confinement but in providing for the child, who cannot be allowed to suffer, and there is yet another child to be reared in unstable surroundings. These considerations should serve further to concentrate attention upon an earlier stage and encourage the promotion of contraceptive knowledge.

## Youthful marriages

That the youthfulness of the parties to a marriage may of itself be a contributing factor to its risk of breakdown has already been made clear. It would seem to follow that policy should be framed to discourage marriages being entered when the parties have not yet, or have only barely, attained adulthood. Since 1966 there has been a slight drop in the proportion of brides marrying under twenty. In that year about 29 per cent of all brides were under twenty. In 1968 this had fallen to 25 per cent. It is probably too high a social and personal risk that a quarter of all marriages should be of this kind. Does legal policy seek to discourage such marriages?

In 1929[16] the minimum age of marriage was set at sixteen for both sexes. Previously it had been fourteen for boys and twelve for girls, the ages fixed by canon law. This was a desirable reform, but would prevent only the very rare case of extreme abuse and had no effect whatsoever on the rising flood of marriages of parties under twenty-one. Unfortunately, the prohibition, though desirable, is extreme and inflexible. The present provision, which is contained in the Marriage Act 1949[17] declares that any 'marriage' where either of the parties is under sixteen at the time of the ceremony is void. It must, then, be treated as if it had never taken place. But this could lead to hardship if, for example, after years of ostensible married life it was found that a genuine mistake has been made about the age of one of the parties at the time of the wedding. Or it might be found that the bride had concealed her true age. The law then says that the couple must be treated as if they never had been married. If one of them dies, the other is not legally a widow or widower. This could have had disastrous effects on the survivor's economic security. After 1971, however, the survivor of such a union is given a certain degree of protection. If he entered into the marriage in good faith with the

16. Age of Marriage Act 1929.
17. Marriage Act 1949, s. 2.

deceased spouse he will be treated as a dependant for the purpose of the Inheritance (Family Provision) Act 1938. If it would have been reasonable for the deceased spouse to have provided for the survivor's maintenance, the court then may, on application of the survivor, make an order for such provision to be made out of the estate, whether the deceased died leaving a will or not.[18] This will not apply, however, to a party who misrepresents his age on marriage and he may pay heavily for that deception. Fortunately the children will be considered legitimate unless both parents knew their marriage was invalid.[19] These results could equally well be obtained by forbidding the solemnization of a marriage where either party is under age, but saving the validity of the marriage should it take place in contravention of the prohibition. This is the position taken in New Zealand.[20] Alternatively, many countries consider marriages contracted below the minimum age to be voidable rather than void. That is, they can be set aside by a party (usually the innocent one) within a certain time from its celebration. Unless this is done, the party who enjoys all the advantages of the union will be bound by it. However, the Law Commission (1970) has recommended against altering the law. It was thought to be inconsistent and impracticable to allow these marriages to be validated when the criminal law forbids sexual intercourse with a girl under sixteen. How can a marriage be valid if it is a criminal offence to perform the obligations it imposes? But once the girl is sixteen this objection falls away. If the man was under twenty-four and reasonably believed the girl was over sixteen when he married her, a prosecution will fail. Why should the marriage be struck down? Even if he is convicted, should this necessarily affect the marriage any more than conviction for making a false declaration to the superintendent registrar? Perhaps such a marriage should be capable of being repudiated by either of the parties or by the action of a third party while either of them is under sixteen, but should be considered to have become validated when they have both reached that age.

If the parties are over sixteen they may marry. However, if either has not yet attained to age of majority and is not a widow or widower,

18. Law Reform (Miscellaneous Provisions) Act 1970, s. 6. Family provision is discussed in greater detail below, p. 218 *et seq*.
19. Legitimacy Act 1959, s. 2.   20. Marriage Act 1955, (N.Z.), s. 17.

English law, in common with most other systems, requires certain specified persons to consent to the marriage. These persons are the parents of the party still a minor if they are living together. If they are divorced or separated, only the parent who has custody need consent. If a parent has been deserted by the other, only the deserted one need consent, and the same is true with respect to a surviving parent unless a guardian has been appointed, in which case he too must consent. The guardians or guardian must also consent if both parents are dead. If the minor is illegitimate, his mother or guardian must consent. The Marriage Act 1949[21] provides that if the superintendent registrar or ecclesiastical authority issuing the licence to marry is satisfied that the consent of a person cannot be obtained because that person is absent or inaccessible or under some disability, then, if the consent of some other person (e.g. the other parent) is required and obtained, the first consent can be dispensed with. But if there is no other person whose consent is required, then the permission of the Registrar General or of a court must be obtained. Also, if a person whose consent is required refuses to give it, the court may do so instead. 'Court' in this context includes the High Court, county court or a magistrates' court, and in practice most applications of this kind are made to magistrates. However, since decisions by magistrates' courts are not officially reported and there is no provision for appeal it is unfortunately not possible to discover on what principles applications of this kind are decided.

If a marriage takes place without the proper consents, it is still a valid marriage, and it is expressly provided[22] that, if the validity of the marriage is later called into question, this cannot be done by giving evidence that the required consent had not been given. The object is to give every opportunity for the consent requirement to be complied with before the marriage takes place but if this fails, then to accept the marriage as accomplished. So, if the marriage is to take place in the Church of England and is preceded by banns, a person whose consent is required may 'openly and publicly declare or cause to be declared, in the church or chapel in which the banns are published, at the time of publication, his dissent from the intended publication'. Upon the enactment of that dramatic scene the publication of the banns becomes void and no valid marriage can take place

21. Marriage Act 1949, s. 3.   22. *ibid.*, s. 48(1).

if both parties 'knowingly and wilfully' go through with it.[23] If the person who dissents is rather more discreet and privately communicates his dissent to a clergyman this will not, it seems, be sufficient to prevent the marriage taking place, although it is improbable that a clergyman who knows of this will solemnize it. If the marriage is by common licence (see p. 66) one of the parties applying for it must swear that the required consents have been obtained or have been dispensed with or that there is no person whose consent is required. It is open to the grantor of the licence to satisfy himself of the truth of the oath but should it be false, this does not affect the validity of the marriage. If one of the parties admits to being under the age of majority, the practice of the Faculty Office, from which common licences are issued, is to require the witnessed consent of the parents, but there is no legal requirement for this. It is also possible for *anyone* to enter a *caveat* against the grant of a common licence stating why he objects to its grant, and if this is done the matter raised must be investigated. But usually the licence issues promptly, the authorities relying on the good faith of the parties.

If the marriage is not to take place in accordance with the rites of the Church of England, it is necessary for the certificate of a superintendent registrar to be obtained and, on applying for it, one of the parties must make a solemn declaration in writing that, if one of the persons to be married is a minor and not a widow or widower, the requisite consents have been obtained or properly dispensed with. Since 1970 a superintendent registrar may require written evidence of that consent, or that it has been obtained.[24] There is no legal provision requiring birth certificates to be produced, although if the superintendent registrar is suspicious as to the age of the parties he may ask for them or for other evidence of age, or he may check official records. Here, too, a *caveat* may be entered stating objections against the granting of the certificate. There is an additional provision that anyone whose consent is required may forbid the issue of the certificate by writing 'forbidden' opposite the entry of the notice of marriage in the marriage notice book. This has the effect of rendering notice of the marriage and all proceedings following on it void.

When the Family Law Reform Act 1969 lowered the age of legal

23. *ibid.*, ss. 3(3) and 25(c).   24. F.L.R.A. 1969, s. 2(3).

majority from twenty-one to eighteen as from 1 January 1970, all the legal provisions concerning consents were from then limited to marriages where one or both of the parties was over sixteen but under eighteen. It may be greatly doubted whether the existence of this cumbersome apparatus is justified as a deterrent during only two years of a minor's life. Nevertheless, the majority of the Latey Committee, impressed by evidence of earlier physical maturity among young people than formerly, recommended the reduction from twenty-one to eighteen of the age at which marriage without parental consent could be entered. This it did in the face of the evidence of the instability of these marriages, of opposition to such a reduction by sample polls of youthful opinion and of the evidence of foreign laws, which almost unanimously retain the age of twenty-one, at least for men. The majority accepted that the refusal of parental consent prevented a 'great many' unwise marriages taking place, but felt that 'it is the force of parental persuasion that does the trick, not the stick which the sanction of the law puts in the parent's hand'. This is probably true and it is unlikely that the alteration of the law will lead to a significant increase in the number of youthful marriages. On the other hand there may have been a relatively large number of individual cases in which legal support for the parental action led to desirable results. Prior to 1970 an average of 600 applications a year were made to courts for parental consent to be dispensed with, and these succeeded in just over half the number of cases. There were, therefore, about 300 instances a year where courts supported parental decisions. We do not know in how many of these cases the applicant was between eighteen and twenty-one. Nor do we know how many more marriages were postponed in that age group as a result of parental refusal. But postponement undoubtedly happened – sometimes, it may be assumed, beneficially. The dissentient minority of the Committee, in opposing the reduction of the age, stated: 'The importance of the law is that it defines the terms on which the generations consult and negotiate with each other. To move the frontier across which the argument is conducted would be to effect a decisive change in the balance of power.' There seems to be much good sense in this observation for it is inevitable that the concept of parental persuasion is weakened when advice can be countered by the retort that the child is now legally an adult, for this is to assert, correctly, that the community has recognized that at that age the child is capable of independent judgment. It was inconsistent for the majority to have endorsed the value of parental persuasion and then to have removed community approval of it. It may be that legal provision can do little to discourage teenage sexual experience; but it can discourage teenage marriage and it is unfortunate that the majority report led to its withdrawal from this function.

## Other forms of marriage regulation

It is often remarked that, while stringent conditions must be fulfilled for qualification into many fields of occupational status, those for entering that of matrimony are very weak indeed. Suggestions for imposing more exacting requirements upon those contemplating marriage were made to the Royal Commission on Marriage and Divorce (Morton Commission) (1956). The Commission considered that this matter fell outside its terms of reference, but nevertheless expressed concern on the urgency of the problem and advised the Government to set up at an early date a suitably qualified body to review the marriage law and the existing arrangements for pre-marital education and training. Fourteen years later the Law Commission was entrusted with this task, and its views are awaited.

The suggestions to the Royal Commission related to imposing brakes upon hasty and ill considered marriages. We have seen that length of engagement appears to have some association with the degree of marital stability. In so far as brief engagement implies brief acquaintance, it might be argued that legal steps should be taken to stipulate some minimum period of engagement as a safeguard against impetuous marriages. But there is little reason to suppose that whirlwind marriages happen as often as romantic authors would like us to suppose. Pierce (1963) surveyed the length of acquaintance before marriages of couples married from 1930 to 1959, and found that from 1940 only about one-third married within one year of acquaintance. This was, however, a substantial increase on the corresponding proportion for couples married in the 1930s, where only some 13 per cent married within the first year. Nevertheless, among the one in three couples who marry before they have known each other a year there may well be a number for whom the added formality provided by an official waiting period between registration of intent to marry and actual ceremony might be of benefit in emphasizing to them the solemnity with which society views the occasion. Now that the wardship jurisdiction and parental restraint against marriage end at eighteen, some form of substitute restraint, perhaps limited to persons under twenty-one, might be of positive value in some individual cases. The Latey Committee considered a suggestion for a brief compulsory betrothal period, but rejected it. The Committee was impressed by the practical difficulties it would involve; 'couples about to go abroad; couples who suddenly get the chance of a lease or a flat to rent; or . . . the young man who gets offered a good job in a different part of the country.' Hardship would also be caused if the woman was pregnant. With the exception of couples about to go abroad, for whom exception might be made, delaying a wedding hardly seems onerous in those circumstances. As for marriages precipitated by pregnancy, delay in those cases might be highly desirable. The description of a brief pause between the registration of intent to marry and the marriage as a 'betrothal period' would be unfortunate and inaccurate. But it would be a regulation with a rational objective however imperfectly it may be attained.

When we examine the present English law relating to formalities prior to marriage it is difficult to see to what purpose relevant to modern conditions much of it is directed. The starting point is Lord Hardwicke's Marriage Act of 1753. Prior to its enactment no formalities whatever were required for the formation of a valid marriage. The parties need only exchange promises, either immediately to become husband and wife (*per verba de praesenti*) or to do so on consummation (*per verba de futuro*). This was the so-called 'common law' marriage. The presence of a priest as a witness was not even necessary. Nevertheless it was customary for a priest to be present. This, however, did not prevent clandestine marriages taking place for unscrupulous purposes because certain renegade priests were prepared to witness them at a moment's notice. There was no difficulty about age, provided that the boy was above fourteen and the girl above twelve. These clandestine marriages were of particular concern to rich families. Marriage, in that period, was of paramount importance in determining to whom money and property was to pass and clandestine marriages might be used by the ambitious to establish a claim to the family wealth of their spouse. The 1753 Act was draconian in its solution. It required *every* marriage, with the exception only of those of Quakers and Jews, to be solemnized in accordance with the rites of the Church of England. The ceremony had to be preceded either by the publication of banns in the local parish church of the parties 'upon three Sundays preceding the Solemnization of the Marriage', or by the grant of a 'special' licence by the Archbishop of Canterbury or of a 'common' licence by an authorized clergyman. No clergyman was bound to publish banns unless, seven days before their first publication, notice *in writing* had been delivered to him by the parties giving details of their names, addresses and residence. In the case of a 'common' licence, this could ordinarily only be issued to authorize solemnization of the marriage in the church or chapel in the parish or chapelry within which one of the parties had been resident for four weeks. This did not apply, however, to a 'special' licence which was, and still is, governed by an Act of 1533 entitled 'An Act concerning Peter-pence and Dispensations', otherwise known as the Ecclesiastical Licenses Act. It was part of Henry VIII's anti-papal legislation and simply provided that henceforth applications for licences were no longer to be made to the Pope but to the Archbishop of Canterbury.

The motivation behind the 1753 Act was to protect, not the institution of marriage, but the property of the rich. Only the rich members of the religious establishment were able to arrange for marriages to be conducted by Church of England ceremony. No exception was made for Roman Catholics or Protestant Dissenters. The poor were not considered. Most of them could not write and therefore could not give the required notice. In Parliament, the Bill was roundly attacked as a measure which would encourage extra-legal unions. It would, said Henry Fox, virtually put an end to marriage among the poor 'lest the daughter of a noble or rich family should marry a footman or sharper, or the son a chamber maid or a common strumpet'. But the system lasted for eighty years. The Marriage Act 1836 eventually provided an alternative method of contracting marriage. It conferred upon the superintendent registrars of births and deaths the additional function of issuing certificates and licences to marry and of officiating over marriages solemnized in their offices.

Notice of marriage was to be given to the superintendent registrar in the district where each party (if living in different districts) or both of them (if living in the same district) had resided for not less then seven days. The parties might then apply for a licence, which would cost them £3 in addition to the value of the necessary stamps, and then, after seven days, the superintendent registrar was bound to issue the certificate. If the parties were not prepared to pay for a licence, they had to wait for twenty-one days before receiving the certificate. The licence would be granted only if one of the parties to be married swore or affirmed that either of them had been resident for fifteen days immediately preceding the grant of the licence in the district within which the marriage was to be solemnized.

These, substantially, remain the provisions in the present day. The main changes are that if a marriage is to be celebrated by Church of England rites on the authority of a 'common' licence, the licence can only be issued for solemnizing the marriage in the parish church of the parish or the authorized chapel of the ecclesiastical district in which one of the persons to be married has had his or her usual place of residence for fifteen days immediately before the grant of the licence or which is the usual place of worship of both of them. One of the parties must swear on oath that the residence requirements has been fulfilled, but a false oath does not invalidate the subsequent ceremony, although it opens its maker to prosecution for perjury. A marriage must be solemnized within three months from the completion of publication of banns or grant of common licence.[25] None of these requirements applies to a marriage by 'special' licence, which may take place anywhere at any time according to Church of England rites. A 'special' licence costs £25. A 'common' licence costs £4·50.

If a marriage is not preceded by banns or ecclesiastical licence, it must be authorized by superintendent registrar's certificate, with or without a licence. A licence now costs £2·25. Without the licence, the certificate issues after twenty-one days; with the licence it must be granted one day after the day on which notice of marriage was given. Such a marriage can be solemnized in any Church of England church or chapel in which banns could have been published within the registration district or which is the usual place of worship of either

25. Marriage Act 1949, ss. 15 and 16.

of the parties, or it can take place in the superintendent registrar's office or in a registered building. Registered buildings are usually places of worship of religious denominations other than the Church of England, and marriages within them must take place in the presence either of the registrar of marriages of the local registration district or of an authorized person, who is usually a minister of religion of the denomination concerned; his name and address must have been communicated by the trustees or the governing body of the registered building to the Registrar General and the local superintendent registrar.[26]

The spirit of the 1753 Act still dominates the provisions as they operate today. That Act was designed to combat clandestine marriages. Its main purpose, therefore, was to ensure as much *publicity* to marriages as it could. When the 1836 Act introduced the civil ceremony as an alternative, fears were expressed that this would result in a resurgence of clandestine marriages. This explains the obsession for publicity in the rules laid down. Banns are to be published 'in an audible manner'. Whether the marriage is in accordance with Church of England rites, or in a registered building, or in a register office, there must be at least two witnesses present in addition to the official celebrating the marriage. The ceremony must take place between 8 a.m. and 6 p.m., and anyone knowingly and wilfully solemnizing such a marriage at any other time is liable to *fourteen years imprisonment*. The building in which it is solemnized (except in the case of Church of England marriages) must keep its doors open throughout the ceremony, although this has been interpreted as meaning that access to the part of the building in which the ceremony takes place must not be prevented.[27] But the modern problem is not one of profligate priests officiating over the marriages of young heiresses in dimly lit rooms. It is to create sufficient solemnity for the occasion to draw the attention of the couple to the seriousness of their step. It does not appear that the regulations achieve this. The maximum periods of delay from notice of intention to marry to ceremony are the three weeks which occur in the case of marriage by banns (taking into account the seven days'

26. *ibid.*, Part III.
27. Registration of Births, Deaths and Marriages Regulations 1968, sch. I, Form 22.

notice to the clergyman before their first publication) and where the marriage is by superintendent registrar's certificate without licence. The purpose is to provide for publicity of the notice of marriage. But on the payment of the appropriate sum a licence can be obtained and this reduces the waiting period to virtually nothing. It is difficult to see what purpose is served by this. Concern for publicity would similarly appear to underlie the requirement for seven days' residence in the district of the superintendent registrar to whom notice is given. But in urban areas it is unlikely that the parties will become known in that time. In any event the requirement does not cause any delay in the case of couples who ordinarily reside in the district. Nor do the present provisions make any attempt to draw the attention of the parties to the type of legal obligations to which the contract they are about to enter will bind them nor, a matter of growing importance, to the effect marriage may have on their property. It is improbable that reforms in this direction will result in any significant change in general attitudes to marriage, but the fact that they may be of benefit in even a small number of cases justifies their consideration.[28]

## Health

Unknown to one, or even both, of the parties, one of them may be suffering from serious ill health at the time of the ceremony. If this becomes evident only afterwards, a severe strain may be imposed upon the union. In addition, children may be born into a family weakened by chronic ill health. The high degree of ill health in problem families has been referred to earlier. Wallis and Booker's marriage guidance counsellors (1958) mentioned health problems second after personal defects as a major factor in marital difficulties, and it may well have accounted for the instability of income which Goode (1956) associated with his broken marriages. Were the law to require production of health certificates by the prospective spouses this might be regarded as detracting from the personal nature of marriage and assimilating it too closely to a commercial transaction

28. The Kilbrandon Report on the Marriage Law of Scotland (1970) recommended against the introduction of provisions for delay in that country. This is in line with the general approach of the Committee in advising greater freedom to marry in accordance with diverse religious rites.

where defects should be disclosed. Yet many jurisdictions require this. In any case, for certain diseases the present law does allow a remedy after marriage which is closely parallel to repudiation of defective goods in commercial law.

In the case of marriages taking place after 31 July 1971, if one of the spouses was, at the time of the ceremony, suffering from a mental disorder within the meaning of the Mental Health Act 1959 of such a kind or to such an extent as to be unfitted for marriage or, unknown to the other party, was suffering from venereal disease in a communicable form, or was pregnant by a person other than the petitioner, the other party may have the marriage annulled. Proceedings must commence within three years of the wedding and are subject to the defence of approbation (see p. 180).[29] A recent High Court decision[30] has interpreted references to unsoundness of mind and mental disorder as requiring a very extreme degree of disability so as to make a person not simply *unsuited to*, but in effect *incapable of* marriage. It will be very rarely that such a person will marry without the other spouse realizing his condition. It may therefore happen that one party suffers from a concealed condition at the time of the ceremony which subsequently becomes manifest revealing him to be a person very different from his appearance at the time of the marriage and probably someone quite unsuited to marriage. The other spouse will not be able to annul the marriage and must therefore look to the law of divorce to terminate the marriage should he wish to do so. The provision for divorce will be discussed at a later stage, but it is quite probable that the party seeking divorce in such a situation might have to live separately from the other for five years before being entitled to a divorce.

The decision in *Bennett* v. *Bennett* is defensible on the ground that a wider definition of mental disorder could lead to attempts to get marriages annulled on vague allegations of mental instability. But it adds weight to the suggestion that spouses might be advised to be forewarned about the mental health of their future partner. Where

29. Nullity of Marriage Act 1971, ss. 2 and 3. Where the marriage was before 1 August 1971, proceedings must start within a year of the wedding and sexual intercourse must not have taken place since the discovery of the condition. See Matrimonial Causes Act 1965, s. 9(2); N. of M. Act 1971, s. 3(4).

30. *Bennett* v. *Bennett* [1969] 1 All E.R. 539.

the afflicted spouse suffers from venereal disease, to give a right to annul the marriage after that fact is found out as the law presently does may be to attempt a cure after irreversible damage has been done. A syphilitic child may have been conceived. It is true that the number of cases of this kind which come before the courts is extremely small. In 1966 and 1967, out of a total of 1,558 nullity decrees, only twenty-six were given on the grounds of unsoundness of mind or epilepsy, and seven on the ground of venereal disease. But it will be appreciated that these figures give no indication of the numbers of marriages which may have been put under heavy strain by the presence of these conditions but which did not result in a decree of nullity, either because the healthy spouse did not wish to bring those proceedings or because he could not do so owing to the effluxion of a year since the marriage or the occurrence of sexual intercourse after discovery of the affliction. So a compelling argument can be made for pre-marital certification of freedom from these complaints. Most of the states in the United States have legislation requiring parties who intend to marry to undergo some form of serological blood test for the detection of communicable syphilis and marriage licence will be refused if the disease is present. Oregon goes further and requires applicants for a marriage licence to produce a medical certificate testifying to medical examination and laboratory tests showing that the applicant 'is not infected with syphilis in a communicable stage and is free from other communicable venereal diseases, feeble-mindedness, mental illness, drug addiction or chronic alcoholism'.[31] In Washington, marriage rights are denied to persons suffering from pulmonary tuberculosis in its advanced stages.[32] Unless the disease was such as to be transmissible to children it may be considered excessive to refuse a marriage licence. But it may be thought desirable that a medical report is submitted so that the parties are at least forewarned, as is done in France.[33]

*Persons unsuited to marriage*

Lord Devlin has pointed out (1965) that divorce not only dissolves a marriage but gives the parties their freedom to remarry. He suggested

31. Oregon Revised Statutes (Supp., 1963), 106.071.
32. Washington, Rev. Code Ann. (1961), s. 26.04.030.
33. Code Civil, Article 63.

that the divorce process might be used to require the parties to convince the court of their respect for the married state before that freedom is allowed to them. To disallow a marriage because the judge thought one or both the parties did not have the right approach to marriage would be novel indeed and would confer upon the judiciary a power of moral supervision over the population which many would consider invidious and intolerable. However, until 1 January 1971, judges did exercise a degree of moral censorship of this kind. Under the divorce law operating before that date, a decree could be refused even when the respondent had flagrantly repudiated the marriage if the judge thought that the petitioner's own conduct showed that he, too, had not shown sufficient respect for the institution of marriage. A particularly striking example occurred in *Williams* v. *Williams*.[34] The marriage of the husband, who was the petitioner, had initially run into difficulties when, after five years of marriage, his wife deserted him in favour of an adulterous relationship which lasted two years. However, he took her back when that was over, but shortly afterwards she left him again and, by the time he sought a divorce, she had been living in adultery again for six years. Yet he was refused a decree. The reason was that, after his wife's second desertion, the husband had had casual relations with many women and, although he had now met a woman whom he wished to marry, he had had intercourse with her and had not revealed to her that he was a married man until a few days before his planned wedding with her. In spite of this, the woman said that she wished to marry him 'more than anything'. In the Court of Appeal it was said that it had been 'plainly right' that he had not been given a divorce. It is impossible to see what was to be gained by this refusal and the removal of this power of moral censorship by the judiciary by the Divorce Reform Act 1969 is arguably the most worthwhile of its reforms.

*Three-year bar to divorce*

An important and characteristic feature of the English divorce law is that no petition for divorce may be presented within the first three years of marriage except with the leave of the court. Leave may be given only if the case is one of 'exceptional hardship suffered by the petitioner or of exceptional depravity on the part of the respon-

34. [1966] 2 All E.R. 614.

dent'.[35] The Law Commission (1966), which recommended that this restriction should remain in the reformed divorce law, considered that it was a useful safeguard against irresponsible or trial marriages and a valuable external buttress to the stability of marriages during the difficult early years.

Assuming that it is correct that the provision may have some effect in causing people to think more carefully about a contemplated marriage, this can only happen if it is known to them. This, therefore, is another piece of information which could usefully be communicated to parties who give notice of marriage. Parties should know that if they are not serious about marriage or if they are unfortunate enough to have made a mistake they cannot rely on a quick and simple return to square one. But there may well be cases where the withholding of the decree for three years would be so unduly detrimental to the parties that the harm done to one or both of them outweighs the general deterrent value of the delay period. Hence, it would seem, the proviso excluding cases of exceptional hardship. Unfortunately, the proviso has been unhappily worded and this has led to questionable interpretation. Suppose the couple have separated and are unlikely to meet again. Is an exception to the three year rule made out if one party can prove that the parting was due to a particularly unpleasant act by the other, even though it will not be repeated? There is authority that it is.[36] The section refers to 'exceptional hardship *suffered* by the petitioner'. It is not necessary for the hardship to be continuing or to be likely to be repeated. Yet, if the purpose of the section is to deter from rash marriages, why should those who have made a particularly serious mistake escape from the deterrent provision if they are put in no special danger by the delay period? Fortunately, the courts have not confined themselves to considering past conduct, and have asked themselves whether exceptional hardship will result in the future if the remedy is postponed.[37] This, it is suggested, should be the *only* relevant criterion. And there is another point. It has been stated in the Court of Appeal[38] that the hardship

35. Matrimonial Causes Act 1965, s. 2.

36. *Bowman* v. *Bowman* [1949] 2 All E.R. 127; *Brewer* v. *Brewer* [1964] 1 All E.R. 539.

37. *W.* v. *W.* [1966] 2 All E.R. 889.

38. *Sanders* v. *Sanders* (1967) 111 Sol. Jo. 618.

alleged should ordinarily flow from the conduct of the respondent spouse. Only in a 'very strong' case would hardship suffered by the petitioner unconnected with the respondent's conduct justify an early decree. This is surely entirely wrong. If, as in *Sanders* v. *Sanders*, the petitioner's own mental state is such that to fail to grant the decree would aggravate his instability, there is no point maintaining the three year ban in his case as a deterrent to other persons. The availability of the proviso should not be regarded as a form of compensation due to one party as a result of the particularly heinous conduct of the other but as an emergency escape clause to be used in cases where the deterrent value of the period must be tempered by individual mercy.

# Chapter 2
# During Marriage:
# The Matrimonial Home
# and other Assets

Once the marriage has started it is of course true that it stands or falls upon the relationship between the spouses. Legal rules are unlikely to have much influence upon its ultimate success or failure. While the partnership is a happy one, there is little or no need to pay attention to any legal code. It has been out of recognition of this fact that English law has taken its traditional attitude of non-interference in domestic matters. In a famous passage, Lord Justice Atkin has said:

The common law does not regulate the form of agreements between spouses. Their promises are not sealed with seals and sealing wax. The consideration that really obtains for them is the natural love and affection which counts for so little in these cold courts. The terms may be repudiated, varied, or renewed as performance proceeds, or as the disagreements develop, and the principles of the common law as to exoneration and discharge, and accord and satisfaction are such as find no place in the domestic code. The parties themselves are advocates, judges, courts, sheriff's officer and reporter. In respect of these promises each house is a domain into which the King's writ does not seek to run, and to which his officers do not seek to be admitted.[1]

Most European lawyers, looking at the complex provisions relating to domestic finances and property to be found in their codes would be astonished by this attitude, and even in English law it is not completely valid today. The European codes do not, to be sure, import ideas belonging to the commercial world into family arrangements, but legal principles are certainly to be found operating there. The view that is taken is that even when the marital relationship is successful, a possible area of friction is reduced by having the rights between

1. *Balfour* v. *Balfour* [1919] 2 K.B. 571.

the parties clearly stated so that they both 'know where they are'. And, of course, if disagreements were to develop, there must be some coherent principle upon which the rights between the parties can be decided, and this becomes particularly important if the marriage is broken by separation, divorce or death. Many European lawyers would go further and claim that the very statement by the law of the principles governing fair management between the spouses has an effect on their conduct. Renauld (1966) puts it this way: 'Without doubt it is for the most part a question of atmosphere and goodwill rather than direct legal intervention, but to neglect the role the law can and should play is to ignore the very real indirect influence which the positive affirmation of certain principles and the establishment of codes of conduct can have on individual behaviour.'

English practice, however, has been to refrain from formulating general principles as to how families should be managed. It has preferred to wait until something has gone wrong and then to provide some form of remedy for the aggrieved party. The law on this will be examined in some detail in the light of the criterion of its effectiveness in minimizing the breach between the parties and encouraging continuance of the relationship. In other words, it will be asked how far the existing law contributes to the security which spouses seek in marriage, for, in so far as it does so, it is combating one factor associated with proneness to divorce and is thereby encouraging family stability.

## Occupation of the matrimonial home

The rules governing the security of the spouses in occupying the matrimonial home depend upon their respective property rights in it. They will therefore be considered in three possible situations; (a) where only one spouse has property rights in the house; (b) where they share its legal ownership and (c) where one is legal owner and the other has an interest in it, to be explained later, called an equitable interest.

But first it should be pointed out that the law provides no clear guidance as to which spouse should provide the home or by whom a dispute about its location should be resolved. The matter is to be decided pragmatically by applying the principle that each is under a duty to cohabit with the other under reasonable conditions. So if a wife owns a house and unreasonably refuses to allow her husband to live in it with her, she may be compelled to admit him.[2] But normally it is reasonable to expect the man to provide the home, and if he fails to provide reasonable accommodation his wife need not live with him.[3] He cannot be legally compelled to acquire an acceptable place to live, but if he does not do so, his wife can obtain a maintenance order against him covering her accommodation costs. But it is not very satisfactory to wait until a crisis has arisen and then to ask who has acted reasonably. For example, there may be a genuine disagreement when neither is unreasonable. In such a case, neither may be in desertion, and the wife may be forced to pay for her own accommodation. It should be the husband's duty to see to his wife's shelter unless it would be unreasonable for him to do so.

### Where one spouse alone has a legal or other interest in the house

If one spouse alone legally owns the house, or occupies it under any other property or contractual interest, then the right of the other spouse to occupy the home depends entirely on the duty of the owner to permit cohabitation. The right of cohabitation of the spouse without any property or contractual interest is secured in a number of ways. (In the following it will be assumed that it is the husband who owns the house, for this is usually the case. But the principles apply equally if it is the wife who is the owner.) The owner-spouse may not evict her. If she is out of occupation the law will not, of course, assist the owner in keeping her out unless she has forfeited her right to cohabitation. If she finds her entry into the home barred, she may apply to the High Court for an order securing her entry. The court may order this under the powers conferred on it by the Matrimonial Homes Act 1967. If, however, the house is one that has never in fact served as the matrimonial home of the parties, then the Act does not apply. If, for example, the wife were to be absent from the home and the husband sells the house and purchases a new one in her absence, the courts may be unable under the Act to compel him to permit her to enter the new house.

2. *Shipman* v. *Shipman*, [1924] 2 Ch. 140.
3. *Fletcher* v. *Fletcher*, (1945) 61 T.L.R. 354; *Dunn* v. *Dunn*, [1948] 2 All E.R. 822.
4. *Lindwall* v. *Lindwall* [1967] 1 All E.R. 470.

In *Gurasz* v. *Gurasz*,[5] however, Lord Denning claimed that the courts, or, at any rate, the High Court, has an inherent power apart from the Act to secure the entry of a wife into the matrimonial home by way of enforcing the husband's duty to provide her with shelter. Lord Denning's judgment in this case is important not only in the event of a situation occurring as has been described, but in other possible contexts. Let us suppose that a husband who is the sole legal owner of the house behaves so outrageously towards his wife that she finds it impossible to live there with him. She may certainly leave the house, and it will be her husband, not herself, who will be in desertion. But is she to be rendered homeless by his conduct? The Matrimonial Homes Act can again be of assistance to her, for this Act allows the High Court or a county court, on application by her, to 'regulate' her husband's right to occupy his own house. He may be restricted to using certain rooms or even, perhaps, to using the house only at stated times.[6] But it is unclear whether the Act allows a court to *expel* the husband from the house. In *Maynard* v. *Maynard*[7] it was held that the right of owner-spouse to occupy cannot be *terminated*, no matter how outrageous his conduct. On the other hand, the right of the *other* spouse to occupy under the Act *could* be terminated if the court thought it necessary. But even if the Act does not permit the expulsion of the owner-spouse, it may be that this may be done anyway under the powers which Lord Denning claimed for the court in *Gurasz* v. *Gurasz*. It must be observed, however, that Lord Denning's remarks on this point are wider than justified by the authority on which he relies, for it had previously appeared that a spouse would be excluded from his own property only if this was necessary to protect the other in the conduct of legal proceedings which had been instituted, or where it was necessary in the interests of young children.[8] In *Gurasz* v. *Gurasz* the order was clearly justified on the latter ground. However it is thought that Lord Denning's statement is defensible as the court would be acting in support of a recognized legal right of the aggrieved spouse, namely, to live in the matrimonial home in tolerable conditions.

5. [1969] 3 All E.R. 822.

6. He may be prevented from occupying it for a limited time or until further order of the court: *Tarr* v. *Tarr*, [1971] 1 All E.R. 817.

7. [1969] 1 All E.R. 1.          8. See *Montgomery* v. *Montgomery* [1965] P. 46.

The position of a spouse who has no property interest in the home as against the one who has such an interest is particularly insecure where there is the possibility of the sale of the house by the owner-spouse to a third party. If the other spouse hears of this in time, she may prevent the sale to the third party if she fears that it would result in her eviction. But to do this, application to the High Court or county court is necessary. The court may allow the sale to take place if suitable alternative accommodation is provided by the owner-spouse.[9] The danger is, of course, that the sale may take place without the knowledge of the wife. It was in order to protect a deserted wife from being evicted as a result of a sale over her head that Lord Denning at one time tried to establish that a deserted wife's right not to be evicted by her husband was of such a nature that it operated also against her husband's trustee in bankruptcy[10] and even against third parties to whom the husband sold or mortgaged the property provided that they had notice of the wife's rights. This doctrine appeared to place persons taking conveyances or mortgages of property under a duty to inquire whether the sellers or mortgagors (if married men) had deserted their wives, and the House of Lords eventually held that a deserted wife had no such rights as Lord Denning had sought to create for her.[11] The only occasion where she would have rights against a third party was where the sale was a mere 'sham' arranged by the husband and a friend for the sole purpose of ejecting the wife from the premises.[12]

Lord Denning had not, however, campaigned in vain and, two years after the decision of the House of Lords, the Matrimonial Homes Act 1967 was passed. The Act contains special provisions under which a wife, whether deserted or not, can protect herself against sale of the house to a third party. The spouse who does not have a legal share in the ownership of the house is given special statutory rights of occupation and these may be protected against third party transferees if, in the case of registered land, a notice or caution is entered under the Land Registration Act 1925 or, if the property is not registered land, the rights are registered as a land

9. *Lee* v. *Lee* [1952] 1 All E.R. 1299.
10. *Bendall* v. *McWhirter* [1952] 2 Q.B. 466.
11. *National Provincial Bank* v. *Ainsworth* [1965] A.C. 1175.
12. See *Miles* v. *Bull* [1968] 3 All E.R. 632.

charge under the Land Charges Act 1925. This is certainly a useful provision for a spouse who has no interest in the property of the other. However the solution is not completely satisfactory. Before any protection is acquired, registration or the entry of notice or caution is necessary. This casts on the non-owning spouse the burden of taking a formal step (for which solicitors will have to be consulted) in order to be protected. When should this be done? Should the spouse be advised to do this immediately the house is bought, or, if one of them already owns a house when the couple are married, at the time of the marriage? There is much to be said for the view that the step should be taken when all is blissful between the parties rather than to wait until a crisis arises, by which time it might either be too late, for the property might already have been disposed of, or the atmosphere too emotional for parties to be expected to have in mind the provisions of the Act. Furthermore, if relations between the parties are strained, it can hardly be regarded as a friendly act conducive of reconciliation if one party instructs a solicitor to register his or her rights of occupation. If cautionary registration is considered desirable, this may be something about which parties should be told when they give notice of intention to marry.

A very important limitation on the protection which registration or entry of notice or caution affords is that, even if it takes place, it is of no avail against the owner-spouse's trustee in bankruptcy. If the owner-spouse goes bankrupt, the house can be sold in order to satisfy his creditors.[13] In this respect the Act falls short of the protection which Lord Denning had attempted to provide for a deserted wife by his manipulation of judicial doctrines. The protection of a spouse against the consequences of improvidence by the other raises difficult considerations of weighing the interests of family security against the rights of creditors. It is a matter to which English matrimonial property law pays very little heed, and will be discussed in general at a later point (see p. 105 ff).

In one respect, however, the Matrimonial Homes Act has made a contribution to the security of a spouse deserted by the owner of the matrimonial establishment without the necessity of a formal step being taken. Section 1(5) states that a spouse who has rights of occupation under the Act may either make or offer to make payment dis-

13. Matrimonial Homes Act 1967, s. 2(5).

charging any liability with respect to the property by way of rent, rates, mortgage payments or 'other outgoings' and this shall be effective as if made or offered by the owner-spouse. This does not meet the problem of transfer to a third party or of the situation arising on the bankruptcy of the owner-spouse, but it does give the non-owning spouse an opportunity, if she has the means, to buy time by staying in possession while discharging the obligations of the other.[14]

The principles outlined above will apply whether the owner-spouse holds freehold title to the house or holds a lease. If the tenancy is protected by the Rent Act 1968, the protection of the other spouse requires special provision. This is because the Rent Act is designed to protect from eviction a tenant who is in occupation of the premises at the time when his contractual lease expires and who remains in occupation thereafter. The landlord cannot evict him unless the court is satisfied that this would in all the circumstances be reasonable and that one of a stated number of conditions exists. These conditions include cases where the rent is not paid, or the premises are being improperly used, or where suitable alternative accommodation is available for the tenant, or where the landlord resided in the premises before letting them and wishes to resume residence. The Act only applies to certain classes of dwelling being, in general, confined to unfurnished premises the rateable value of which does not exceed (in London) £400 or (elsewhere) £200. It therefore gives a considerable degree of security to a married couple whose flat or house falls within its provisions. But it is common that the tenant is the husband alone. If he has deserted his wife, he may not be in occupation at the relevant times so as to secure the protection of the Act. This does not matter, however, as the law imputes his wife's continued occupation to him, so she can obtain the protection to which he would have been entitled as occupying tenant. The law goes even further to protect her. If a deserting husband communicates to the landlord that he intends to revoke his wife's implied authority to remain in occupation on his behalf, his act has no effect, for this would be tantamount to eviction of the wife by a deserting husband, which will not be allowed.[15] These safeguards were created by the judges from common-law principles, and for this reason were subject to a startling

14. See *Hastings and Thanet Building Society* v. *Goddard* [1970] 3 All E.R. 954.
15. *Middleton* v. *Baldock* [1950] 1 K.B. 657.

exception. If the husband had discovered that the wife had committed adultery, even a single act, he could revoke her authority to occupy the premises and she would lose her protection against the landlord.[16] The rule from which this conclusion was drawn sounds sensible enough, for it simply states that a husband is not obliged to support an adulterous wife. But it jars in this context because the husband may long have lost interest in his wife. Her protection is, in any case, primarily against the landlord. Why should the law attach so much importance to a single sexual act by a deserted wife? Her need for security for herself (and probably the children) remains unchanged. The answer is that this exception was one of the numerous traces of the ecclesiastical origins of English matrimonial law. The divorce courts were the direct successors to the ecclesiastical courts, which exercised a power of moral censure over litigants. This power permeated the divorce law until 1971, and it would be quite anomalous for it still to appear in the context of the Rent Act. There is, however, good reason to suppose that this exception is no longer applicable because the principle by which the spouse in occupation is held to continue the possession of a deserting spouse who holds the protected tenancy has now been given statutory form.[17] No reference is made to an exception in the case of an adulterous wife and none should be imported.

### Where spouses are joint legal owners

If the house has been conveyed to the spouses in their joint names, they will each have a legal interest in it. Each will, therefore, be entitled to occupy it by virtue of this interest. For this reason the Matrimonial Homes Act 1967 does not apply. This is, however, unfortunate, for it means that the enforcement of occupation rights between spouses who are joint legal owners rests on a different basis from that where only one is the legal owner. So if one spouse is denied access to the house, he may be able to obtain an injunction against the other if this is genuinely necessary to protect his property interest,[18] a matter which it may not, however, be easy to establish. He may also be able to rely on the general powers of the court asserted by Lord Denning in *Gurasz* v. *Gurasz*. But if Lord Denning's view of

16. *Wabe* v. *Taylor* [1952] 2 All E.R. 420.       17. M.H.A. 1967, s. 1(5).
18. See *Des Salles d'Epinoix* v. *Des Salles d'Epinoix* [1967] 2 All E.R. 539.

the court's powers fails to win judicial acceptance, the anomaly might be reached that, without the Matrimonial Homes Act 1967 to assist him, a spouse who is joint legal owner with the other has his right to occupy less well protected than a non-owning spouse. Whether a co-owning spouse can apply to the court for the other to be expelled also depends on the correctness of Lord Denning's dictum. Even if that dictum is upheld in later cases, it must be open to doubt whether the court, under its inherent power, may 'regulate' the right to occupy of a spouse who has joint legal ownership in the same way as, under the Act, it can regulate the right to occupy of a spouse who is sole legal owner.

As regards the dangers of a possible sale to third parties, a spouse who is a joint legal owner is in a strong position. Conveyance of the property cannot take place without his consent. The necessity for registration does not, therefore, arise and it is impossible for one spouse to dispose of the property behind the back of the other. But the situation may well arise that one spouse wishes to sell, but the other objects. If the parties were strangers the courts would normally compel the objecting party to agree to the sale. But where they are married to each other and the property in issue is the matrimonial home, the view has been adopted that, as the parties had initially agreed to use the house as the matrimonial home, it would be wrong to compel a spouse to agree to the sale if the house can still serve that purpose.[19] But where the marriage has broken down in fact, though not yet in law, the Court of Appeal has held in one case[20] that sale should normally be ordered because the house was no longer being used as the matrimonial home. It was said that a spouse should not be allowed to live rent free in a house half of which belonged to the other, even though he had taken over payment of the mortgage instalments. In that case it was the wife who had left her husband and who wanted the house sold. If it was reasonable to expect the husband to find alternative accommodation, the order for sale can be justified. But the reasoning is dangerous. A spouse, especially a wife, expects to find security by entering marriage. So long as the relationship lasts, legal rules safeguarding that security are of secondary importance. It is precisely when the relationship breaks down when the

19. *Jones* v. *Challenger* [1961] 1 Q.B. 176.
20. *Rawlings* v. *Rawlings* [1964] 2 All E.R. 804.

rules deriving from the fact of marriage assume first importance. They should ensure the security hitherto provided by the relationship. If a man deserts a woman, the fact that she is his wife should operate to prevent him from depriving her of shelter. The reasoning of the Court of Appeal ignores this and treats her as a stranger. Its results can be seen in *Jackson* v. *Jackson*.[21] After forty years of marriage a husband left his sixty-five year old wife. He wanted to sell their jointly-owned home and the judge ordered the wife to consent to the sale. It may have been fair to allow the husband to realize his property, but the fact that the judge said that he expected the wife to make her own arrangements for her future accommodation completely undermines the expectation and entitlement of a wife in that situation that her husband shall provide her with reasonable accommodation.

A spouse who is joint legal owner is also in a better position than one who has no legal interest in the home if the other spouse becomes insolvent. His share in the house, which will usually amount to half its value, will be safe from the creditors. Nevertheless, this may be of little comfort, for it will probably be far more important to a wife and children to stay in undisturbed possession of a house than to receive a capital sum which may be too small to put towards another house. Yet the only way in which the creditors can be satisfied is for the house to be sold. Whether to order the wife to permit the sale raises again the question whether the law gives priority to security of the home or to satisfaction of creditors. As in the case of the policy adopted by the Matrimonial Homes Act 1967 where only one spouse is legal owner (see p. 80) here also the law favours the creditors. The courts will order sale. It is, however, most unfortunate that in one case where sale was ordered[22] the judge suggested as an additional reason for ordering it the fact that the wife had been deserted and that the marriage had broken down. As has been suggested above, this consideration should, if relevant at all, be a factor *against* ordering sale. But here too the courts have a fairly wide latitude in the exercise of their discretion and sale may be postponed to allow the spouse in question to make the best arrangements for alternative accommodation which the circumstances allow.

21. [1970] 3 All E.R. 854.
22. *Re a Debtor, ex p. the Trustee* v. *Solomon* [1966] 3 All E.R. 255.

*Where one spouse is legal owner and the other has an equitable interest*

The situation can arise where, although one spouse alone has legal title to the house, the other is not without some form of property interest in it. This happens where the spouse without legal title has acquired an equitable interest in the property. The manner in which this comes about will be explained shortly (see p. 88) but in this context it is necessary to note only the effect such an interest has on the spouses' rights to occupy the house.

Where a spouse has an equitable interest in the home, the technical position in law is that the other holds the legal title as a trustee for each of the spouses. As will be seen, a spouse might acquire an equitable interest comparatively easily, so there must be thousands of spouses holding legal title to a house who are, in the eyes of the law, in the position of trustees, little though they themselves may realize this. The legal consequences which flow from this state of affairs are complex. In the first place, the spouse who only has an equitable interest in the house has a right to occupy the house by virtue of that interest which is distinct from her general right to cohabit with the other spouse.[23] But in most cases she will not need to rely on that interest if she wishes to enforce her right to occupy the home because, unlike the spouse who is the joint *legal* owner, she is given rights of occupation under the Matrimonial Homes Act 1967 which may be enforced by an order under that Act.[24] But her equitable interest may still be of importance if she has it in respect of a house which has not yet served as a matrimonial home, for then the Act does not apply.

Where the house is threatened with sale by the spouse who is legal owner, the fact that the legal owner is trustee creates difficulties. A trustee who is sole legal owner should not sell unless an additional trustee has been appointed, so if the spouse who is not the legal owner hears of the impending sale, she can obtain a court order delaying the sale until an additional trustee is appointed.[25] But if an

23. *Bull* v. *Bull* [1955] 1 Q.B. 234.
24. M.H.A. 1967, s. 1 as amended by Matrimonial Proceedings and Property Act 1970, s. 38.
25. *Waller* v. *Waller* [1967] 1 All E.R. 305.

additional trustee were to be appointed there is no guarantee that this person will be favourable to the interests of the spouse without legal title and, although the trustees must 'consult' her about the sale, they need only give effect to her wishes if her share of the value of the house is greater than that of the legal owner.[26] As the extent of that share may be very difficult, if not impossible, to tell at that time, this test is hardly satisfactory. In any case, this is very remote from reality, for spouses in this situation are hardly likely to be familiar with the technicalities of the law of trusts. There must in practice be many sales by a spouse who is sole legal owner which are technically breaches of trust but, unless the purchaser knows the sale is in breach of trust (which is unlikely), he takes good title. Moreover, if the purchaser takes a legal interest in the property (either, for example, by way of conveyance of the legal title to him or by execution of a formal mortgage in his favour) and he has no knowledge of the existence of the equitable interest of the other spouse, he will take the property free of that interest. In other words, the equitable interest which the one spouse had in the house and which gave her a right to occupy it, vanishes. If the house has been sold and purchase money has been received, the equitable interest now attaches itself to the money. But this will be of little comfort if the main concern of that spouse is to remain in occupation. It is also of no use if the house has not been sold, but has been legally mortgaged to a third party who now wishes to redeem his security. This was the situation in *Caunce* v. *Caunce*.[27] The husband, who was sole legal owner, had created three legal mortgages over the house in favour of a bank, which now sought to sell the house. The wife had an equitable interest in it and argued that, as she had been in occupation when the mortgages had been created, the bank should be deemed to have had knowledge of her interest. Her counsel pointed to a rule of law that mortgagees are under a duty to investigate whether anyone who is in possession of the mortgaged property has an interest in it and that, if they fail to do this, they take the property subject to the interest.[28] But the judge refused to apply the analogy. The rule, he said, applied only where the fact that someone other than the mortgagor was in possession would raise suspicion that that person had an equitable

26. Law of Property Act 1925, s. 26(3), as amended.
27. [1969] 1 All E.R. 722.          28. *Hunt* v. *Luck* [1902] 1 Ch. 428.

interest in the property. This did not, he said, apply where a wife was in occupation, for it was only to be expected that she would be living with her husband. It raised no suspicion that she might have an interest in the property.

The reasoning in *Caunce* v. *Caunce* illustrates with the utmost clarity how alien it is to English legal thinking to conceive of the possibility that a wife might have an interest in the property of her husband simply because she is his wife. Indeed, had Mrs Caunce been a stranger (a mistress or a male friend of her husband), she would have been in a stronger position because the mortgagee would have been on his guard as to whether the stranger was in possession under some interest in the property. It is difficult to find enthusiasm for a law according to which the holding of the married status not only fails to achieve security of occupation in relation to dealings with it by the other spouse but is a positive disadvantage to the person concerned. The Matrimonial Homes Act 1967, however, provides some measure of assistance for a spouse who has an equitable interest. She is now[29] given rights of occupation under that Act which she may register in the same way as a spouse who has no interest whatsoever in the home, and if she does this she will receive the protection given by the Act to persons who register their rights in the manner described above (see pp. 79–80).

## Share in assets

In addition to security in the matrimonial accommodation, economic security involves the acquisition of assets. Where a long standing marriage breaks up and it is necessary to distribute the property accumulated over these years, each spouse is likely to feel entitled to a share in it. This can be of particular importance to a wife. She may have been withdrawn from economic activity for many years while she has run the home and cared for the family. During that time she may have accumulated little or no capital of her own. She may find it particularly difficult to return to the area of work in which she was competent before her marriage. For this reason knowledge that some at least of the acquisitions of the family during

29. She was not able to do so under the Act as originally passed: *Gurasz* v. *Gurasz*, above; M.P.P.A. 1970, s. 38.

the marriage legally belong to her may be very important to a married woman.

## The matrimonial home

In most families the only asset of any substance is the matrimonial home. Where the spouses are joint legal owners, their respective shares are settled by an express declaration in the conveyance, which usually gives them equal shares. Unless there is fraud or a mistake, this is conclusive.[30] Joint legal ownership is therefore the most desirable method of ensuring not only occupation of the home for each spouse but also participation in the fruits of its realization. But if the husband alone is legal owner, the wife, at first sight, is not entitled to any share in its value. If she applies to a court, as she may do, for an order determining what her property interests in the home are, the court has no power to create for her any interests in the house no matter how much it might feel her efforts during the marriage in its management would, in justice, have earned her that reward.[31] Unless it is granting a decree of divorce, nullity or judicial separation, a court has no power to alter the respective property rights of the spouses.

But although the court may not alter the property rights of the spouses during the marriage, it is bound to ascertain what those property rights are, and, although the usual result of one party alone holding legal title is that that party alone is entitled to the proceeds of sale of the house, this need not necessarily be the case. It will not, for example, be the result if, when the legal title is transferred to a husband, he takes it expressly subject to an agreement that the right to its value shall belong to his wife. In such a case the husband will hold the legal title as trustee for his wife, and it is she who is entitled to its value. She has, as is said, a 'beneficial' or 'equitable' interest in the house. But the law goes even further than that. It might not be possible to discover an express agreement between the spouses as to whether the wife should have a beneficial interest in the house or, if she is to have one, whether it should be an interest in the whole of its value or merely some portion of it. Nevertheless, the conduct of the

30. *Re John's Assignment Trusts, Niven* v. *Niven* [1970] 2 All E.R. 210.
31. *National Provincial Bank* v. *Ainsworth* [1965] A.C. 1175; *Pettitt* v. *Pettitt* [1969] 2 All E.R. 385.

parties may lead to the conclusion that there was in fact such an agreement. In this case, too, a trust will be imposed on the holder of the legal title in favour of the other to the extent to which the agreement indicates.

The most difficult case, however, is where there is neither an express agreement about the beneficial interests nor can there be found sufficient evidence that there was *actual* agreement. The spouses may never have addressed their minds to the question as to what shares they should have in the property should it be sold and a dispute arise. Even so they may have treated the house in such a way that, had they thought of the matter, any reasonable person would say that they would have considered that the beneficial interests in the house should be shared in some way. Suppose, for example, the husband becomes sole legal owner of a house which costs £1000. He pays £900 and his wife £100. It is not unreasonable to suppose that, had the question of their respective shares in the value of the house been drawn to their attention, they would have said that the wife was to have one tenth share and the husband the rest.[32] The courts have, therefore, been prepared to hold that, in some situations, a spouse acquires a beneficial interest in the property merely by acting in a certain way. The determination of what these situations are has been a major source of legal controversy in recent years, and it is necessary to appreciate the history of this controversy in order properly to understand the position of English matrimonial property law today.

In legal decisions shortly after the last war it was recognized that a spouse could acquire an equitable interest in the property by making a direct financial contribution to its purchase. If this was by way of assisting in the repayment of mortgage instalments, a process which posed insoluble problems in determining the extent of the contribution of each spouse, the extent of the respective shares was decided by applying the 'palm-tree' method of justice – the spouses would share equally.[33] The importance of this doctrine in the development of matrimonial property law cannot be overrated. Henceforth it could be decided that any wife who had helped in the repayment of the mortgage had thereby acquired an equitable interest in the house and

32. *Re Rogers' Question* [1948] 1 All E.R. 328.
33. *Rimmer* v. *Rimmer* [1953] 1 Q.B. 53.

was entitled to a share in the proceeds of its sale. Invariably she would be entitled to a half share. The only qualification which left some room for judicial discretion, was that the contribution had to be 'substantial'. Simply to pay the occasional instalment over a period of several years would not be sufficient.

Building on this idea, some judges, in particular, Lord Denning, sought to extend the occasions where a spouse (usually the wife) would acquire an interest in the property of the other. In 1957 Lord Denning said that it was not necessary for the wife's contribution to be in the nature of direct cash payments. If she goes out to work and pays for the household expenses, the children's clothing and so on, and this enables her husband to devote a greater part of his income to the repayment of the mortgage, she is, in Lord Denning's view, contributing to the purchase just as effectively as she would be if she handed over her earnings directly for the repayment of the mortgage. In fact, the couple would be acquiring the house by their joint efforts, and where they applied their joint efforts to the acquisition of family assets, they would be assumed to have equal shares in those assets.[34] But at first the courts were reluctant to accept the proposition that *indirect* financial contributions of this kind would suffice to acquire for the contributor a share in the property. In *Allen* v. *Allen*[35] the Court of Appeal decided that indirect contributions could only be taken into account if they first went into a joint pool of the spouses's earnings from which the purchase money was drawn. This is open to the criticism that it would be deplorable if the determination of the wife's interest in the home depended on the chance arrangements of the mechanics of keeping the domestic money. However, it now seems that the majority opinion of the House of Lords in *Gissing* v. *Gissing*[36] favours the view that an indirect contribution, provided that it is financial and substantial, will be sufficient for these purposes.[37]

Once the principle has been admitted that a spouse might acquire an interest in the property of the other by making some positive contribution to it, its potential scope is very wide. This can be seen in *Appleton* v. *Appleton*.[38] Two successive houses had been bought,

34. *Fribance* v. *Fribance* [1957] 1 All E.R. 357.
35. [1961] 3 All E.R. 385.   36. [1970] 2 All E.R. 780.
37. *Falconer* v. *Falconer* [1970] 3 All E.R. 449.   38. [1965] 1 All E.R. 44.

each in the wife's name. The husband, who was a professional wood-carver, had done a considerable amount of work on each house by way of alterations and additions. He had constructed a shed by the side of the second house and he did his work there. It was admitted that the parties had formed no common intention about rights in the ownership of the house, but this did not deter the Court of Appeal from deciding that the husband was entitled to a share in the proceeds of the sale of the house proportionate to the value of the work he had done on it. The same conclusion was reached in *Jansen* v. *Jansen*.[39] In *Button* v. *Button*[40] Lord Denning explained that the kind of work which would 'earn' a spouse a share in the property was the type which one would usually require a contractor to do. It was not enough simply to do the 'do-it-yourself' jobs which spouses often do. This created a very uncertain boundary line and it became very difficult for lawyers to advise clients whether they had an interest in the matrimonial home, or if they did so, what was its extent. This extension of the doctrine in *Rimmer* v. *Rimmer* was eventually tested in the House of Lords in *Pettitt* v. *Pettitt*.[41] The majority opinion re-asserted the general principle that a spouse (or, indeed, anyone else) does not acquire an interest in property legally owned by another unless an intention common to each of them that this should be the case could be proved. The *only* exception to this, it was held, was where there had been a financial contribution to the purchase price. Simply to show that one of the parties had made improvements to the property was not enough unless it could be proved that this was carried out as a result of an *actual agreement* about the sharing in the property, which would be a very rare occurrence.

The Law Commission (1969) thought that the decision in *Pettitt* v. *Pettitt* was too restrictive and that the law should adopt the position stated by Lord Denning in *Button* v. *Button*. A section was therefore incorporated in the Matrimonial Proceedings and Property Act 1970 which states that 'where a husband or wife contributes in money or money's worth to the *improvement* of real or personal property' which belongs to one or both of them, he or she shall, 'if the contribution is of a substantial nature and subject to any agreement between them to the contrary express or implied', be treated as having

39. [1965] 3 All E.R. 363.
40. [1968] 1 All E.R. 1064.
41. [1969] 2 All E.R. 385.

acquired a share or an enlarged share in the property to the extent agreed or, if there was no agreement, 'as may seem in all the circumstances just.'[42] How a solicitor is to advise spouses of their property rights when these may depend on a court's view of what is 'just' is unclear. The requirement that the contribution should be substantial retains the uncertainty which was an unsatisfactory feature of Lord Denning's test. It seems that the Law Commission, which drafted the section, had in mind the very same distinction which Lord Denning made between 'do-it-yourself' jobs (which would not suffice) and more substantial work (which would). But it is to be noted that the section requires the *contribution* to be substantial, not the *improvement*. The contribution may be in 'money's worth', which means labour. Does this mean that a husband who spends a substantial amount of time on minor improvements acquires an interest in the house under the section? This is unlikely, but even if he were to do so it is probable that the extent of his interest would be related to the value of the improvement (or to the increased value of the property after the improvement) rather than to the amount of time spent in making it. There is another reason why a spouse who spends a substantial amount of time making minor improvements will probably not qualify within the section. This is because if he did so, a great injustice would be created between the position of a husband and that of a wife. Most wives spend many hours running the home and maintaining it in general. Although some remarks of Lord Justice Phillimore in *Gissing* v. *Gissing* in the Court of Appeal suggest that a wife might acquire an interest in the home simply by performing her housekeeping tasks, this view did not win acceptance in the House of Lords. If a wife is not rewarded by a share in the house by doing the type of work wives normally do it would be very unfair if a husband acquired an interest in it by spending a large portion of his time making the kinds of improvements husbands normally try to make in the home.

There is, however, one situation apart from making improvements, by which a spouse, by labour, may acquire an interest in the home. This is where he or she assists in the business of the other without reward but does the kind of work which would normally attract wages.

42. s. 37.

By doing this, a spouse will acquire an interest in the value of the business, and if the business, or its premises, is sold, and a house is purchased out of the proceeds, the spouse will acquire an interest in the house proportionate to his contribution to the business. This seems to be the result of the decision of the Court of Appeal in *Nixon* v. *Nixon*.[43] It was stated that free labour of this kind was 'equivalent' to a direct financial contribution. This particular extension of the doctrine of *Rimmer* v. *Rimmer* has not been tested in the House of Lords and may not be consistent with the view of the law taken by that House in *Gissing* v. *Gissing*. It would certainly be a novel proposition if a stranger, or even some other close relative, who worked in a firm without receiving wages acquired a property interest in the business assets. It may be that such a person would be entitled to some form of remuneration under an implied contract or some similar legal basis, but for him to acquire an interest in the property of the firm would be a different, and startling result. So if the doctrine applies at all, it applies only between spouses. For this reason alone it is somewhat suspect because in both *Pettitt* v. *Pettitt* and in *Gissing* v. *Gissing* the House of Lords was at pains to emphasize that there were no special rules relating to the acquisition of property rights as between husband and wife and that the legal principles properly applicable were those of a general nature equally valid between parties who were strangers.

The overall picture with respect to the determination of property rights between the spouses in the matrimonial home may be summarized as follows. If the property is conveyed to the spouses jointly, then, unless it is expressly stated otherwise, each will hold the property on trust for the other as equal beneficial owners. If it is conveyed to only one of them, the existence and extent of the beneficial interest of the other will depend primarily upon agreement between them at time of the conveyance. In the absence of evidence that such an agreement actually existed, the other spouse may nevertheless acquire a beneficial interest in the property (a) if he has made a substantial monetary contribution, direct or indirect, to the purchase. (His interest will be proportionate to his contribution, but if this cannot be clearly quantified, it will be a half interest. Unpaid work in the business of the other spouse may be considered equivalent to

43. [1969] 3 All E.R. 1133. See also *Muetzel* v. *Muetzel* [1970] 1 All E.R. 443.

making a direct monetary contribution); and (b) if he has made a substantial contribution by money or work to the improvement of the property, in which case he acquires such beneficial interest, or enlarged beneficial interest as agreed or, if there is no agreement, as the court thinks just. It is worth noting that the circumstances mentioned under (a) apply to contributions to the purchase of property acquired *before* marriage by parties who intend to marry and who afterwards do marry,[44] whereas it is doubtful if those stated under (b) apply to improvements made to a house before the marriage takes place.

*Other assets*

The most important assets in most families other than the matrimonial home itself will usually be the household furniture, a car and various forms of savings. There is in principle no reason why the doctrines considered above in connection with the matrimonial home should not apply to these items too. Indeed, some judges, notably Lord Denning and Lord Diplock, have sought expressly to single out a class of assets which they have termed 'family assets' to which these doctrines should apply. Lord Diplock has used that expression to include property, whether movable or immovable 'which has been acquired by either spouse in contemplation of their marriage or during its subsistence and was intended for the common use and enjoyment of both spouses or their children, such as the matrimonial home, its furniture and other durable chattels.'[45] Thus defined, the expression would not extend to investment property, to which different rules might apply. The purpose of classing certain types of property as family assets is to assist in the practical application of the general principles already discussed to specific items. So where both spouses are earning, it soon becomes very difficult to ascertain which of the household articles have been acquired by direct purchase by one of the spouses, which have been purchased from joint contributions from each and to which a spouse may be considered as having made an indirect contribution (as, for example, by paying the electricity bill to enable the other to purchase a carpet).

44. See *Ulrich* v. *Ulrich* [1968] 1 All E.R. 67.
45. *Pettitt* v. *Pettitt* [1969] 2 All E.R. 385 at p. 410. It should be noted that the M.P.P.A. 1970, s. 37 (see pp. 91–2) covers improvements to movable as well as immovable property.

The 'doctrine' of family assets simply states that if each are making financial contributions, direct or indirect, to the common household property falling within that class should be considered to be owned jointly. In *Pettitt* v. *Pettitt* some members of the House of Lords criticized the creation of this class of assets as something alien to English law. This is hardly justified, however, because the categorization is only a useful tool to enable judges to apply principles generally recognized by the House of Lords to a complex fact situation. If this approach were eventually to win general judicial acceptance, a working wife who made a substantial financial contribution to the running of the home might acquire not only an interest in the house itself, if her contributions helped the husband in paying the mortgage, but also in its contents and possibly also in the family car.

But where one spouse makes no financial contribution to the running of the home he may find himself with no interest at all in the assets accumulated over the years. The Royal Commission on Marriage and Divorce (1956) recognized the particularly severe injustice this caused in the case of savings and eventually the Married Women's Property Act 1964 sought to remedy it. The Act contains only one section, which reads:[46]

If any question arises as to the right of a husband or a wife to *money derived* from any *allowance made* by the *husband* to the wife for the expenses of the matrimonial home or for *similar purposes*, or to any property acquired out of such money, the money or property shall, in the absence of any agreement between them to the contrary, be treated as belonging to the husband and wife *in equal shares*.

Not only is this section extremely limited in its scope but it is also very imperfectly drafted. It operates, for example, only where the husband makes an allowance to his wife and not where she pays one to him. This may be a rare case, but there seems no reason why the result should not be the same where it occurs and, indeed, this is what the Royal Commission had recommended. The Act only applies to money (or property acquired out of it) which is *derived from* the allowance. Suppose a husband hands his wife £8 on Friday. On Wednesday she spends £2 on the purchase of a candlestick. Is the £2 derived from the allowance? If so, the candlestick is commonly

46. Important words italicized.

owned. But if the £2 is held not to be derived from the allowance but to have *constituted* part of the allowance, then it will belong to the husband. If the former interpretation is supported, it would follow that all the household articles purchased out of the allowance, including perhaps personal effects of the wife, are commonly owned, in which case there exists in English law a degree of community of property more extensive than that prevailing in most European countries. But if the latter interpretation is correct, it becomes difficult to decide precisely at what point money ceases to be part of the allowance and becomes derived from it. If, for example, the wife had saved £2 a week from the allowance for four weeks and then purchased a candlestick worth £8, this would probably be considered as being purchased from money derived from the allowance and thus as being jointly owned. Although there is something anomalous in regarding the first candlestick as belonging to the husband and the second one as belonging to each in common, it is probable that this latter view is correct as the Royal Commission had clearly intended that common ownership should apply only to *savings* from an allowance and purchases made from such savings. There is also doubt as to the extent of the expression 'similar purposes', for the expenses of which an allowance may be made within the Act. Finally, it seems that the type of co-ownership imposed by the Act is one of common ownership whereby, if one party dies, his share does not accrue to the survivor, but passes with his estate. This could cause inconvenience in the case of savings and household articles and probably is not what the spouses would have wanted. The Act is a particularly unfortunate example of the inadequacy of piecemeal legislation as a solution to the fundamental problems of matrimonial property law. At the end of a long marriage it will be impossible to discover out of which moneys particular household articles were purchased and accordingly, for practical purposes, the Act is a dead letter when household effects are distributed at the winding up of a marriage.

Where moneys are accumulated in joint bank accounts, special principles are applicable. Much will depend on the nature of the account, and these principles are subject to the details of arrangements in individual cases. The general presumption will be that the spouses are joint owners of any moneys in the account at any given time. This will be so even where the husband alone pays into the account because he will be presumed to be making a gift of half of it to his wife, a doctrine, it may be observed, standing in sharp contrast to the position where he furnishes a house which is to be the matrimonial home of the parties.[47] The presumption of joint ownership of the moneys may be rebutted, however, by showing that the account was in joint names merely for convenience. This will not be an easy proposition to establish.[48] If a spouse draws money from the account and makes a purchase, the usual result will be that the purchase belongs to him or her alone.[49] This, it will be noticed, is a different rule from that applied by the Married Women's Property Act 1964 with respect to property acquired out of moneys derived from a housekeeping allowance. In certain circumstances, however, purchases from moneys drawn by one spouse from a joint account will belong to each spouse jointly. This will happen if the joint account is intended to serve not simply as a kind of 'clearing house' from which each spouse may draw money for his or her own benefit, but as a common pool in the character of joint savings. If the new acquisitions can be regarded as the conversion of those savings into a different form, the spouses will continue to own them jointly.[50] If one spouse dies, his or her half share will accrue to the other. This is clearly a sensible rule where savings are concerned and is again to be contrasted with the rule regarding savings from a housekeeping allowance. But it only applies where the savings have been put in a joint bank account. If this is not done, and the Married Women's Property Act 1964 does not apply, savings to which only one spouse has contributed will remain in his ownership no matter how much, in fact, the other relied upon them as being savings for both of them.

## General comments and comparative review

Throughout the complexities and inconsistencies of the law of matrimonial property in England as it stands today there runs a basic, and very questionable, philosophy. This can be described as an attitude of *commercialism* towards the determination of domestic rights. This is well illustrated by the comment made by Lord Justice

47. The furniture remains his: *re Cole* [1963] 3 All E.R. 433.
48. *Re Figgis*, (*dec'd*) [1968] 1 All E.R. 999.
49. *Re Bishop* [1965] 1 All E.R. 249.
50. *Jones* v. *Maynard* [1951] Ch. 572.

Davies on the outcome of the appeal in *Bedson* v. *Bedson*.[51] This was a case where, after eleven years of marriage, the husband retired from the army and bought premises consisting of a shop with a flat above it, in which the family lived. For four years the wife helped her husband in the shop, receiving only a nominal salary from him. Then she left him. The premises had been paid for entirely by the husband, but the conveyance had been into the names of both parties and it had been declared that they held the property jointly. Holding that the conveyance established conclusively that the spouses were to share in the property equally, the Lord Justice remarked that he came to this conclusion 'regretfully' because the husband had paid for the whole of it and the wife had contributed 'not one penny'. The law on the acquisition by a spouse of an interest in family assets legally owned by the other betrays the same concern that the spouse claiming the interest must have 'earned' it, either by making cash contributions, or by performing other tasks which were more than a spouse would normally be expected to do and which, therefore, entitled him to the interest.

At this point it may be instructive to contrast the attitude to matrimonial property widely taken in those European countries which operate some form of community of property system. In many of those countries it is the *fact of marriage* which entitles each spouse to an equal share in the family property. The right rests, not upon *effort*, but upon *status*. As Renauld (1966) observes, the wife of a rich man may spend her time at leisure, and yet she would be entitled to an equal share in the common property. The assumption that lies behind this is that it is fundamental to the nature of the conjugal union that not only are the lives and experiences of the spouses shared on a personal level, but that this applies also to material possessions. Property acquired for the family is to be shared not only in fact but in law. Since this is the common attitude most people would take, where spouses in those countries wish to arrange their property rights differently, it is necessary for them to direct their minds specifically to doing so and to make express provision for it.

In comparing the English approach to matrimonial property law with that of European systems it is also necessary to make another

51. [1965] 3 All E.R. 307.

very important distinction. This is between the *ownership* of property and the *management* of it. It may have been a failure by early English lawyers to appreciate this distinction which led to the great difference between the subsequent development of matrimonial property law in this country and its development in Europe. In both England and Europe, medieval law and custom regard it as axiomatic that the husband should have sole power to manage the family property. A wife was under severe legal disabilities and could perform few legal acts without the consent or cooperation of her husband. But this was not inconsistent with the possibility that she might have a share in the ownership of the property so that if, for example, the marriage came to an end by the death of her husband, she could take away from it her share of the property. This indeed is what happened in early English law. But the division of property on death took place in the ecclesiastical courts. These courts existed side by side with the courts of common law and, in the ambit of their jurisdiction, operated a different system of law. The lawyers of the common law courts, therefore, paid little attention to the division of property on death, unless it was land, and concentrated on the property rights existing during marriage. There they saw the husband with full powers of management, and they therefore attributed to him a very wide range of ownership, which even extended over property which had belonged to his wife before marriage. He had complete ownership of her personal property comprising movable property and money and, with slight restrictions, over her leasehold property. The wife, however, retained ultimate ownership of her freehold land, but her husband had the right to use and occupy it during marriage. This right was seen as an *estate* in the land (a form of ownership) which he could dispose of to others. Indeed, he even held his estate (for his own life) after his wife's death if a child had been born of the marriage.

In the course of time the legal position of the husband came to be seen as giving the husband and his family an unfair dominance over the property which had come from the wife or her family. As Kahn-Freund (1955) points out, this friction became particularly acute when personal property began to assume an economic importance which approached that which land had always held. A method was gradually devised which would keep the control of movable assets deriving from the wife's family out of the hands of the husband. Where property was transferred to her for her separate use, it was said that the husband, while still legally owner of it, held it on *trust* for her. This was a device of the courts of equity, and a wife in this position would be considered to be the *equitable owner* of the property, although her husband retained legal ownership of it. So the concept of *ownership* was used to wrest *control* away from the husband. Initially this device was confined to property which had been transferred to the wife expressly subject to her separate enjoyment of it, but when it was decided in 1882 to allow the wife to have independent control over *all* property which she had brought in to the marriage, the technique adopted was to give her separate ownership of it.[52] Of course the husband retained ownership over property which he brought into the family. The result has been that, just as in early English law domination by the husband in management of a family property was reflected by his virtual monopoly in ownership of it, so by the end of the nineteenth century independence of management was matched by separate ownership of the property. Marriage of itself created no property rights in the assets belonging to the other spouse.

In European systems, however, no difficulty was seen in allowing a wife property rights in family goods while nevertheless retaining in the husband sole power of management of it. He would even be able to dispose of it. Usually there would be safeguards so that if, for example, the husband's administration was so incompetent or profligate that it endangered his wife's property she could obtain a court order terminating his management and releasing to her the share in the assets which was hers at the time of the order. By doing this a wife's property holding could be improved when she married because it was usual to allow the wife a half share in the combined assets of the parties. No attempt can be made here to describe the richness of detailed variation in these systems, but throughout there runs the distinction between ownership and control. Throughout, also, is to be found the domination of the husband in controlling the property. For this reason these systems have, over the years, come under heavy strain. The wife's subordinate position became inconsistent with growing ideas of equality between the sexes. As wives increasingly

52. Married Women's Property Act 1882.

brought cash income into the family, modifications were introduced to protect a wife's earnings from her husband's management. She was given greater powers to enter into transactions on her own behalf and to participate in decisions relating to the community. More recently, solutions of a radical nature have been devised largely to protect the wife from debts imposed on the community by her husband.

In the present context there may be two functions which a community system can perform which are relevant. One is to contribute to the security of the marriage during its subsistence by giving each spouse an interest in some or all of the family property while the marriage is still a 'going concern'. But whether the security of a marriage is enhanced by doing this can probably never be ascertained. Does a wife feel security if she knows that the matrimonial home and its contents are legally jointly owned by herself and her husband from the moment she marries or acquires them? Or is she really only concerned, consciously or subconsciously, that, irrespective as to how the property is currently owned, important items of family property cannot be disposed of without consultation with her and that, if anything were to go wrong with the marriage, she would be certain to retain a fair share of the property? It is probable that most wives would not be much concerned about the technical position as to legal ownership at any particular time and that it is the substance of the matter which counts. Concurrent legal ownership can lead to many complexities and a number of European countries where it once prevailed have now either abandoned it or substantially modified it and have sought to secure the economic protection of each spouse during marriage by other means. A brief sketch will be given of four systems, one of which retains common ownership, another which abandons it, and two which adopt compromise solutions.

The Netherlands is one of the few remaining European countries which imposes full community of property taking effect on marriage unless the spouses have expressly provided otherwise. The community consists of all the property (with special exceptions) which belonged to each spouse at the time of the marriage, and property which is brought into the marriage afterwards is added to it. It is regarded as a natural consequence of this universal sharing of assets that debts too should be shared. With special exceptions, they are payable out of community property. The damage which the debts of one spouse may inflict on the community is potentially heavy, so the community can be suspended by a court on a number of grounds, amongst which is levity in incurring debts. One or even both of the spouses may renounce the community when it is dissolved, and if he does so he will not be responsible for the debts incurred by the other. But in return, his share in the community assets accrues to the other side and he will be liable for the whole of any community debts he himself has contracted. The system is somewhat extreme and unsatisfactory and has recently been subjected to two important modifications. The spouses may now contract out of it and opt for a system they find more suitable even *after* they married under the system. Secondly, during the marriage each spouse is now free to deal with those items of the community which he or she has brought into it. Thus, for the purposes of management, the community assets are treated as if they are still separately owned. So for all practical purposes, the fact that they are theoretically commonly owned during the marriage becomes of importance only when the community is terminated, for then they are shared out.[53]

In practice the Dutch system approaches those which have abandoned the idea of common ownership during marriage, but impose it only when the partnership between the spouses breaks up. Such a system is the Danish, which closely resembles the systems of the other Scandinavian countries. Each spouse retains ownership over his or her property during the marriage and may deal with it freely. Only when the partnership is dissolved (or on other specified events) is all the property which each party owns (whether acquired before or after the wedding) shared equally between them. Debts, however, are not shared as they are in Holland. Each spouse pays his or her own debts from his or her own assets. It is the balance (if any) which is shared. Where postponement of the division would weaken a spouse's chances of obtaining a fair share (e.g. if he has been deserted by the other) the court may, on application, order an immediate division.[54]

A compromise between the full community of Holland and the

53. *Nieuwe Burgerlijk Wetboek*, articles 93–115.
54. Danish Act concerning the Legal Effects of Marriage 1925; see Pedersen (1965).

deferred community of the Scandinavian countries is to be found in the provisions imposed upon French spouses who marry without making alternative provision. As in Holland, these result in actual joint ownership, but, in contrast to the Dutch system, the range of assets covered is very limited. Only acquests acquired *after* the wedding are included, provided that they have been acquired as a result of the joint efforts of the spouses or from industry or savings of each (even though these savings might have derived from income from non-community property). Certain types of property of a particularly personal nature, for example, clothing and pensions, are excluded from the community. The community assets are ultimately liable for debts incurred in the maintenance of the home and the children. They may also have to satisfy other debts contracted during the marriage by either spouse, but in that case the debtor spouse must compensate the community. The management of the community is entrusted to the husband, but the consent of the wife is required for certain important transactions, such as dealings in immovable property or the making of gifts, and she may freely spend her earned income. The husband is also liable to account for gravely defective management.[55]

The West German system, like the French, covers only a limited range of assets, but, unlike the French (but following the Scandinavian pattern), does not create joint ownership over this property during the marriage. It is simply shared out on dissolution of the marital partnership by an event other than death. The property falling for division is confined to joint acquests during the marriage, and this is calculated by determining the difference between the total net assets at the end of the marriage and their total value when the marriage began. During the marriage each spouse manages his or her separate property.[56]

It can therefore be seen that not all modern European systems have found it necessary to impose concurrent ownership of matrimonial property as their standard matrimonial regime. Where this is done, problems arise about the management of the commonly owned property. The Dutch solution to this is so drastic as virtually to nullify the effect of the co-ownership. The French solution retains the pre-eminence of the husband. Eastern European systems, in

55. Code Civil, articles 1400 *et seq.*; loi 13 juli 1965.
56. Burgerliches Gesetzbuch, articles 1363–1407.

which common ownership is usual, generally allow *either* party to administer the property as the agent of the other, though this is usually restricted to movables. It would seem that the security of spouses is not significantly advanced by the imposition of concurrent ownership. What is probably far more important in achieving this is the power given by all these systems to each spouse to restrain the administration of the other. In the Netherlands the community can be terminated if one spouse is incurring unreasonable debts (even on his own behalf), or if he squanders the community property or if he unreasonably fails to provide information about his dealings with it to the other spouse.[57] So, also, in France separation of the community property can be ordered in the event of maladministration. Indeed, it is even provided that the dealings of a spouse in his or her *separate* property may be suspended if they are of such a nature as to endanger the interests of the family.[58] Similarly Scandinavian and German law require spouses to deal with their separate property with the interests of the whole family in view and if this is not done and the value of the combined family property is imperilled, the other spouse may apply for immediate dissolution.

The European systems also provide additional safeguards relating to special items of property. In the Netherlands, for example, hire purchase transactions involving standard household articles must be completed by the spouses jointly. Dealings in the matrimonial home in which both spouses are living, or in which one is living alone, require the consent of the spouse who does not have the right of management of it. Third parties must satisfy themselves that these requirements are met, and if they are not met the transaction may be nullified.[59] A French husband is under similar restrictions with regard to dealings in immovable property[60] and the Scandinavian countries also protect the matrimonial home in this way. Germany is an exception, for there the consent of the other spouse to the sale of the matrimonial home is required only if the home is all the vendor spouse has in his estate. But household *articles* are protected.[61] A device found in the United States and Canada directed at protecting the matrimonial home is to allow a dwelling house to be registered

57. B.W., article 109.  58. C.C., articles 220–21; 1429; 1443.
59. B.W., articles 87–9.  60. C.C., article 1424.
61. B.G.B., articles 1365, 1369, 1370.

as a 'homestead'. The effect of this is not only to require the cooperation of both spouses in any dealings with the house, but also to protect it within certain limits against execution for debts incurred by either spouse. A similar technique is to be found in the Joint Family Homes Act 1964 of New Zealand.

With the exception of the right to prevent the sale of the matrimonial home, an English spouse enjoys no protection if he or she fears that the other party is dealing with his own property in such a way as to endanger the security of the family. Even with respect to the home, the position is hardly satisfactory. Unless a spouse is joint legal owner with the other, or has registered his rights of occupation, he may not even get to know of the disposition. The facilities for registration approach most nearly to the 'homestead' legislation in North America and in New Zealand. But it falls short of that legislation inasmuch as this registration has no effect against the creditors of the other spouse, and nothing can be done to prevent that spouse from running up inordinate debts. It is, besides, a negative, almost hostile act in contrast to the positive step whereby each spouse registers a house as a 'homestead'. But the most fundamental distinction between the systems which have been reviewed lies between those which require some form of registration and those which do not. Where protection is confined to registered property, the position of third parties dealing in dwelling houses is considerably eased. On the other hand it may be strongly argued that third parties acquiring a property interest in a house which is clearly a dwelling house ought reasonably to inspect it (either personally or through an agent, such as a surveyor) and in this way it will usually be discoverable whether the vendor has a spouse in occupation. If this were discovered, or was reasonably ascertainable, it may not be unfair to require the third party to ensure that that spouse has consented to the transaction. It is largely a question of what is considered as normal in a community, and clearly this would take some time to win acceptance in England. By way of compromise, a scheme similar to the homestead legislation whereby formal registration of the home will create joint legal ownership is more likely to prove acceptable to current legal thinking.

Where the owner spouse goes bankrupt it becomes largely a matter of policy whether rights of creditors are given greater weight than protection of family assets. In this situation a spouse who is joint owner of family assets is in a stronger position than a spouse who simply has a claim to half the net assets on dissolution, as under the Scandinavian systems. His half of the property should, theoretically, escape the creditors. But even in systems of concurrent co-ownership, once one spouse has incurred debts, it is rare that the community can escape the consequences entirely. Dutch spouses, it was pointed out, share debts, and in France the community has to satisfy them, subject to a right of compensation. Homestead legislation does, however, confer a limited degree of protection over the house as against creditors. Such legislation clearly raises very complex issues which would affect the practice of granting credit in the economy as a whole. In any case common ownership will involve some degree of sharing of debts, even if this is confined to debts associated with the common property. Distinctions of this kind can lead to excessive complexity, and this consideration alone gives favour to a scheme of the Scandinavian kind. Each spouse would be liable for his or her own debts which would be levied against his or her own property. There would be no question of executing against the property of the other spouse unless, perhaps, the debt was of a household nature (see p. 127). On termination of the community the other spouse would have a claim only to what was left, if anything, after satisfaction of the first spouse's creditors. The Ontario Law Reform Commission (1967, 1969) has suggested a scheme of this kind for Ontario, and it has much to commend it. Where the only substantial asset is the home, which the debtor spouse either owns alone or jointly with the other spouse, the conflict between protection of creditors and the family becomes acute. Again, a reversal in the present policy of favouring the creditors would raise very broad issues. But a small step in favour of the family could be taken by extending the existing area of discretion to order sale from cases where the spouses own the house jointly to cases where one of the spouses has no more than a right of occupation under the Matrimonial Homes Act 1967, and then by exercising the discretion in a humane way so that a spouse who has had no benefit from the debts is not cast upon the streets without having had a full opportunity to make alternative arrangements.

But a more important way to protect a spouse whose security is threatened by the improvidence or misbehaviour of the other is to entitle that spouse to apply to court for an order vesting half the matrimonial property in him or her, thereby placing it beyond the reach of the other's future creditors should bankruptcy or desertion occur. This is the essence of the 'deferred community' of the Scandinavian countries. Its introduction would, in fact, require little change in the present English law. At the moment the courts have wide powers to redistribute the property of the spouses between them when the marriage is terminated by decree of divorce or nullity. But, except in the rare cases of judicial separation, the courts have no powers to alter property interests when a dispute arises *during* marriage, although they may order a husband to make a lump sum payment to his wife by way of maintenance (see pp. 112, 150). As Kahn-Freund (1970) has remarked, there is no difference in principle between a maintenance application during marriage and one taking place in divorce proceedings which requires that the powers of the courts dealing with a crisis situation falling short of divorce should be limited in this way. If the courts were to be given this power, its effectiveness would be greatly assisted if each spouse were allowed the right to information about the financial dealings of the other. While this would not be a right which would be easily susceptible of legal enforcement, it is one which could be expected, in the course of time, to influence the behaviour of married people on this matter. In these ways, without going as far as to relegate creditors to a position subordinate to the family, the law can go some distance to protect a spouse and the children against the threat of homelessness and want brought about through the action of the other.

# Chapter 3
# During Marriage: Financial Security and Assistance

## Support

Apart from sharing in the assets, an important element in the security which the law can ensure for a spouse is regularity of income for the family. It must be decided upon whom and to what extent the obligation to meet household expenses falls. If one spouse is failing to make his proper contribution to the day-to-day running of the house, whether in cash or by services, what remedies are available to the other? Which of the spouses must meet the debts incurred in the running of the household? These are questions to which the law must provide an answer. It should give guidance on the general principles to be applied in answering them and specify, to the extent considered appropriate, the detailed application of those principles. It is, however, difficult to find clear statements of principle on these matters in English law. But two points can be made with certainty. A husband is in general liable to support his wife. A wife, on the other hand, will normally be in the position of manageress of the household and will therefore be able to bind her husband to pay for household expenses as his agent. But the detailed implications of these statements and the means of ensuring their enforcement are so haphazard that they present a picture of entanglement and obscurity.

The lack of guidelines appears most clearly if a case is considered in which a husband alleges that his wife is failing to make a proper contribution to the running of the household. Perhaps she is falling short in her management of it, or perhaps she is failing to make a cash contribution which would be reasonable in the circumstances. The law provides no clear statement as to what a wife's household duties are. The law of matrimonial cruelty, however, provides some assistance. It has been held that a husband who is 'bone idle' may be guilty of cruelty if this causes injury to his wife's health.[1] There is no reason why this should not also apply to a slovenly wife if her idleness led to an intolerable situation which was injurious to the husband's health. If this were to happen, it would be open to the husband to apply to a magistrates' court which can then order the wife to pay him a weekly sum of money, but only if the court thinks it reasonable to do this 'by reason of impairment of the husband's earning capacity through age, illness or disability of mind or body'.[2] Alternatively, he could leave her and petition for divorce. It is, therefore, only by bringing charges of cruelty or instituting divorce proceedings[3] that legal guidance about a wife's duties in this respect can be elicited.

If the husband thinks the wife ought reasonably to be making some (or more) cash contributions to the household expenses, he may bring proceedings against her in either the magistrates' courts, or in the High Court or county court, alleging that she is wilfully neglecting to provide reasonable maintenance for himself and the children. Again this only applies if his earning capacity has been impaired, so that a wealthy woman is able to escape any obligations to make cash contribution to the household if her husband is fit to work. Her husband will not even be able to make her liable to pay for debts he has entered into in providing for the household. Even if an order is obtained against the wife it will, if made by a magistrates' court, be unenforceable against her, and no liability will accrue against her while the parties are living together.[4] This last restriction does not, however, apply in the case of an order of the High Court or a county court.

It must be obvious that there are grave defects in a system under which the duties of the spouses to each other can only be ascertained in the context of hostile proceedings between them. Substantial duties which, in most people's minds, the spouses owe morally to each other, become confused in a mesh of procedural niceties. The restrictions upon the occasions when a husband may obtain a maintenance order against his wife impose undue rigidity on a situation where it is

1. *Gollins* v. *Gollins* [1964] A.C. 644.
2. Matrimonial Proceedings (Magistrates' Courts) Act 1960, ss. 1 and 2.
3. Or proceedings for judicial separation, but these are very rare.
4. M.P.(M.C.)A. 1960. s. 7.

generally considered that each spouse owes the other an equal moral duty of support. In the normal case it will indeed be the husband who is breadwinner. But there may be many where a cash contribution from the wife can be reasonably expected. The law is, therefore, poorly adapted to assist a husband who complains that his wife is failing properly to fulfil her household duties. The position of the wife who makes a similar complaint against her husband is rather better and that is the main area in which maintenance law operates. But even here the law is in a very unsatisfactory state and its reform is becoming an urgent necessity. It is, therefore, necessary to consider it in some detail.

Where the husband is handing over to his wife insufficient money to run the house, she is able to involve him in liability for purchases she makes which are necessary for the household. This is obviously a practical matter and will depend on a tradesman's readiness to extend credit in this way. If ready cash is required, there is another avenue open to the wife if she can arrange it. She may borrow urgently needed money from a friend who can then reclaim it from the husband. The reason why these possibilities exist is that a wife is, in the normal course of things, the person who looks after the day-to-day running of the house and therefore she has the implied authority of her husband to bind him for the costs necessary for her to carry out her function as household manager. But there is no implication that a husband can similarly bind his wife, nor that she has any share in the debts which she incurs on behalf of her husband. The rule was developed in a context where a wife had no legal power to contract on her own behalf, and in any case might have no resources of her own to meet any liabilities. The husband was the only person to whom the tradesman could effectively look to obtain payment. Neither of these propositions is true today. The rule is further weakened by the fact that it is an application of the ordinary law of agency and in no way arises out of the matrimonial relationship. It would apply, for example, whether or not the woman acting as 'household manager' was married to the man. It is also subject to express revocation by the man. The husband need only tell his wife that she may not use his credit and the agency vanishes.[5] Since a trader has no means of knowing whether this has happened or not, in law he could be in a very weak position if he grants credit to a married woman.

5. *Debenham* v. *Mellon* (1880) 6 App. Cas. 24.

Why did the common law give the husband the right to revoke his authority and as a result to starve his wife of an adequate housekeeping allowance? Reasons for it were advanced by Chief Justice Erle in *Jolly* v. *Rees*.[6] He said that if a wife could contract for her husband against his will, this would encourage improvident spending by wives 'not only in the ranks where wealth abounds . . . but also in the ranks where the support of the household is from the labour of the man, and where the home must habitually be left in the care of the wife during his absence at work'. But the liability would only cover goods necessary for the running of the household, so the chances of 'improvidence' appear remote. The Chief Justice also objected to the fact that, if the husband were not allowed to revoke his authority, a jury would have to decide on what was a reasonable allowance for a husband to make to his wife. This expression of the traditional non-interventionist attitude of English law in family matters cannot be supported any longer. It is the judge, not the jury, who would now decide the question and judges and magistrates often have to decide similar questions when fixing the amount of maintenance a husband should pay his wife under a maintenance order.

However, in one respect the old common law did mitigate the wife's hardship. If her husband had turned her out, or had deserted her or forced her to leave by reason of his misconduct, he could not further deprive her by forbidding her to support herself at his expense. She had what was known as the 'agency of necessity'. It was, however, subject to restrictions. It would be lost if the wife committed a single act of adultery. It would fail to arise if the wife could support herself from her own resources, a rule which effectively allowed a husband to oblige his wife to look after herself.[7] Worst of all, it seems to have arisen only after the parties had separated, not before, because, as we have seen, while they were sharing the same household, the husband could forbid his wife to pledge his credit. Nevertheless, rusty though it was, the doctrine served some useful purpose. For example, it operated in favour of a wife whose maintenance order against her husband proved inadequate, and it enabled a wife's costs in legal proceedings against the husband to be recovered from him. But the Law Commission (1969) was more impressed by its archaism, and as a result of its recommendations the

6. (1864) 15 C.B. (n.s.) 628.
7. *Biberfeld* v. *Berens* [1952] 2 All E.R. 237.

agency of necessity has now been abolished.[8] It was argued that other remedies for the wife would be more effective. These must now be considered.

If the wife seeks redress in the High Court or county court she is in a fairly strong position. She may allege that her husband has wilfully neglected to provide her with reasonable maintenance or to provide or make proper contribution to a 'child of the family' for whose maintenance it is reasonable to expect him to provide (see p. 152 for explanation of this term). If the court thinks she or any such child is in immediate need of financial assistance it may make an immediate interim order in her favour even before it has made a final determination of the issue. A wide range of orders may be made including a lump sum which can cover necessary expenses incurred by the wife before she made the application. Orders for periodical payments may be ordered to be reinforced by security, and secured orders may last as long as the wife lives or, if she should get divorced, until she remarries.[9] This is certainly an advance on the old law. The provision for payment of a lump sum to offset emergency expenses which the wife had met whether by drawing on her own savings, by incurring credit or by borrowing is vastly to be preferred to the institution of proceedings by third parties under the old agency of necessity.

However, applications in the High Court or county courts are few indeed when compared to those made in magistrates' courts. In 1969 there were only 149 applications made in the former courts compared with 26,753 made for maintenance orders by married women before magistrates. When applying for maintenance before magistrates, a wife must allege one or more of a specified number of 'offences' committed by her husband against her or other stated persons. The offences are that

1. He has deserted her; or
2. He has been guilty of persistent cruelty to her or a minor child of hers or of his who has been accepted into the family; or
3. He has been found guilty of assault on her or of certain sexual offences; or
4. He has committed adultery; or
5. He has had sexual intercourse with her while suffering from venereal disease which he but not she knew about; or

8. M.P.P.A. 1970, s. 33.   9. M.P.P.A. 1970, ss. 6 and 7.

6. He has been for the time being an habitual drunkard or a drug addict; or
7. He has compelled her to submit herself to prostitution; or
8. He has wilfully neglected to provide reasonable maintenance for her or a dependent child of the family.[10]

The reason for the presence of the offences 2–7 is that in these cases the wife can obtain, together with a maintenance order, a further order which relieves her of her obligation to cohabit with the husband, and which deals with the custody of the children. But a non-cohabitation order would be inappropriate in cases 1 and 8. These are the common grounds upon which maintenance alone is claimed, the last one being parallel to the ground upon which maintenance may be claimed in the higher courts. Yet there are differences in the type of relief the magistrates can offer. Like the higher courts, magistrates' courts may order weekly cash payments to be made and, since 1968, these may be of any amount,[11] but magistrates cannot order them to be secured against any capital asset the husband might have. They may, however, make an interim order if the hearing is adjourned for more than a week. But it is doubtful whether the order, when made, can be back-dated to the period between making the complaint and the first hearing, and even more doubtful with respect to the period between the time the husband stopped supporting the wife and her complaint to the court. It is in covering these periods that the powers of the higher courts to award lump sum payments are so useful. No court will make an order in favour of a wife who has committed adultery[12], but if she commits adultery after it is made, magistrates are *bound* to revoke the order whereas the higher courts simply *may* do so.[13] There is also no rule for the higher courts, as there is for magistrates, that liability under an order fails to accrue while the parties cohabit, so those courts may make an order determining the proper amount of housekeeping money a husband should pay his wife while he is living with her. This was done by the High Court in *Caras* v. *Caras*.[14]

10. M.P. (M.C.) A. 1960, s. 1.
11. Maintenance Orders Act 1968.
12. *West* v. *West* [1954] P. 44; M.P.(M.C) A. 1960, s. 2(3)(b).
13. *Spence* v. *Spence* [1964] 3 All E.R. 61; *ibid.*, s. 8(2).
14. [1955] 1 All E.R. 624.

The position is unsatisfactory enough when these differences exist between the approaches adopted by the higher courts and the magistrates' courts. But it is made even worse by the fact that the grounds upon which a complaint can be made in court may involve consideration of extremely complex technical rules relating to matrimonial misconduct. If the complaint is made in the magistrates' court on the ground of desertion, it becomes necessary to decide whether the circumstances of the separation amount to desertion in law and, further, if the complaint is contested by the other party, which of the two is in fact the deserter. If the complaint is on the ground of persistent cruelty, the court must be aware of the complicated law about matrimonial cruelty. It is also open to a defendant in proceedings based on adultery or cruelty to claim that, even if he is guilty of either of these offences, the other party should not be allowed to hold them against him because they were either connived at by the other party or have since been condoned. Even if the complaint is only on the ground of wilful neglect to provide reasonable maintenance, issues of this kind may arise. A husband can only be guilty of wilful neglect to maintain his wife if he is under a common law duty to maintain her. He will not be under a duty to maintain her if she has deserted him or is guilty of some other matrimonial offence *unless*, of course, he has connived at it or condoned it. In this way the law as to matrimonial offences can also arise in apparently straightforward 'wilful neglect' cases.

In a later chapter the reformed law of divorce will be discussed in detail (see ch. 9). The fundamental purpose of the reform was to change its basis from one resting upon a determination of matrimonial *guilt* as between the parties to one resting upon the *fact* of marriage breakdown. It is therefore both confusing and impracticable for the whole weight of the law relating to matrimonial offences, which has been significantly reduced in the law of divorce, to be retained in maintenance proceedings which mainly take place before magistrates. This is not to state that the principles upon which divorce petitions should be decided should be exactly the same as those applicable to maintenance proceedings. When it is necessary to decide whether a spouse should make payments to the other, some assessment of conduct is generally thought to be necessary. But the extreme complexity and technicality of the law relating to matrimonial offences make it entirely unsuitable for application in magistrates' courts, and, indeed, in any court deciding a maintenance claim because it is of prime importance that the powers of the court should be of maximum flexibility. The unsatisfactory state of maintenance law has been drawn to the attention of the Lord Chancellor by Mr Leo Abse M.P. and it was recognized that this was a matter which required attention.[15] Reform in this area is, therefore, to be anticipated. Nevertheless, an account of the law relating to matrimonial offences should be given, not only because it does in fact represent the law applicable in maintenance proceedings as at 1 January 1971, but because it formed the foundation of the divorce law ever since the introduction of judicial divorce in this country until the reform of that law on 1 January 1971. A proper appreciation of the modern divorce law requires understanding of the system which it has superseded, and the account given below will assist in this.

## Desertion

It is not only the spouse who leaves home who may be in desertion. If he has been forced to leave as a result of the misconduct of the other, then the one who remains behind will be the deserter. The latter is said to be in 'constructive' desertion. If the circumstances which led to the separation were not due to misconduct by either, but nevertheless they justified the separation (as where, for example, one spouse suffers from severe mental illness putting the other in danger) then neither will be in desertion. The drawing of these distinctions in different factual situations has provided some of the most difficult and least satisfying problems in matrimonial law. Let us take the situation where a wife leaves her husband and alleges that his conduct has driven her to doing this. If she is to succeed in proving desertion against her husband she must show two things. First, a factual situation of such a 'grave and weighty' nature that she could not reasonably be called upon to endure it; second, an intention on the part of her husband to bring the cohabitation permanently to an end. The same of course applies if it is a husband alleging constructive desertion by his wife.

Whether the first requirement is met in any given case clearly

15. *The Times*, 9 November 1970.

offers scope for great divergence of opinion. The courts can only lay down broad lines of guidance. In earlier cases a very high 'level of endurance' was expected. Reference has already been made to the case of *Buchler* v. *Buchler* where the Court of Appeal decided that a wife was not justified in leaving her husband despite the humiliating nature of his neglect of her in preference for the company of his pig man (see p. 43). A different, and far more flexible, approach was laid down in *Hall* v. *Hall*,[16] but only after a sharp conflict of judicial opinion. The marriage in that case had been unhappy as a result of the husband's drinking habits. The wife alleged that he came home drunk on most nights of the week, but this led to no more than the usual kind of disturbance which results from a drunken man returning home. The wife eventually left the home without warning and claimed that he should maintain her. The magistrates decided that this was conduct which she could not be expected to endure and found the husband guilty of constructive desertion. The Divisional Court reversed this finding. Mr Justice Cairns said that, in his view, drunkenness with its ordinary accompaniments of rowdiness and inconvenience for those who have to deal with the drunkard could not be considered such that a reasonable man would not expect his wife to stay and put up with it. 'Unfortunately,' he said, 'there are many drunken husbands and many wives who suffer the unhappiness of living with them.' But this view was in its turn reversed when the case was taken to the Court of Appeal. There it was pointed out that the decision of the magistrates was 'thoroughly sensible' and that it was 'not surprising' that the wife had left. Lord Justice Diplock made the significant observation that the question as to whether a spouse should be called upon to endure certain conduct was simply one of fact and one which magistrates were particularly suited to decide in the light of their knowledge of the social background of the parties. If this approach is the correct one, it means that magistrates and judges deciding this element of the offence must not do so by applying *their opinion* as to whether the conduct was intolerable, but by deciding what *in the neighbourhood* would be considered behaviour justifying a spouse leaving the house.

The second element required for constructive desertion is an intention on the part of the deserter to put the marriage to an end. But

16. [1962] 3 All E.R. 518.

this does not mean that a man can treat his wife intolerably and then defend himself from a charge of constructive desertion by saying that he enjoyed maltreating her and never intended her to leave. It is enough if he persists in conduct which a reasonable man would realise is bound to result in the wife's departure. In such a case he will be presumed to have intended to break up the marriage, no matter how much he may assert to the contrary.[17] But if the party whose conduct has led to the separation is not responsible for his actions, he cannot be said to intend to bring the marriage to an end. He will not, therefore, be in desertion of the other, and if his condition is sufficiently serious, nor will the spouse who has left the home be in desertion, for he or she will have sufficient excuse for having done so. Although this will deprive both parties of one of the grounds for claiming maintenance against the other specified in the Matrimonial Proceedings (Magistrates' Courts) Act 1960, a claim may, in these circumstances, be made on the ground that the party against whom the claim is made is wilfully neglecting to provide the other with reasonable maintenance. As neither are in desertion and the separation has been forced on them, the husband's duty to support his wife will remain.[18] A husband suffering from mental disorder may even be able to obtain an order from his wife since his earning capacity will probably be impaired by reason of his illness. But although the husband's obligation to his wife will continue, it is not clear how far a mentally ill person can be said to have neglected to provide maintenance 'wilfully'.

There is another situation in which parties living separately may nevertheless not be in desertion of each other. This is where the separation has taken place as a result of a mutual agreement to live apart. The agreement need not be formal. It is sufficient that the parting was understood to be what both parties wanted. What is particularly important about a situation of this kind is that there appears to be a rule that, where spouses have separated by consent, neither party is under any obligation to maintain the other unless an agreement to this effect was expressly made at the time of the separation or can be implied into the circumstances. This 'rule' is of

17. *Lang* v. *Lang* [1955] A.C. 402; *Hall* v. *Hall*, see p. 116; *Saunders* v. *Saunders* [1965] 1 All E.R. 838.
18. *Tickle* v. *Tickle* [1968] 2 All E.R. 154.

dubious authority, but has been accepted as good law by the Court of Appeal.[19] The soundness of the rule is rendered particularly suspect by the fact that, if there was an agreement that, for example, the husband should pay a sum to his wife after their consensual separation, and in the course of time this sum becomes inadequate, the husband is liable to be ordered to pay his wife a larger sum.[20] It is extremely odd that no such order can be made if they parted on the understanding that he would pay her nothing or if they simply did not address their minds to the question (because, perhaps, at the time the wife was sufficiently provided for from other sources). It is also a very undesirable rule in itself. The dividing line between desertion and separation by consent can often be very difficult to draw.[21] The right to support should arise from the status of the parties and not from technical niceties of this nature. Of course, the circumstances of the separation, the events which have happened since that time (for example, any change in the health of the parties) and other matters, should always be taken into account in deciding what is the proper sum to award.

### Persistent cruelty

In the context of maintenance law, the term 'cruelty' bears the same meaning as it did in divorce law before 1971 with the modification that, to provide a successful foundation for a maintenance claim, the cruelty must be 'persistent'. It is, therefore, necessary to prove that the complainant has suffered injury to health.[22] This is fairly easily satisfied as evidence of nervousness and anxiety will often suffice. But if injury to health cannot be established, the charge must be one of constructive desertion. But it is not any conduct that damages health which amounts to cruelty. It must be of the same severe character as that which is required to justify a spouse to leave. If, therefore, a charge of cruelty is dismissed on the ground that the facts alleged do not disclose a sufficiently 'intolerable' situation, it will not be open to a claimant to allege the same facts as a basis for a

19. *Northrop* v. *Northrop* [1967] 2 All E.R. 961.
20. *Tulip* v. *Tulip* [1951] P. 378.
21. See *Nutley* v. *Nutley* [1970] 1 All E.R. 410.
22. *Russell* v. *Russell* [1897] A.C. 395.

charge of constructive desertion against the other spouse.[23] On the other hand, if a charge of constructive desertion fails because the necessary intent cannot be established (because, for example, the person against whom the charge is made is mentally ill), a charge of cruelty may well succeed. The reason for this distinction is that, in *Williams* v. *Williams*[24] the House of Lords decided that matrimonial cruelty referred to a *state of affairs* which was intolerable and not to a morally reprehensible *state of mind* in one of the spouses. It was not necessary to pay any attention to the respondent spouse's state of mind if the situation created by his conduct was sufficiently unendurable. Therefore an insane spouse, or one who acted under irresistible impulse, could be 'cruel' for the purpose of matrimonial law.

Although a decision of the House of Lords is authoritative in our judicial system, it must be doubted, however, whether the decision in *Williams* v. *Williams* can be relied on as a certain guide to a court's interpretation of matrimonial cruelty. The reason is that, although the decision makes it clear that the House of Lords considered that henceforth questions of *moral blameworthiness* were no longer relevant for determining whether the 'offence' of cruelty had been established, three subsequent decisions of the Court of Appeal have re-introduced the requirement that a person cannot be said to be 'cruel' in matrimonial law unless he is to some extent at fault.[25]

Two of those cases arose out of the consistent failure of one spouse to afford sexual relations to the other, and the reaction of the judges is a remarkable illustration of the degree to which conscious or subconscious feelings on matters concerning sexual behaviour can overcome the normal rational processes. For, although it is clear that refusal to have sexual intercourse with a spouse can amount to cruelty if it is wilful, it is equally clear that, in *Williams* v. *Williams*, the House of Lords laid it down that henceforth wilfulness was not an *essential* factor in proving matrimonial cruelty. Nevertheless, in these two cases the Court of Appeal insisted that the conduct would only amount to cruelty if it was indulged in wilfully and callously. It could not be cruelty if it resulted from a physical or psychological affliction.

23. *Ogden* v. *Ogden* [1969] 3 All E.R. 1055.   24. [1964] A.C. 698.
25. *B.(L)* v. *B.(R)*. [1965] 3 All E.R. 263; *Le Brocq* v. *Le Brocq*, [1964] 3 All E.R. 464; *Sheldon* v. *Sheldon* [1966] 2 All E.R. 257.

These cases can only be supported, if at all, on the ground that where this particular form of conduct is relied on as constituting cruelty, the sting that makes it unendurable lies not so much in the effect in being deprived of sexual relations but in the vicious intent behind it.

### Condonation

In addition to desertion and cruelty, a complainant in maintenance proceedings in a magistrates' court may allege the offence of adultery. But neither adultery nor cruelty may be relied on if they have been 'condoned'. In the same way, it is no defence to a claim alleging wilful neglect to provide reasonable maintenance to say that the other party has committed 'cruel' conduct or adultery if that cruelty or adultery has been condoned. Condonation arises where the wronged party reinstates the other into his role as a spouse and forgives him for having committed the offence. Forgiveness, however, does not necessarily imply that the offended spouse no longer feels the hurt done. In this context it is used in a legal, not a psychological sense. It means that the person wronged has given the other spouse to believe that he will not take any legal proceedings against the other as a result of the offence.[26]

The rationale behind condonation as a bar to an allegation is that once a matrimonial offence has been committed against the innocent party, this amounts to a repudiation of marital obligations by the guilty party and automatically gives the innocent party the right to seek certain remedies. It is thought to be unfair to the guilty party to allow the innocent spouse to take advantage of the remedy while at the same time affirming that the matrimonial relationship still exists by continuing to accept the guilty party as a spouse. This is a perfectly reasonable doctrine when applied to commercial transactions. A party cannot take benefits under a contract and at the same time allege that he has no obligations under it because the other side has repudiated it. He cannot, it is said, both approbate and reprobate. But to apply this doctrine to marriage is to ignore the fact that marriage is far more than a contractual relationship. It is a personal relationship. Adultery by one party is not equivalent to breach of contract. It may be the outcome of a deterioration in the relationship and may severely shake it. But it will not necessarily lead to its

26. *Hearn* v. *Hearn* [1969] 3 All E.R. 417.

collapse. A relationship of this kind is a continuous process, not divisible into cut and dried legally defined sections like a commercial arrangement.

Yet the law of condonation is riddled with legalism. Suppose a husband has been guilty of adultery. The wife, still in love with him, continues (or resumes) cohabitation in an attempt to save her marriage. After a time it becomes clear he no longer cares for her and she realises the relationship is irretrievably broken. She would be held to have condoned his adultery and would have to await his commission of another offence in order to obtain a remedy. By 1963 the realisation that this rule penalized a spouse who attempted reconciliation led to statutory intervention and it is now provided that 'adultery or cruelty shall not be deemed to have been condoned by reason only of a continuation or resumption of cohabitation between the parties for one period not exceeding three months, or of anything done during such cohabitation, if it is proved that cohabitation was continued or resumed, as the case may be, with a view to effecting a reconciliation.'[27] From 1971 this provision will be irrelevant in divorce cases, for condonation as such has been removed as a bar to divorce under the new divorce system introduced by the Divorce Reform Act 1969. However, it is still operative in relation to allegations of adultery and cruelty in claims for separation or maintenance orders in magistrates' courts.

The purpose of the 'reconciliation' provision introduced in 1963 seems clear enough. If the relationship between the parties does not immediately terminate on the commission of the offence but survives, though wounded, the law will allow three months grace for the parties to decide whether the offence has finally destroyed it. But nothing so simple has emerged from judicial interpretation of the subsection. The first qualification put upon it was in *Brown* v. *Brown*.[28] Although profoundly upset by the discovery of the wife's misconduct, the husband, in a genuine attempt to save the marriage, expressly forgave her and tried to resume normal married life. But the wound had gone deeper than he had thought and within a short time he left her. She now claimed financial relief against him through the

27. Matrimonial Causes Act 1965, s. 42(2), re-enacting Matrimonial Causes Act 1963, s. 2(1).
28. [1967] P. 105.

magistrates' court. His defence was that her adultery justified his departure, but she argued that he had condoned it. The Divisional Court upheld the finding of the magistrates that he had condoned the adultery and that the 'reconciliation' clause did not apply. Sir Jocelyn Simon, the President of the Divorce Division, said that the evidence showed that, as the husband had expressly forgiven his wife before going back to her, the resumption of cohabitation *resulted from* reconciliation and was not instituted *with a view to effecting* reconciliation, which was what the clause required. This decision is little less than disastrous and almost completely nullifies the effect of the clause. An attempt at reconciliation does not start propitiously if the offended party hedges his forgiveness with legalistic reservations as to his rights should the resumption prove a failure. The President argued that to allow one party a reconciliation with the possibility of recanting afterwards would be to 'destroy the effect of the reconciliation' and would in fact prejudice its chances. This is fallacious. The guilty party has nothing to lose by partaking in the reconciliation even if the innocent one may withdraw within three months. But the innocent party, on the President's interpretation, will be deterred from making true reconciliatory gestures. Nor is it unfair on the guilty party to keep his position open for this short time. If the reconciliation truly succeeds then there is nothing more to be said. If it fails within that time he or she is in no worse position than if no reconciliation had been attempted. The reasoning of Sir Jocelyn Simon was, however, approved by the Court of Appeal in a later case.[29]

Let us assume that the parties are not in fact completely reconciled on resuming cohabitation because one of them has not unreservedly forgiven the other. He has wanted the marriage to continue, but, perhaps dubious whether it could do so, saw himself as giving the other spouse a 'last chance'. The attempt at reconciliation fails. Has he condoned the offence or will the 'reconciliation clause' apply? *Quinn* v. *Quinn*[30] holds that it does not apply. It is true that the spouses are not fully reconciled in the sense that they were held to be in the *Brown* case, but, it was held, it is not enough for one of them to have 'mental reservations' about the resumption of marital life. He must communicate these to the other party. There should be mutual agreement between the two that the resumption is to be in

29. *Herridge* v. *Herridge* [1966] 1 All E.R. 93.     30. [1969] 3 All E.R. 1212

the nature of a 'trial period'. This decision is astonishing. It is in direct contradiction to the view of Sir Jocelyn Simon in the *Brown* case that the clause was *not* designed to permit a 'trial' period. This view is in fact highly dubious, but Sir Jocelyn and the Court of Appeal in *Quinn* cannot both be right. But far more serious is that it closes even the small gap for operation of the clause left by the decision in *Brown*. The only situation in which it can operate now appears to be where the spouses *expressly* agree that they will live with each other in a spirit of probation, being careful not to give the impression that the past offence has been forgiven. Anything more remote from the true workings of human nature is hard to imagine and these decisions should be swept away when the entire law of maintenance is reviewed.

*Connivance*

Passing from condonation to connivance, it is to be noted that connivance applies only to the offence of adultery. Magistrates' courts therefore may be required to consider the defence when separation or maintenance orders are claimed on that ground. Connivance differs from condonation because, while the latter defence deprives a party of a remedy on the ground of his failure, subsequent to the offence, to repudiate the relationship, the former deprives him of the opportunity to complain of it because he has actually instigated it. This is perfectly straightforward and acceptable in any context. But even so simple an idea is not free from difficulty. What is to happen if a spouse gives the other limited licence to commit adultery? A wife thinks that if she allows her husband to sleep once or twice with a girl with whom he is infatuated, this will cure him. He in fact goes away and lives with the girl. Has she connived at the further consequence of the adultery? In so far as the justification for the defence rests upon the claimant's implication in the offence it would appear that it should be limited to the extent of that implication. Consequences following from it which were not intended, indeed, vehemently opposed, by the claimant spouse can hardly be said to be connived at by him. But if this is the reasonable view, it was nevertheless the one rejected by the House of Lords in *Godfrey* v. *Godfrey*.[31]

31. [1965] A.C. 444.

In that case the husband bitterly fought to retain the affections of his wife who was in love with another man. At one point she invited the other man to the house. The husband, under the strain, returned home the worse for drink and discovered them embracing. In despair he challenged them: 'If you two want to go to bed together, why the hell don't you?' This they did, but before morning the husband had turned the other man out. His wife then left to live with her lover. The husband, it was held, could not complain of his wife's initial or continued adultery because he had connived at it. In law, therefore, a spouse will be taken to have instigated acts causally related to an initial act even though consent may have long since been withdrawn. While perhaps appropriate where it is alleged that the complainant's misconduct conduced to the offence (a separate defence), this test seems inappropriate to the nature of connivance. Some cases[32] suggest that this consequence can only be avoided if the complainant subsequently 'condoned' the initial act of adultery. There appears to be some confusion of thought in this suggestion. It is very difficult to see how a spouse who reinstates a partner who has committed an offence which he has encouraged can properly be said to 'forgive' that offence. He certainly is not giving up any rights of action with respect to it, for he has none. Also, condonation operates to deprive a spouse of a remedy against the other; on this suggestion it would have the unusual effect of serving as a condition giving him a remedy. The true explanation of the cases holding that connivance is broken by an intervening 'condonation' must be that the acts which are said to be amounting to 'condonation' of the initial act are really indications that consent to subsequent acts was withdrawn. If this is so, the decision of the House of Lords in the *Godfrey* case cannot be supported.

### Other defences

The Matrimonial Proceedings (Magistrates' Courts) Act 1960[33] expressly states that adultery may not be relied on if the party relying on it has 'by wilful neglect or misconduct conduced to' the adultery Although it is not stated explicitly in the Act, analogy with the law

32. *Gorst* v. *Gorst* [1952] P. 94; *Richmond* v. *Richmond* [1952] 1 All E.R. 838.
33. S. 2(3)(a).

of divorce before the reform suggests that these defences would also be available to a party against whom desertion or cruelty were alleged. This contemplates situations where, for example, a husband so neglects or ill treats his wife that she is forced into prostitution. It would be obviously unjust for one party to allege as an offence against him by the other conduct to which his own behaviour has led. But cases are not always clear cut. If a husband develops an affection for another woman, will this be misconduct which conduces his wife's adultery? There may well be a causal link between the two.[34] If desertion is the offence charged, any misconduct which has conduced to it will probably be sufficient to have entitled the alleged deserter to leave, in which case desertion will be negatived. But in one case[35] it was said that there could be a class of acts which, though not serious enough to have entitled a spouse to leave the other, might nevertheless be of sufficient gravity to be held to have conduced to his departure. If cruelty is in issue, the form which this defence takes is slightly different. It is said that the complainant spouse so acted as to bring the cruelty upon himself; in effect, that his conduct *provoked* it. In 1952 it was said in the House of Lords that 'when a husband and wife have reached the stage of unending accusations and recriminations, the wife's satisfaction in inflicting pain may be the reflex of the bitterness and pain suffered by her'.[36] The reasoning here is that one cannot blame a person for acts which would otherwise amount to cruelty if they are a reaction to one's own conduct. There is a good deal of interaction between the personalities of married people, and the consequence of this reasoning is that the greater the intensity of the conflict, the less either side is to blame, and, consequently the less likely is the conduct of either to fall within the legal definition of cruelty. The logic of this conclusion can, however, be avoided by application of the decision of the House of Lords in *Williams* v. *Williams*[37] where, as has been remarked earlier, it was held that legal cruelty was to be discovered by looking to the facts rather than the morality of the parties. But it was observed that there has been judicial defection from that decision, and it is regrettable

34. See *Brown* v. *Brown* [1956] P. 438.
35. *Postlethwaite* v. *Postlethwaite* [1957] P. 193.
36. *King* v. *King* [1953] A.C. 124.
37. [1964] A.C. 698; see p. 119.

to note that at least two cases subsequent to the *Williams* case have ignored its implications on the defence of provocation in cruelty.[38]

## Comparative review

It may not be an unjust comment on the law of maintenance as it operates between spouses that its deficiency in providing a clear exposition of the duties of the spouses towards each other and the common household is matched by the excessively technical and obscure nature of the rules for determining the balance of guilt between them. The position in the European civil codes is exactly the reverse. The sections of those codes dealing with the duties of the spouses to each other commence with general statements of principle setting out the mutual obligations of the spouses, followed by detailed rules as to how, in normal circumstances, those obligations are to be apportioned between the spouses. The enforcement of these duties depends on the conduct of the spouses, but there can be found little or nothing in the way of detailed rules for assessing the rights and wrongs of marital conduct.

The statements of principle establish the duties of maintenance and support as a fundamental incident of marriage ('*régime base*'). Unlike matrimonial property systems, these cannot be modified by agreement between the parties. It is stated that these duties are *reciprocal*. It is not found necessary to limit a wife's duty to support her husband in cases where he is under an earning disability. Naturally the cash income will usually be provided by the husband and the wife will discharge her contribution by the management of the house, but this kind of detail as to the form the contribution takes is open to variation by the parties.[39] In principle they should both contribute to the costs of the common household and related expenditure (such as holiday debts). The Dutch code lays down in detail the sources from which payment should be made. First, the money is to come from joint income; then, in equal proportions, from their separate incomes; next from communal property; and finally from separate property. If debts have been incurred in respect to the household, each will be liable in full no matter which party contracted the debt,

38. *Safier* v. *Safier* (1964) 108 Sol. Jo. 338; *Stick* v. *Stick* [1967] 1 All E.R. 323.
39. See C.C., articles 212–4 (France); B.G.B., article 1360 (W. Germany).

although in certain circumstances a court can free a spouse from this liability. It is expressly stated that these principles of equal responsibility are to apply even though the parties are living apart by mutual agreement. If, however, the separation was due to unreasonable conduct by one of the spouses, these reciprocal duties are replaced by an obligation which rests upon the guilty spouse alone to contribute to the subsistence and needs of the other. No distinction is drawn in this context between the husband and the wife.[40]

The problem of support may be divided into two stages. The first involves specifying upon whom the obligations fall and to what extent. The second concerns the conditions upon which one or other of the spouses forfeits, wither wholly or partially, the rights marriage would normally confer upon him against the other spouse. English maintenance law fails to make this distinction. It is primarily concerned with the second stage. The obligations of spouses towards each other only emerge incidentally and in a piecemeal fashion as a result of decisions about the conditions which justify their forfeiture. Although the contribution to actual marital stability can only be marginal, if anything, it is probably better that the mutual obligations of spouses are ascertained by reference to a positive statement of principle by the legislature than by considering whether one of the spouses has committed an offence against the other. It certainly would contribute to simplicity of exposition. The rights and duties, so stated, should be reciprocal, though it should be recognized that they may be fulfilled in different ways. They should continue even where the spouses have separated by agreement and should be enforceable even while they are living together.[41] They should be regarded as inevitable incidents of the marital status. If each spouse is under a duty to contribute in some form to the household, it would seem to follow that each should be liable to meet debts contracted for its day-to-day management. This, too, would rest on the status of the parties and would be preferable to the present common law position which is simply an application of the commercial law of agency. The Law Commission (1967) tentatively suggested that support duties between spouses should be shared equally, but in its later

40. B.W. articles 84–86.

41. The latter is expressly stated in New Zealand maintenance law: Domestic Proceedings Act 1968, s. 30.

proposal (1969) it adopted 'for the time being' the more restrictive approach to be found in the Matrimonial Proceedings (Magistrates Courts) Act, 1960.

The failure of English law to lay down positive duties on the spouses regarding their contribution to running the home, leaving them to resort to the crude procedures of the courts to obtain a matrimonial order, may account for the deeply curious fact that the recipient of a sum paid under a maintenance order is liable to tax on the amount received. Conversely the payer (usually the husband) is entitled to tax relief on the payments. Were the wife's receipt of the money to be seen (as it should be) as the acquisition of her share in the family income which the fact of *marriage* allocated to her as her proper entitlement, it would be difficult to see how she could justifiably be taxed on it. A wife who in normal circumstances receives a housekeeping allowance from her husband is not taxed on receipt of it, and nor is he entitled to relief in respect of the payments. If the maintenance law is reviewed with a view to founding the obligations on the fact of marriage rather than the circumstances of the separation, this particular incident of the tax law should be reconsidered.

With regard to the second stage referred to above, which concerns the conduct of the parties, the Law Commission's tentative suggestion was that a court should review that conduct in a flexible way, untrammelled by the technical rules of the law relating to matrimonial offences. This would be a most welcome reform and would do no more than to extend to maintenance proceedings during marriage the present practice of the divorce courts when they decide on maintenance matters ancillary to granting a divorce decree.

*Enforcement process*

Where a wife is receiving insufficient cash support, her remedy lies in seeking a maintenance order either in the High Court or county court or in a magistrates' court. The requirement that, for liability to accrue under a magistrates' court's order, the parties must separate has already been criticized. But there are other problems about this remedy which bring into question its effectiveness as a means of safeguarding the economic security of a married woman. Of the 26,753 applications for maintenance in magistrates' courts by married women in 1969 only 17,424 were successful. Some of the dismissals may have resulted from the reconciliation of the parties before the hearing was concluded, but it is probable that many were due to the technical restrictions surrounding the law of maintenance which have been discussed. It must also be remembered that an application which is not dismissed may nevertheless be only partially successful, for the wife's claim may fail, but that on behalf of a child may succeed.

But even where the wife's application succeeds, the sums awarded are, on average, extremely low. A sample of orders made in September and October 1966 which was taken by the Home Office showed that the average order made in the first instance was £2 19s in favour of a wife on her own and £3 2s if she had one child, and rather less if she had more than one. The average amount payable for each child was £2 if there was only one child, the sum getting smaller for each additional child. The paucity of the amounts ordered by magistrates was revealed by the report of the Select Committee on Statutory Maintenance Limits (Graham Hall Committee) (1968) and this illustrates the difficulties facing magistrates when they try to do justice to deserted families where there is insufficient money to go round. They are well aware that orders which are too high cannot be enforced. This was confirmed by the Graham Hall Committee which received evidence that, of all orders live on 1 January 1966, 38 per cent were in arrears by amounts which represented six weekly payments or more and 24 per cent by amounts representing payments of six months or more.

The Attachment of Earnings Act 1971 contains measures which attempt to improve the methods by which payment by reluctant spouses can be enforced. A system whereby a notice was served upon a debtor-spouse's employer requiring him to deduct a certain sum from the spouse's wages and pay this direct to the court was instituted by the Maintenance Orders Act 1958. This worked less effectively than had been hoped, largely because a debtor-spouse determined to avoid payment could keep out of reach by constantly changing his job. It is difficult to prevent frustration of the system in this way. However, the new Act does what little is possible by requiring the debtor to notify the court when he leaves employment or becomes employed or re-employed and also requiring an employer who takes a man into employment and knows that there is an order against him, to inform the court that he is the debtor's employer.[42] The order no longer terminates with a change of employment; it simply lapses and can be easily revived. Also, it is no longer necessary to wait for four weeks of default before applying for an order attaching earnings. This may be done now if fifteen days have elapsed since the making of the order and the debtor has wilfully or culpably failed to make one or more payments under it. An unusual innovation is the provision which allows the debtor himself to apply for an order to be made against his own earnings – a provision useful for willing debtors who wish to avoid the inconvenience of handing over the money each week. This provision, in effect, enables them to transfer the administrative chore to the employer. Indeed, widespread use of the attachment procedure is likely to impose a heavy burden on employers.

No matter what enforcement mechanism is devised, it is impossible in the majority of cases for one man adequately to support two households. How a cake not large enough for two families is to be fairly divided between them is a matter no one can solve with complete satisfaction. The Divisional Court has made an heroic attempt to formulate some principles which should guide magistrates when faced with problems of this kind, and these may be summarized as follows:

1. An attempt should be made to keep the former family (or wife, if there were no children) at the standard of living it (or she) enjoyed before the separation. If it is to be lowered, this should be no more than is inherent in the circumstances of the separation.

2. It would be futile to make an order depressing the husband below subsistence level. The former family should not be set at a standard significantly higher or lower than the husband's present family.

3. In determining the standard attainable by each family, the courts should pay attention to the inescapable expenses of each family, especially where this involves maintaining children. So the husband's obligations to his new family will not be ignored.

4. The court is also to take into account the wife's actual or potential earning capacity. This is only to pay attention to realities.

42. A.E.A. 1971, s. 15.

5. These considerations apply equally whether the husband's second family is legitimate or not. If, in order to maintain his former wife at a standard comparable to that which she enjoyed during the cohabitation, the husband is not able to provide his mistress or second wife with the income she expected, that is irrelevant since she had to accept him subject to his existing obligations.

6. In all cases the court should realize that it is futile to make an order beyond the husband's capacity on which he would probably default.[43]

Despite these efforts, the chances of a family broken by the desertion of the breadwinner falling below subsistence level are extremely high. In 1965 there were 104,000 separated wives who were in receipt of national assistance. 41 per cent of these had a court order in their favour, and in half of these cases the court order was regularly complied with. Yet their income was insufficient to fend off poverty as then defined. It is therefore quite clear that the magistrates' courts procedure does not prevent the breakdown of a family from throwing thousands of women each year on to social security benefits. Indeed, in some senses a woman who fails to obtain an order against her husband and relies on supplementary benefit is in a better position than her counterpart who is in receipt of a marginally adequate maintenance payment because the collection of the supplementary benefit is simpler and more certain than that of maintenance payments. Where supplementary benefits are payable to separated wives, sections 22–4 of the Ministry of Social Security Act 1966 operate to permit that Ministry to recover a contribution from the husband provided that he is under a duty to maintain his wife. The common law rules as to a husband's liability to support his wife are applicable at this point, with the exception of the controversial rule that the duty does not arise where the parties have separated by agreement.[44] In this situation, a wife claiming through the supplementary benefits commission procedure is at an advantage. She may also be better off under that procedure if she has committed adultery. This, as we have seen, will debar her from obtaining a maintenance order against

43. *Ashley* v. *Ashley* [1965] 3 All E.R. 554; *Attwood* v. *Attwood* [1968] 3 All E.R. 385; *Roberts* v. *Roberts* [1968] 3 All E.R. 479.
44. *National Assistance Board* v. *Parkes* [1955] 2 Q.B. 506.

her husband. It will not debar her from obtaining supplementary benefit, however, and it is arguable that, while it will be a relevant circumstance to be considered when deciding whether the commission can reclaim from the husband, it is not an absolute bar against such a claim.[45] The utilization of the supplementary benefits machinery in this context resembles its use by unmarried mothers and, as in those cases, its use has led to the suggestion that state machinery might be used much more extensively so as to underwrite a level of maintenance for all separated wives higher than the supplementary benefit flat rate and to collect contributions from the husbands by adjustment of their PAYE coding. The merits of this contention are considerable where the separated wife has children to support, and it is difficult to refute Wynn's plea (1966) that a 'fatherless children's allowance' should be payable at no less a rate than the sums paid to strangers to bring up foster children. Children have to be provided for somehow, and if they are not to be taken into state-supported institutions, with the consequent risk of them becoming a lifelong charge on the community due to later inadequacy or delinquency, the only alternative is to provide the means for their adequate rearing in a family, even a fatherless one. The case for this approach is certainly strong enough to merit serious consideration, and a committee under Mr Morris Finer Q.C. was set up in November 1969 to consider it. The issues to be examined involve very broad questions of social policy and the welfare services, and on 1 January 1971 the committee's report was still awaited.

### Other financial assistance

The section on support obligations was primarily concerned with the extent to which the rights of each spouse to look to the other for financial support during the marriage is legally recognized and how they are enforced. There are, however, further ways by which the operative family unit may be underwritten by legal provision. This is done by so structuring state and other schemes which confer financial benefits on individuals that they operate to the advantage of the family unit. Some examples of this policy will be considered in this section.

45. *National Assistance Board* v. *Wilkinson* [1952] 2 Q.B. 648. However she will receive no benefit if she is *cohabiting* with a man.

*Family allowances and family income supplement*

The purpose of family allowances is to make provision for state assistance on a family basis. It is to supplement the income of the breadwinner and to provide the housewife with additional cash for household expenditure. For this reason, when they were introduced by the Family Allowances Act 1945, family allowances were made the property of the wife. This assistance, it should be observed, is not confined to legal families, for a family for these purposes includes not only a man and his wife living together, but also a single man or woman, or a man or woman separated from his or her spouse, and that person's children or such children as he or she is maintaining.[46] As it is considered of primary importance to assist large families, the allowance is payable only if the family consists of two or more children. Children are covered by this, however, only if they are under the upper limit of compulsory school age or, if above it, until they are sixteen and prevented from obtaining regular employment by reason of prolonged disability, or until they are nineteen if they are undergoing full-time instruction or training.[47] The provision regarding disability will become redundant when, in 1973, the upper limit of compulsory school age is raised to sixteen.

Family allowances are paid in cash through the Post Office. The sum payable had remained at the level fixed in 1956 throughout the twelve following years, despite inflation, until they were twice raised in 1968. The immediate impetus for the increase was the report of the Ministry of Social Security (1967). The Report was based on a sample of families in receipt of family allowances in the summer of 1966. It therefore excluded single child families. The report showed that of the 3·9 million families with two or more children in receipt of these allowances, 345,000 (with 1·1 million children) had resources less than the basic minimum supplementary benefit scale laid down in 1966. Of those families, 125,000 could not receive supplementary benefit because the father was in full-time work and 20,000 could not receive the full benefit because of the wage stop, the rule which depresses the benefit to a sum below the recipient's potential earnings rate. The government reacted by proposing a rise in family allowances of 7s, but later supplemented this by an additional 3s

46. Family Allowances Act 1965, s. 3.    47. *ibid*. ss. 2 and 19.

to offset the price increases expected as a result of the devaluation of sterling.[48] As from October 1968 the rates are fixed at 18s (90p) for the first child entitled, and £1 for each subsequent child.

It is also the policy of this legislation to assist families for whom the need is greatest. The method adopted by the government is to make family allowances payable to all families with children which qualify but to recoup from the richer families by means of taxation. In particular it was the intention to confine the increases of 1968 to poorer families. Therefore it was decided to reduce the child relief allowance on taxable income (see below) for all who were in receipt of family allowances in such a manner that persons paying income tax at the standard rate would in effect be repaying in taxation the increases in family allowances. Persons paying no tax or tax at reduced rates would benefit from the increase in accordance with their means. The way this works was explained by the Joint Parliamentary Secretary to the Ministry of Social Security:

A married man with two children under 11, earning £12 per week – £624 per year – would pay no tax in 1968 and will get an extra £22 family allowance, that is, about 8s 6d a week averaged over the year. If he earns £15 per week – £780 a year – the extra tax he will pay will be about £11 per year. In other words, he will pay back about half the extra allowance in tax on the take-back system. The family will end up with about 4s 3d. per week more. At £20 per week he will pay something like £17 extra tax on the additional allowance and the take-back, leaving the family about 2s a week better off. At £22 per week – £1,444 per year – the family will derive no benefit from the extra allowance.[49]

This method of repaying the increase in family allowances is sometimes referred to as 'clawback'. It was largely due to objection to this technique of confining the benefits of an increase in family allowances to the poorer sections of the community which determined the Conservative administration returned in 1970 to abandon their proposals made while in opposition to increase family allowances and instead to provide aid for the poor by way of family income supplements.[50] It was pointed out that a general increase in family allowances, a large amount of which would be reclaimed

48. Family Allowances and National Insurance Acts 1967–1968.
49. H.C. Deb., vol. 762, col. 293.
50. Family Income Supplements Act 1970.

from the husband by means of the clawback, would do no more, in those cases, than forcibly to transfer the sum involved from the husband (who paid the tax) to the wife (who received the benefit)[51]. In so far as this can be regarded as a guaranteed minimum house-keeping allowance for the wife, this is probably a desirable process. But leaving that point aside, the proposals for family income supple-ments have been strongly criticized on the ground that they will benefit only a marginal number of families. The proposals entail the establishment of a prescribed income level, which will vary according to the number of children in the family. Thus families with a single child would be included. In so far as the family income falls short of that level, the couple may jointly apply for a sum to make up *half* the difference between the two, but up to a limit of £3 a week. The proposals are designed to provide for families who are not in receipt of supplementary benefit, either because the wage earner is in full-time work or, if not, because supplementary benefit is not payable owing to the 'wage stop'. The new 'prescribed income level' could therefore become a new 'poverty line' drawn at a level lower than the present subsistence level for supplementary benefit purposes. But a more immediately serious objection to the scheme is that benefits are payable only on application, which will involve an assessment of family income. It has been estimated that this may deter as many as 50 per cent of potential recipients, who, in any case, constitute no more than approximately 1 per cent of working households.[52] Nevertheless, the scheme is to be linked to other concessions to the poor (e.g. exemption from prescription charges) and was introduced as a first step in an overall scheme to alleviate family poverty where it is most serious.

*Income tax benefits*

The family is regarded in many respects as a single unit for revenue purposes. A husband and wife will have their income aggregated for the purposes of determining the total income to be assessed and, although each may apply for separate assessment, this does not affect the overall rate of taxation.[53] The Finance Act 1968, in section

51. H.C. Deb., vol. 806, col. 220 (Sir Keith Joseph).
52. See *The Times*, 10 November 1970.
53. Income and Corporation Taxes Act 1970, s. 37.

15, carried further the concept of treating the family income as a whole for taxation purposes by treating as part of the parents' income the *unearned* income accruing to a minor child so long as he remains unmarried and is not in regular employment. The purpose was to prevent monies nominally going to children from being used to finance the family as a whole, and, accordingly, payments which are in a special way personal to the child are excluded. Examples are damages for personal injuries (such as those awarded to 'thalidomide' children) and affiliation payments to unmarried mothers.[54] In contrast to the case where there are only two persons constituting a *de facto* union, which is not recognized in law, the law does recognize a *de facto* union for these purposes when a child is born, so that if the parents have an illegitimate child, the relevant income of the child will be aggregated with that of the mother.

Before they marry, single persons are entitled to personal relief of £325 which reduces their taxable income by that amount. When they marry and the incomes of the spouses are combined the husband is entitled to £465 personal relief.[55] The whole married man's allowance is allowable only if the man has been married throughout the whole year of assessment. If he is married during part of it, he is only entitled to an increase in personal allowance proportionate to the length of time during the year of assessment during which he was married. It will be observed that the married man's relief is less than double the relief available to each of the parties had they remained single. Marriage would therefore appear to increase the tax liability of a couple who are both wage earners. This is not so for most people, however, because a married man is entitled to additional reliefs with respect to his wife's *earned* income. If he is living with her, he is entitled to an additional relief of seven-ninths of that income or £325, whichever is the lesser sum. Family allowances, though generally regarded as earned income of the wife, are, however, not so regarded for these purposes.

The result is that, by the combination of the husband's married relief of £465 and the relief on his wife's earned income, a married couple will usually obtain greater tax relief on their combined income than they would if treated separately. But this will not be

54. I.C.T.A. 1970, s. 43. See however p. 137, footnote 56.
55. I.C.T.A. 1970, s. 8 as amended by Finance Act 1970, s. 14(1)(a).

true in cases where the combined income of the spouses reaches a large total, because when this becomes liable to surtax (at about £5500) the rate of taxation increases considerably, so that parties whose income is aggregated at this level incur heavier taxation than they would if taxed separately. An adverse tax position can also result if the wife is in receipt of *unearned* income, as this, too, is aggregated with the husband's income, but is not subject to special relief in the same way as her earned income. There is therefore a progressive family taxation system which imposes heavier tax liability on the richer families than on the less well off. This policy is underlined by the assimilation of the unearned income of a minor child to the husband's total income. The Royal Commission on the Taxation of Profits and Income (1954) justified the policy of aggregating the income of husband and wife on the ground that a family should be treated as a single unit for fiscal purposes and that it would be wrong if the incidence of its taxation depended on how the contributions to it were divided between the spouses. The Commission was sceptical whether people allowed these considerations to influence their decision whether or not to marry. It is improbable that any significant number of people are deterred from marriage for this reason, but this difficulty could be met by extending the principle of aggregation to *de facto* units, a development which would be consistent with the theory behind the policy and analogous to the aggregation of the unearned income of an illegitimate minor child with his mother's income. However, the policy is coming under some criticism and it is expected that it will be re-assessed by the present government.[56]

Further advantages accrue to families by way of tax concessions where they qualify for child relief. Persons who qualify are entitled to £115 relief with respect to each child under eleven, £140 for children under sixteen and £165 for children over that age provided they are receiving full-time education or are undergoing vocational training on a course lasting at least two years. A person qualifies for the relief

56. In the 1971 Budget it was announced that from 1972 spouses would be permitted to elect to be taxed as if they were separate individuals and that the unearned income of a minor child would no longer be aggregated with that of his parents. These reforms will give taxation benefits to the higher income groups. Surtax is to be abolished in favour of a graduated tax for all incomes.

if he proves that there is a 'child of his' within the above categories living at any time within the year of assessment or if 'he has the custody of and maintains at his own expense a child (other than a child of his)' who falls within those categories.[57] Although the statute is not entirely free from ambiguity, illegitimate children are clearly intended to be included within the category of children with respect of whom relief can be obtained and, indeed, an unmarried mother may claim an *additional* relief of £100 with respect to an illegitimate child of hers with respect to whom she was entitled to ordinary child relief.[58]

The provisions for tax relief on proof of maintenance of certain dependants other than the taxpayer's wife and children affords a comparatively rare example in English law of the recognition of the 'extended' family. A taxpayer who maintains a relative of his or of his wife is entitled to relief if that relative is incapacitated by old age or infirmity from maintaining himself, unless the relative is his own or his wife's mother, in which case relief is claimable whether she is incapacitated or not. The amount of relief claimable is adjusted according to the income of the 'relative', a term which is left undefined, but which would seem to include any blood relation.[59] It should be emphasized that, while the availability of tax relief for sums used to maintain relatives is an example of legal recognition of moral duties, English law, unlike many other systems, imposes no legal obligation upon persons with means to support members of their extended family. Indeed, there is not even a legal obligation upon a child to maintain his aged parents, and, as will be seen a parent's duty to maintain his children is subject to severe restrictions (see p. 149).

## Social welfare and insurance

It is not possible to give a detailed review of the social services upon which a family in ordinary circumstances may draw. These include

57. I.C.T.A. 1970, s. 10. It was announced in the 1971 Budget that child allowances would be raised by £40 each. This goes some way in meeting the criticism by Wynn (1970) that the taxation system takes insufficient account of the expenses involved in bringing up children. It does not, however, benefit the families of those whose incomes are below the tax threshold.

58. I.C.T.A. 1970, s. 14 as amended by F.A. 1970, s. 14(1)(f).

59. I.C.T.A. 1970, s. 16.

services provided by local health departments, especially in regard to expectant and nursing mothers and the provision of an adequate midwifery service. The school health service, operated by the local education authority, provides attention for the health of children over five in the same way as the local health authority does for children under five. A more detailed examination of child welfare legislation follows in the next part. Other forms of social service, such as school meals and milk, medical, dental and other supplies are subject to fluctuation according to central government policy. This, at the beginning of 1971, was oriented towards imposing limited charges for facilities of this kind with provision for exemption for people who cannot afford them.[60] Wide publicity is promised of the exemptions available.

Pecuniary assistance for the family is provided through the national insurance scheme. The principal benefits relevant in this context are the sickness, unemployment, industrial injuries and maternity benefits and retirement pensions. The scheme was established by the National Insurance Act 1946 and is based on flat-rate insurance contributions which, if the required number are made, entitle the insured to certain benefits. These, too, are paid at a flat rate. When fixing the level of contribution it is necessary to avoid an amount which would be unduly burdensome on the lower income groups. Consequently in such a scheme, the benefits are spread very thinly, and a large percentage of beneficiaries, in particular old age pensioners, have been obliged to supplement the benefits payable to them under the insurance scheme by supplementary benefits. An attempt to remedy this position was made by the National Insurance Act 1959. This superimposes above the flat-rate scheme an earnings-related contribution which entitles the contributor to correspondingly higher pensions. This does not apply to self-employed persons, and persons employed by organizations operating an approved occupational pensions scheme are exempted if the organization 'contracts out' of the graduated state scheme. The National Insurance Act 1966 has extended the method of supplementation introduced for pensions by the 1959 act to other insurance benefits, but employees cannot be contracted out of these graduated contributions. In return, supplements are payable on an earnings-related basis for up to six months

60. H.C. Deb., vol. 805, cols 37 *et seq.*

of unemployment, sickness or injury after the first fortnight. Benefits payable during the first six months of widowhood are likewise supplemented.

The 'two-tier' system of compulsory flat rate contributions and additional payments with earnings-related supplements grafted upon them appeared unsatisfactory to the last Labour government. The flat-rate retirement pension was itself insufficient and about two million pensioners were obliged to seek 'supplementary pensions'. The National Superannuation and Social Insurance Bill sought to introduce a general, compulsory, earnings-related pension and social benefit scheme. The pensions and benefits payable would approximate more closely to the earnings received by the beneficiaries. This would, of course, entail the payment of higher contributions by those with higher incomes. The scheme was also to be redistributive. The lower paid contributors would receive a benefit which was proportionately larger in relation to their contributions than those in the higher groups who would, to that extent, have been subsidizing the lower income groups. It was not proposed that private occupational schemes should be supplanted. But as the state scheme would have been compulsory, contribution both to a private scheme and to the state scheme would have been excessive for many people. To avoid over-insurance in this way it was proposed that partial contracting out, or abatement of, the compulsory contributions should be permitted.

The Bill failed to reach the statute book before the dissolution of Parliament, which was followed by the return of the Conservative administration. The new government has not proceeded with the scheme. It is, however, proposing to make a complete review of the national insurance system and may itself put forward an earnings-related scheme of some kind. As an immediate measure, however, the National Insurance (Old Persons' and Widows' Pensions and Attendance Allowance) Act 1970 was passed. This provides for pensions to be paid to persons who were over pensionable age when the national scheme commenced in 1948. These people will now be over eighty. A single person is entitled to £3·60 a week, with an additional £2·20 if he is a man and his wife is living with him. If the recipient is already in receipt of supplementary benefit, this will be reduced to the extent of the pension. The provision is therefore of real benefit only to persons over eighty who are not drawing supplementary benefits. The other provisions of the Act concern widows' pensions and are not relevant in this context (see p. 224).

The retirement pension becomes payable to a man at sixty-five and to a woman at sixty, provided that they have retired from regular work. But when they reach seventy and sixty-five respectively the pension becomes payable whether they are working or not. Before they reach these ages, however, the pension payable will be reduced proportionately to the extent that their earnings exceed £9·50 a week. The basic flat rate of the pension is £6 a week, but the payment to a husband is increased by £3·70 if his wife is living with him, whatever her age, provided that she is not herself in receipt of pension and provided that she is not earning more than the amount of the increase. Additional increases are payable with respect to dependent children within certain categories. £2·45 is payable for the first child, £1·55 for a second child and £1·45 for each additional child.[61] The amount of graduated pension which may be added to the flat rate will depend on the recipient's earnings and the contributions paid.

Sickness and maternity benefits are of particular importance in the family context. The payment of sickness benefit maintains income for the family while the breadwinner is unable to earn it. The flat rate payable is £6 a week, but this is subject to the earnings-related supplement introduced by the 1966 Act. This supplement is payable to those earning more than an average of £9 a week, though this is limited so that the whole benefit (basic flat rate plus supplement) will not exceed 85 per cent of the average earnings of the recipient. The supplement will be paid for six months only, and the benefit will not be payable for the first three days of sickness unless the claimant is off work for twelve or more days within thirteen weeks from his first day's absence. Further supplements for dependents are payable. There are two kinds of maternity benefits. One is the *maternity grant* of £25 to offset some of the expenses of childbirth. If the confinement takes place in the home, additional services (such as midwifery and, possibly, a home help) will be provided by the local health authority. A *maternity allowance* is also payable. It is calculated in the same way as sickness benefit and starts eleven weeks before the expected week of confinement and lasts for eighteen weeks in

61. The amounts given become payable on 20 September 1971.

all. The purpose is to compensate a working woman for loss of income, so the recipient herself must have fulfilled the contribution requirements and should not be working during the period over which the benefit is paid. Both kinds of maternity benefit are available to unmarried mothers.

# Chapter 4
# During Marriage: Protection of Children

To the extent that families receive overall benefit under the legislation described above, the welfare of the child members is enhanced. But the position of the child in the family raises special problems which demand separate attention. The objective of modern family policy with regard to children is to give every encouragement to the family to fulfil its role as the provider for the child of sustenance and protection during its vulnerable years and as the primary agency through which the child is introduced into and adapted for wider society. In so far as families fall short of this task, legal and social means are directed to repair this partial breakdown. This has not always been the policy adopted. When in the late nineteenth century the appalling extent to which poverty had resulted in child neglect began to be appreciated, the policies of the 'progressive' poor law authorities were directed at taking these children outside their home environment, which was regarded as having failed, and rehabilitating them in residential homes. Many of these establishments were admirably managed, often in the form of 'cottage' homes in the form of separate residential units. Strict standards of discipline and hygiene were imposed and the virtues of work were instilled into the children. Later it was thought that the isolation of these groups from the rest of society was a disadvantage and policies turned to placing neglected children in residential homes which were more closely integrated with the surrounding community. Contact with the children's own families, however, was still discouraged, and this policy went as far as to assist these children to emigrate. It was not until after the Second World War that a distinct shift of emphasis took place. The Children Act 1948[1] imposed upon local authorities who received children into their care a duty 'in all cases where it appears to them

1. s. 1(3).

consistent with the welfare of the child to do so (to) endeavour to secure that the care of the child is taken over either by a parent or guardian of his or by a relative or friend of his'. Contacts between children in care and their parents were to be encouraged. For example, the Act[2] gave local authorities power to defray the travelling expenses of parents visiting the children. This duty to restore a child to its home wherever possible provided an incentive to the creation of social services designed to rehabilitate the families from which the neglected children came. It was then but a short step to the present ideal to which family policy aspires and which is expressed in section 1 of the Children and Young Persons Act 1963.

It shall be the duty of every local authority to make available such advice, guidance and assistance as may promote the welfare of children by diminishing the need to receive children into or keep them in care . . . or to bring children before a juvenile court.

It is in the light of this declared policy that the law relating to the protection and welfare of children will be examined.

**General criminal law**

The law of murder and manslaughter is of course available in cases where children are victims of homicide, but there are some special features which are relevant to these cases. The law of murder or manslaughter does not apply to the killing of a child in the womb or in the process of being born. The precise moment when a child is protected by the law of murder or manslaughter may not be easy to determine with exactitude since the legal test is whether the child is existing independently of the mother, a matter which in any particular case may be difficult to establish. However, once the child in the womb is capable of being born alive, its destruction is an offence against the Infant Life (Preservation) Act 1929 and is punishable by life imprisonment. The effect, then, is much the same as for murder with the important distinction that in a charge under the Act the prosecution must prove that the act which caused the death of the child was not done in good faith for the purpose of preserving the life of the mother. This is not a defence which would be available if the charge were one of murder. Nothing in the Abortion Act

2. s. 22.

1967, which legalizes abortion in specified circumstances, affects the offence created by the 1929 Act (see p. 58).

The law of murder has been mitigated in another respect with regard to the killing of very young children. It is provided by section 1(1) of the Infanticide Act 1938 that if a woman causes the death of her own child before it reaches the age of twelve months, but does this when the 'balance of her mind was disturbed by reason of her not having fully recovered from the effect of giving birth to the child or by reason of the effect of lactation consequent upon the birth of the child' then she is to be treated as though guilty of manslaughter but not of murder. This enactment must be seen in the context where conviction for murder required sentence of death, although for these cases it would almost certainly not be carried out. Nevertheless it is hard to see what purpose is achieved by convicting a woman who has acted in the circumstances described by the Act of any crime. It cannot be considered a deterrent to other women from committing acts similarly caused. She herself will require psychiatric treatment, which may not be assisted by the instigation of a prosecution. Yet in recent years about twenty prosecutions a year for this offence have been brought in England and Wales. Since the women convicted were almost invariably put on probation, there seems much to be said for exercising the discretion to prosecute sparingly and to put the woman in touch with the appropriate social and medical services.

In some respects, on the other hand, the law of murder and manslaughter may operate more widely if the victim is a child. This is because, as a general principle, the common law does not impose upon people duties to assist persons in need if they are adult. A striking, and perhaps extreme, example of this attitude is found in the decision of the Court of Crown Cases Reserved resulting from a prosecution for murder in 1862.[3] A mother was indicted as a result of the death in her house of her eighteen year old unmarried daughter who died in childbirth. It was alleged that she had wilfully refrained from calling a midwife. It was decided that she could be guilty neither of murder nor manslaughter because she was under no duty to provide assistance for her daughter who was 'beyond the age of childhood'. But where younger children are concerned, a duty to provide food and other assistance is imposed not only on the parents but

3. *R.* v. *Shepherd* [1862] Le. & Ca. 147.

upon others who have 'charge' of them. In *R.* v. *Gibbins and Proctor*[4] a conviction of murder was upheld against the two accused who had deliberately starved to death Gibbins' seven year old daughter. In fact, it is probable that this clearly recognized duty towards younger children is simply part of a wider general duty imposed upon persons to help those who have become dependent on them and who are 'helpless' unless given some assistance. So parents who failed to look after their ailing and semi-starved daughter of twenty-five were held guilty of manslaughter in *R.* v. *Chattaway*[5] and an earlier case had held that a woman who similarly failed to look after an elderly aunt with whom she was living was also guilty of manslaughter.[6] It is difficult to reconcile *R.* v. *Shepherd* with these cases.

There is a further reason why the law of manslaughter might operate more widely when ill-treatment or neglect results in the death of a child than it would in the case of an adult. This is a result of the doctrine that a conviction for manslaughter is proper in a case where death resulted from an unlawful act perpetrated by the accused against the deceased. By section 1 of the Children and Young Persons Act 1933 it is a statutory offence for a person with custody of a child under sixteen to neglect the child in a manner likely to cause him unnecessary suffering or injury to health, and it is stated that failure to provide adequate food, clothing, medical aid or lodging for the child or to take steps to procure such shall be deemed to constitute neglect. If death results from unlawful contravention of the section a conviction for manslaughter is justified,[7] at any rate if 'all sober and reasonable people would inevitably recognize (that there was) the risk of some harm resulting therefrom, albeit not serious harm'.[8] If death was in fact *intended*, then the charge should be one of murder.

If a child is injured but does not die, the ordinary criminal law as to assault and causing bodily harm is applicable. However, in considering whether the criminal law should be used against parents who have subjected their children to violent injury, extreme caution should be taken. It is now becoming increasingly accepted that many cases where children are 'battered' result from psychological disturbance in the guilty parent. In such circumstances, while it may

4. (1918) 13 C.A.R. 134   5. (1922) 17 C.A.R. 7.
6. *R.* v. *Instan* [1893] 1 Q.B. 450.   7. *R.* v. *Senior* [1899] 1 Q.B. 283.
8. *R.* v. *Church* [1965] 2 All E.R. 72.

indeed be desirable to remove the child from the home by bringing care proceedings (see p. 168), it is highly dubious whether any useful purpose is served by bringing a criminal prosecution against the parent. The problem appears to have been of increasing dimension of late and is currently under review by central and local government. The NSPCC has set up a special department to study it.

## Cruelty and neglect

The main provision of the Children and Young Persons Act 1933, as amended,[9] imposing criminal sanctions for cruelty to and neglect of children was mentioned in the previous section. There it is also provided that neglect likely to cause the child unnecessary suffering or injury to health, wilful assault, ill-treatment, abandonment, exposure or causing or procuring those things may be punished, on conviction on indictment, by a fine of £100 or two years' imprisonment or both, or, on summary conviction, by a similar fine or six months' imprisonment or both. To cause the death of a child under three by suffocation due to overlaying it in bed when drunk is deemed to constitute neglect within the section. Anyone over sixteen who has custody of a child may be liable under the Act and a parent or other person legally liable to maintain it is presumed to have custody. The only way in which a parent can lose this custody is by order of a competent court,[10] so a husband whose wife had deserted him taking the children with her would appear to retain custody for the purposes of the section, but any neglect on his part would be unlikely to be held to be 'wilful'. On the other hand, the rule as to retention of custody has the effect that a husband cannot divest himself of custody by deserting his wife or even by living apart from her with her agreement. The result is that a husband will be guilty of an offence under the section if he wilfully fails to provide adequate food, clothing, medical aid or lodging for his children under sixteen so as to endanger their health, whether he is living with his family or apart from it.[11] This is to be contrasted with the position of a wife seeking a maintenance order on the ground of her husband's wilful neglect to maintain her where, as has been noted (see p. 117), she may be

9. See C.Y.P.A., 1963, ss. 31, 64, 65 and sch. III.
10. *Brooks* v. *Blount* [1923] 1 K.B. 257.   11. C.Y.P.A. 1933, s. 17.

defeated by the fact that the separation was consensual or fail to impose liability on him if he has not left the home. However, the presumption of custody does not seem to apply to the father of illegitimate children, at any rate, not unless an affiliation order has been made against him.[12] But he will be held to have custody if this is evident from the facts.[13]

The Act expressly preserves[14] the right of parents, teachers and other persons with lawful control over a child to punish him, but such punishment is subject to the limits of reasonableness. But it will be no defence against a charge of failing to provide medical aid to say that the accused person had religious or other objection to the use of medicine. However, if the accused person genuinely believes that spiritual rather than scientific means will aid the recovery of the child, it is arguable that his neglect is not 'wilful'. But in *R*. v. *Senior*[15] it was held that 'wilful' simply meant that the act must be done deliberately and intentionally and not by accident. So in that case, where the child died, the accused were held to have been rightly convicted of manslaughter.

Those are the general legal provisions covering child cruelty. Subsequent sections of the 1933 Act create specific offences relating to child welfare. Section 3 concerns children permitted to be in brothels; section 4 covers cases where persons cause or allow children to be used for begging. It is also an offence (punishable by a £10 fine) to give a child under five intoxicating liquor except in the event of illness[16] and section 11 imposes a similar penalty on anyone having custody over a child under sixteen who allows him 'to be in a room containing an open fire grate or any heating appliance liable to cause injury to a person by contact therewith, not sufficiently protected to guard against the risk of his being burnt or scalded without taking reasonable precautions against that risk, and by reason thereof the child is killed or suffers serious injury'. However, if a child were to be killed in those circumstances, a prosecution for manslaughter would also be possible. Other provisions of this Act and of the Children and Young Persons Act 1963 concerning matters relating to safety of children in entertainment and restrictions upon child

12. *Butler* v. *Gregory* (1902) 18 T.LR. 370.
13. *The Liverpool S.P.C.C.* v. *Jones* [1914] 3 K.B. 813.   14. S. 1(7).
15. [1899] 1 Q.B. 283.   16. S. 5; Criminal Justice Act 1967, s. 92 and sch. III.

labour concern child protection in a context wider than the family and need not be considered here.

## Maintenance of children

The ability of a wife to obtain cash maintenance from her husband on her own account and for housekeeping purposes has already been discussed. If she has the children of the marriage with her, her legal entitlement to these payments will clearly add to their security. As we have seen, the wife's rights in this regard, and the means given to her to enforce them, are subject to anomalies and restrictions. There are, however, separate but parallel provisions by which the wife may claim maintenance from her husband on her child's behalf in addition to claiming on her own account. The husband's duties are covered by statute law. Although the point is not entirely free from doubt, it seems that the common law imposed no duty upon a father to maintain his legitimate children. The matter was discussed in *Bazeley* v. *Forder*.[17] A wife who had been deserted by her husband had pledged his credit with respect to clothing necessary for their child. Lord Chief Justice Cockburn, in a dissenting opinion, held that the trades-man could not recover from the husband because, he said, the father was under no obligation to provide maintenance for his child. The only sanction lay in the criminal law of wilful neglect. It was, he added, also not essential for the mother to have kept custody of the child. The majority of the court, however, avoided the barbarity of this conclusion by deciding that clothing for a child was a necessity which the husband was bound to supply his *wife* under the agency of necessity. The tradesman therefore succeeded by reason of the husband's duty to his wife, not to his child.

The agency of necessity has now been abolished.[18] Orders for the maintenance of children can be obtained in the High Court, county courts and magistrates' courts. Sections 6 and 8 of the Matrimonial Proceedings and Property Act 1970 govern the powers of the High Court and county courts. If either the husband *or the wife* have wilfully neglected to provide or make proper contribution towards a child of the family the court, instead of or in addition to ordering the respondent to make periodical payments or lump sum

17. (1868) L.R. 3 Q.B. 559.
18. M.P.P.A. 1970, s. 33; see pp. 111–12.

payment to the applicant of the kinds discussed earlier (see p. 112), may order the respondent to make periodical payments directly to the child or to a specified person on the child's behalf. These payments may be ordered to be secured. They may also be by way of lump sum. Since the age of majority is now eighteen, it is provided that, subject to what is said below, no orders can be made in the first instance for a child who has reached that age. Nor, in the ordinary case, may orders last beyond the date of the child's next birthday after having reached the upper limit of compulsory school age. But if the court thinks it 'right in the circumstances', the order may overrun that age until the child reaches eighteen and can also extend into majority if the child is, or would be enabled to be, undergoing educational instruction or vocational training or if there are other 'special circumstances'. An order commencing after eighteen may be made on the same conditions.

The benefits of these provisions are not confined to children of the respondent, but extend to any 'child of the family for whose maintenance it is reasonable in all the circumstances' to expect the respondent to provide. A 'child of the family' is a child of both parties to the marriage or any other child *who has been treated by both of them as a child of the family* (with the exception of children boarded out with them). But where the child is not a child of the respondent, the extent of his obligation (if any) to that child will be decided by reference to the extent (if any) and basis upon which he assumed responsibility for the child, whether he did so knowing the child was not his own and the liability of anyone else to maintain the child.[19] This formula is a compromise between the interests of a child who has long been supported by a man and the man himself who subsequently discovers the child is not his own. Under the policy of the 1970 Act initial liability of the man is considered as depending not so much on biological relationship but on the fact of the child's dependence. However, justice to the man demands that his position, too, be considered, and this may result in a *reduction* of the extent of his obligation, even though such a reduction may not be the best result from the child's point of view.

It will be recalled (see p. 113) that, while maintenance orders in the High Court may be made while the parties are cohabiting and liability

19. *ibid.*, ss. 5(3), 6(3)(4) and 27.

will arise during this period, the position is different when the magistrates make such orders. Similar differences exist between maintenance orders in favour of children made by the higher courts and those made by magistrates. Two statutory enactments confer on magistrates jurisdiction to make maintenance orders with respect to children. Under section 9 of the Guardianship of Minors Act 1971, the court may, when making an order granting the custody of a child to the mother, make a further order requiring the father to pay a reasonable sum towards the maintenance of the child. The enactment is not confined to magistrates, but when the powers are exercised by magistrates, they extend only over children who are under sixteen, unless the child is 'physically and mentally incapable of self support'. But any order made before the child is sixteen may extend until he reaches twenty-one, and may even be varied after he reaches sixteen.[20] Indeed, once a person in whose favour an order has already been made reaches the age of eighteen, he may apply to the court for an order that the parent against whom it was made makes payment direct to him.[21] But this will stop when he reaches twenty-one. If however, one parent wishes to obtain against the other an order for the maintenance of a child of seventeen, and no order is already in existence or the child is not incapable of self-support, the application must be in the High Court or a county court. This anomaly is simply untidy. There is another which is objectionable. The 1971 Act expressly provides that no order for custody or maintenance made under the Act shall be enforceable or attract liability while the parents cohabit, and shall cease to have effect if cohabitation has lasted three months.[22] This is so no matter which court made the order. It even applies where a child over eighteen but under twenty-one applies for payment under an existing order to be made to him.[23] So again, we see a limitation on a parent's moral obligation to provide for his child, for English law provides a remedy only when a crisis has arisen *between the parents*. This explains the further restriction that a maintenance order under the Act can be made only alongside an order granting custody to one or other of the parents. This clearly contemplates impending total family disintegration. It is wrong that

20. G. of M.A. 1971, ss. 9, 12, 15(2).
21. *ibid.* s. 12(2).   22. *ibid.*, s. 9(3).
23. *ibid.*, s. 12(3).

legal enforcement of the parental duty to support his children should be postponed until this stage.

The other statute relevant to magistrates' courts in this context is the Matrimonial Proceedings (Magistrates' Courts) Act 1960. This empowers magistrates before whom allegations are made on the grounds set out on p. 112 to order either the defendant *or the claimant*, or each of them, to make payment for the maintenance of any 'child of the family'. One of the grounds is that the defendant has wilfully neglected to provide reasonable maintenance for such a child who is, or would but for the neglect have been, a dependant. But if the defendant is the wife, it must additionally be shown that it is reasonable to expect her to make such provision as a result of the impairment of her husband's earning capacity.[24] Unfortunately, the expression 'child of the family' in this context receives a different definition from the same expression as used in the Matrimonial Proceedings and Property Act 1970 with respect to maintenance orders in favour of children made in the High Court and county courts (see p. 150). Under that Act a child is within the definition, even if not a child of the parties, if he has been *treated* by both of them as one of the family. Under the 1960 Act a child who is not a child of the parties is within the definition only if he has been *accepted* by both of them into the family. The difference is important. If, for example, a husband has treated a child as his for some years and then discovers he is not his, he will be held not to have accepted the child[25] and, accordingly, no order at all can be made in the child's favour. Under the 1970 Act, however, the child qualifies for consideration, though any order against a husband in this position may well be *reduced* on account of his misapprehension.

But this is not the only complication. In the High Court or county court an application under the 1970 Act may be made with respect to a child who is under eighteen, and the order may extend beyond that age in certain circumstances (see p. 150). But where the application is to a magistrates' court an application may be made with respect to a child under sixteen or a child over sixteen but under twenty-one if he is undergoing a course of full-time education or training *lasting at least two years*, or if his earning capacity is

24. M.P.(M.C.)A.1960, ss. 1(1)(h)(i) and 2(1)(h).
25. *B*. v. *B and F.* [1968] 3 All E.R. 232.

impaired.[26] Furthermore, where the child is under sixteen, a custody order must have been made because payments must be made to the person to whom the court has committed legal custody of the child, and, as in the case of an order under the Guardianship of Minors Act 1971, liability does not accrue while the parties are cohabiting and the order terminates after cohabitation has lasted for three months.[27]

Although the requirement under each of the statutes governing magistrates' courts' proceedings, that the parties must be living apart before liability accrues, seems to place the liability towards the children on the state of the relationship between the spouses, this is not completely so. An order can be made in favour of a child even if the claimant is barred from obtaining an order in his or her favour on account of having committed a matrimonial offence.[28] This is also true if the defendant has separated from the claimant by consent without making any undertaking that he would provide maintenance for her. The defendant owes no duty to the claimant (see p. 117), but his duty to the child remains unimpaired. However, in *Northrop* v. *Northrop*[29] the Court of Appeal held that, although a claimant in this position was owed no duty by the husband to support her and consequently could claim nothing on her own behalf on the basis of wilful neglect to maintain *her*, she could nevertheless make a claim on her behalf for her loss of earnings occasioned by looking after the child, on the basis of her husband's wilful neglect to maintain the *child*. This decision was of greater practical importance when it was decided than it is now because at that time maintenance orders made by magistrates were subject to a statutory maximum. By making two orders, one in favour of the wife herself and the other in favour of the child on the basis of the husband's single offence (wilful neglect towards the child), the court was able to increase the total sum payable to the mother. But these maxima have been abolished,[30] and it would now be possible to make a substantial order in favour of the child alone which would assist the mother in defraying the expenses of looking after it. But the case may still be relevant, because it might not be proper, when computing the sum necessary for the maintenance

26. M.P.(M.C.)A.1960 s. 16(1).   27. *ibid.*, s. 7(1).
28. *ibid.*, s. 8(2)(b).   29. [1967] 2 All E.R. 961.
30. Maintenance Orders Act 1968.

of the child, to include a sum designed to compensate the mother for her loss of earnings while tending the child. If such compensation were considered necessary, it might still be necessary that the mother claim it in her own right. It should be noted that where a claimant has committed a matrimonial offence and thereby forfeited her right to support, the principle in the *Northrop* case does not apply. In such a case, though the claimant may still obtain an order in favour of the child, none can be made in her own favour.[31]

### Environmental control

The criminal law protecting children against injury is a blunt instrument to keep families intact. The law of maintenance may be of assistance in providing some degree of economic security for children within a family in certain types of conditions. But the causes of child neglect and deprivation are so diverse that the situations covered by those provisions fall far short of the totality of conditions which require attention if the family's duties to its children are to be safeguarded. If the policy of keeping families viable so as to obviate the necessity of having to provide for the upbringing of children outside their own families is to succeed, provisions must exist to enable assistance and supervision to be brought 'to the doorstep' of the home to prevent deteriorating situations from leading to disaster.

The Home Office Committee on Children and Young Persons which reported in 1960 (Ingleby Committee) considered this problem and recommended that local authorities should be obliged to carry out preventive case-work and should be empowered to provide assistance in cash or kind if this was necessary to prevent the suffering of children through neglect in their own homes. Section 1 of the Children and Young Persons Act 1963 implements this recommendation and also empowers local authorities to make arrangements with voluntary associations or other persons for the provision of the necessary facilities. The core of the problem, however, is a matter of organization. There are numerous ways in which the social services might come into contact with families which are at risk. The health visitor from the local health department is a very important source of contact, but officials from the housing department, supplementary benefits com-

31. *Young* v. *Young* [1964] P. 152.

mission, children's department, education department (school welfare officers), general practitioners and probation officers might become involved with families in different ways. In addition, a number of voluntary associations operate in this area, for example the National Marriage Guidance Council, Family Service Units and the NSPCC.

The Ingleby Committee appreciated the extent of the organizational difficulties which this array of services created and suggested, in addition to cooperation between local authorities and the voluntary authorities, that the local authorities should make provision for coordination between their departments in collecting information and making investigations. With regard to the task of investigation and diagnosis, the Committee suggested that a special unit might be set up by local authorities which would serve as a central point of reference for the various services and which would make a comparatively independent assessment of which of them a particular problem required. From this suggestion has developed the establishment of Family Advice Centres. The addition of yet another body of officers might be considered a questionable tactic in view of the confused situation which then existed, and a study of these centres by Leissner (1967) revealed uncertainty about their function. In some cases the emphasis was on an independent and positive role, where the officers of the Centre 'reached out' to assist families in the fringe groups of society (e.g. immigrant families). In others, they adopted a more passive attitude and confined themselves to assisting coordination between other services. The kinds of assistance offered ranged from intensive casework to informal advice, but in the latter case there was danger of overlap with agencies such as the Citizens Advice Bureaux.

A thorough review of the organizational problems behind preventive family casework was made in the Report of the Committee on Local Authority and Allied Personal Social Services (1968) and the implementation of the Committee's recommendations has to some extent removed the rationale for Family Advice Centres. These recommendations were to the effect that local authority social services should be unified into a single department comprising the existing services of the children's department, the welfare services of the supplementary benefits commission, the education welfare services, the child guidance services and certain other welfare services, such as the social work provided by housing departments, and mental welfare work. Only the probation service and the supervision and assistance provided by health departments would operate separately.

The major recommendations of the report were implemented by the Local Authority Social Services Act 1970. The Act requires local authorities to establish a single committee which would replace the children's committee and other welfare committees and would assume the social service functions of the health committee. However, education welfare and welfare services of housing departments are not bound to be transferred to this committee. There will be one Director of Social Services, who will be an important local government officer with responsibility for all the social services of the authority. As a result of this Act, it was only at central government level that a substantial degree of fragmentation of responsibility for family services would be found (in particular, the division of these functions between the Home Office, with its children's department, and the Department of Health and Social Security). But civil service reorganization announced by the Conservative administration in October 1970 included the concentration of these functions in the latter Department. From January 1971 the administrative unification of family services at both central and local level was almost complete.

The assistance which a social case-worker can provide is strengthened if cash and other facilities can be offered. There has been a growing tendency to make cash payments in recent years. In 1965–66, £88,000 were spent in this way, and in 1968–69 this had grown to £261,000 (Home Office, 1967–1969, para. 12). This might appear to impose an undue burden on the public purse, but in fact it can be considerably cheaper to provide a subvention which enables children to stay at home rather than to be put to the cost of receiving them into care. At a rough estimate, the number of children enabled to stay at home through preventive work amounts to about one-third of the cases investigated. Since it costs nearly £9 a week to maintain a child in care, this could represent a considerable saving. Indeed, assistance in cash or kind can avert the necessity of receiving a child into care in many of the circumstances which are the most common in which a child is received into care. The most common situations leading to reception into care are the short-term illness of the mother (one-third of cases in 1968–69), confinement of the mother (about 14 per cent of those cases), death or desertion by the mother (about

11 per cent) and homelessness or unsatisfactory home conditions (a further 9 per cent) (see p. 160).

The provision of day nurseries and arrangements for child minders are especially important for very young children. The Seebohm Committee remarked that it was clear from the evidence they received that 'many children under five are being minded daily in conditions which not only endanger their health and safety but also impair their emotional and intellectual development'. Although the Committee felt that mothers with children under five should not be obliged to go out to work for lack of a reasonable income, this is unfortunately widely necessary, and social services have been slow to provide facilities to ensure that the children concerned are not unduly deprived. Only some 10 per cent of children of the two to four age group attend nursery school. The provision by local authorities of day nurseries fluctuates throughout the country, but in general is insufficient to meet the demand. It has therefore been necessary for most families needing this form of assistance to use the services of daily child minders. The principal legislation governing supervision over the activities of child minders is the Nurseries and Child Minders Regulation Act 1948. This Act requires local health authorities to keep registers both of *buildings* used as nurseries where children under the upper limit of compulsory school are received to be looked after during the day or on a weekly basis (excluding schools and private houses) and also of *persons* receiving children under five into their homes for reward on the same basis. Requirements may be imposed concerning staff, premises and the number of children, and powers are given to the authority to inspect the premises. Over the course of time it became apparent that there were a number of loopholes in these provisions and section 60 of the Health Services and Public Health Act 1968 strengthened them in a number of ways. In particular it extended the provisions to cover situations where children were minded for at least two hours during the day, and compulsory registration was extended to child minders who looked after one child only. The penalties for infringement have been increased and, as a preventive measure, persons applying for registration are required to submit statements about persons they employ or intend to employ in looking after the children and, in addition, about anyone at all over sixteen who is normally resident on the premises where the children will be.

Where it is necessary for children to be cared for away from home for periods longer than six days, an alternative to receiving them into care is provided in the form of private fostering arrangements. It was in this area where conditions of appalling neglect of children were revealed in the second half of the last century, and a series of enactments commencing in 1872 laid the foundation of the modern legislation on child protection. The major relevant Act is the Children Act 1958, but important amendments to it were made by the Children and Young Persons Act 1969. Local Authorities are under a duty to satisfy themselves of the well-being of children fostered in their area and to ensure that they are visited and advised by their officers. Before the amendments of the 1969 Act took effect children were protected by the legislation only if they were being looked after for payment and for periods exceeding a month. But section 52 of the 1969 Act extends the supervision of local authorities to persons undertaking care and maintenance of any child below the upper limit of compulsory school age even if this is free, provided that the person is not a relative or guardian of the child. But if the care is not intended to and does not exceed six days, these provisions do not apply. There is also an exception made for persons looking after children for more than six days but not more than twenty-seven, provided that the person does not do this on a regular basis. Thus parents can leave their children to be looked after by non-related neighbours for up to twenty-seven days without necessitating local authority supervision unless the child-minders' regulations apply, which will happen if two or more non-related children under five are looked after for reward for less than a week.

Persons who take in foster children protected by the legislation have elaborate duties. Before receiving the child, the local authority must be notified, and this notification must be not less than two but not more than four weeks before the reception of the child. An exception is made in the case of emergency, when notification within forty-eight hours of reception (or from the time when a child already in care became a foster child) must be given. By an important modification introduced in the 1969 Act, however, the requirement of notification does not apply to each child received. It applies only when a person first takes in a foster child. Notification regarding subsequently received children is unnecessary if he has had at least one child continuously in care as a foster child from the time of the original notice. Nevertheless when the original notification is given to the local authority, the authority may impose certain requirements which the foster parent must comply with, and these may include giving particulars of any foster child kept on the premises. Officers of the authority have powers to enter and inspect the premises. Persons may be prohibited from keeping foster children, either totally or on certain premises or only with respect to a particular child, but appeal from these prohibitions may be made to a juvenile court.

If a family crisis arises which necessitates the removal of the child from the home, its placement in another family atmosphere, especially if it is one with which the child is already partially familiar, goes a considerable way to lessening risks of disturbance caused by the move. It is an advantage, therefore, if parents can make these arrangements themselves where they see a difficult situation impending. But more often than not parents leave fostering arrangements to be made by the local authority. On 31 March 1969 there were just over 30,000 children who had been boarded out with foster parents by local authorities compared to nearly 11,000 who had been boarded out privately and subject to the child protection legislation. But the latter figure is probably depressed because the number of children covered by that legislation was smaller before the amendments to it were enacted by the Children and Young Persons Act 1969.

When local authority channels are used to arrange for the care of children away from their homes it is necessary for the child to be *received into care* by the authority under section 1 of the Children Act 1948. Usually this is done upon application by one or both of the parents, but the authority is not bound to accede to the application. It can only admit the child if he is under seventeen and the parents (or guardians) are temporarily or permanently prevented by incapacity or other circumstances from providing the child's proper accommodation, maintenance and upbringing, and the intervention of the authority 'is necessary in the interests of the welfare of the child'. But the authority is not obliged to wait until the parents apply, a point of particular relevance with respect to the alternative ground on which a child may be admitted, i.e. that 'he has neither parent nor guardian or has been and remains abandoned (by them) or is lost'. Table 3 gives the principal reasons why children are received into care under the section and the number so received by local authorities in England and Wales during the 12 months up to 31 March 1969. There has been a gradual decline in the total number of children coming into care in recent years as a result of the general policy not to remove them unnecessarily from their home environment.

Table 3

**Reasons why Children came into Care during the Twelve Months to 31 March 1969**

| | |
|---|---:|
| No parent or guardian | 233 |
| Abandoned or lost | 551 |
| Death of mother, father unable to care | 739 |
| Deserted by mother, father unable to care | 5,231 |
| Confinement of mother | 7,162 |
| Short-term illness of parent or guardian | 16,803 |
| Long-term illness of parent or guardian | 1,729 |
| Tuberculosis contact | 63 |
| Child illegitimate and mother unable to provide home | 3,302 |
| Parent or guardian in prison or remanded in custody | 766 |
| Family homeless because of eviction | 1,108 |
| Family homeless through a cause other than eviction | 1,084 |
| Unsatisfactory home conditions | 2,680 |
| Fit person orders – offenders | 1,541 |
| Fit person orders – non-offenders | 3,433 |
| Under s. 36(1) of the Matrimonial Causes Act 1965 | 63 |
| Under s. 2(1) of the Matrimonial Proceedings (Magistrates' Courts) Act 1960 | 82 |
| Other reasons | 4,692 |
| Total | 51,262 |

Source: *Children in Care in England and Wales*, March 1969

Although only children under seventeen may be received into care under the section, once admitted they may be retained (subject to parental rights) until they reach eighteen if their welfare demands it. But authorities are under a duty to endeavour to secure that the child is taken back by his parents, guardians or relations when this will be consistent with his welfare. They are also obliged to attempt to 'further his best interests and to afford him opportunity for proper development of his character and abilities'.[32] Section 13 of the Children Act 1948, as amended by the Children and Young Persons Act 1969[33] lays down the major methods by which local authorities deal with children they have received into care. They may, 'as they think fit', either board them out with foster parents or maintain them in 'community homes', voluntary homes or other homes providing specialized facilities not available in community homes. But leeway is left for special arrangements to be made to fit particular cases as, for example, allowing a child to stay with a relative or friend. Prior to this, boarding out was obligatory unless that would not have been practicable or desirable. Although in the years following the Second World War the percentage of children in care who were boarded out rose sharply, in more recent years this has been declining. In 1963 they represented 52 per cent of the total; in 1969 this had fallen to 48 per cent. It has not been possible for recruitment of foster parents to keep pace with the increase in the number of children being received into care, and the amendments in the 1969 Act give local authorities greater flexibility in deciding how to accommodate children in their care.

Where children are boarded out, the local authority and foster parents must comply with the Boarding-Out of Children Regulations 1955. Children may be boarded out with married couples or single persons, but if the single person is a man he must be either the grandfather, uncle or elder brother of the child. Before boarding out, the child must be medically examined and regular medical examinations must be made while he is boarded out and boarding out must be terminated if it appears that it is no longer in his best interests. There are special provisions if the term of the boarding out exceeds, or is expected to exceed, eight weeks ('a long-stay' boarding out). In such cases the prospective home must be visited by an officer of the Children's Department who is personally acquainted with the child or is fully informed about him, and he must report in writing that the conditions of the home are satisfactory for the particular child. He must also report certain matters concerning the foster parents, including their 'reputation and religious persuasion . . . and their suitability in age, character, temperament and health to have charge of the child'. Visits at regular intervals must be arranged

32. Children Act 1948, ss. 1(3), and 12(1).   33. s. 49.

and the welfare, health, conduct and progress of the child must be reviewed within three months of the placing out and thereafter at least once every six months. The foster parents are required to sign an undertaking to treat the child as they would a member of their own family, to inform the authority of 'any serious occurrence affecting the child' and to permit the stipulated medical examinations and visits. If the stay is expected to be shorter than eight weeks some of these requirements are modified. There must still be a prior visit by the officer but the foster parents are not required to make the undertaking mentioned. They must nevertheless be informed of their obligations. Visits must still be made, but at intervals appropriate to the shorter stay. If in the event the stay lasts longer than eight weeks, the full regulations apply.

How successful is fostering? In assessing answers to this question it is necessary to appreciate that children going to foster parents may often have had a fairly disturbed background. They will have been prised from their own family and may have been accommodated for some time in residential institutions. The research reviewed by Dinnage and Kellmer Pringle (1967) shows that successive breakdowns in fostering arrangements have an adverse effect on the child concerned. As the chances of unsuccessful fostering are higher where the child is disturbed, caution should be exercised over boarding out disturbed children lest a vicious circle of breakdowns, further maladjustment and repeated breakdown should result. On the other hand, the dangers inherent in 'institutionalization' have already been mentioned and a child in care would seem to be faced with risks arising either from the 'total' deprivation of a mother figure while in an institution or from 'serial' deprivation resulting from successive breaches in the development of such a figure. Much will depend on selecting the right child in the appropriate circumstances and on wise placing. Fortunately, research has indicated some factors which are associated with fostering failure or success. If the foster parents have a child of their own the same age or younger than the foster child, this is a factor militating against success. Other adverse factors seem to include cases where the foster child's mother had died before placement and the placement of children over four years old. Foster parents of lower social class tend to be associated with successful fostering.

If fostering is not, or cannot be, arranged for a child in care he will generally be accommodated in a community home. Community homes are, under the scheme introduced by the Children and Young Persons Act 1969, administered by local authorities on a regional basis and comprise establishments which were previously run separately as children's homes and hostels, approved schools, remand homes, and, in so far as they take persons under seventeen, probation homes, detention centres and borstal institutions. Of course within this system children will be accommodated in the particular establishment suitable for them. Voluntary homes such as those run by the Church of England Children's Society and Dr Barnardo's Homes may be integrated into regional system as 'controlled' or 'assisted' community homes, depending upon the degree of independence of management from the local authority.

When a child has been received into care and is either boarded out or in institutional accommodation, it becomes important to determine with clarity the legal position pertaining between the child, parents, local authority and any other persons (e.g. foster parents) who are concerned. First, so long as the child remains in care, the parents must keep the authority informed of their address[34] and are liable to make contributions, either by agreement or under court order, with respect to the cost of maintaining the child. If the child is illegitimate and contribution from the father is required, the local authority must either apply for an affiliation order to be made against him or, if there is one in force, obtain its variation so that payment can be made to itself. In 1968–69 the average contribution per child was 7s 6d a week. However, so long as the child has been merely received into care, the authority's rights over him cease if either parent requests his return unless it takes further steps.[35] One such step is to pass a resolution under section 2 of the 1948 Act assuming parental rights. But it may only do so if *both* parents are dead and there is no guardian, or if *either* parent has abandoned the child, or suffers from permanent disability rendering him incapable of caring for the child or is 'of such habits or mode of life as to be unfit to have the care of the child'. The Children and Young Persons Act 1936[36] extended the situations in which a resolution of this kind can be passed. Where the whereabouts of a parent or guardian have

34. Children Act 1948, s. 10(1).   35. *ibid.*, s. 1(3).   36. s. 48.

been unknown to the local authority for twelve months the child is to be deemed abandoned; parental rights may also be lost by a parent who so persistently and without reasonable cause fails to discharge parental obligations as to be unfit to care for the child, or who suffers from mental disorder with the same result. A parent must be given notice when the resolution is passed. If he objects, the resolution can only stand if confirmed by a juvenile court, and a parent may at any time apply to that court for rescission of the resolution.

If the resolution is passed and not set aside it may last until the child becomes eighteen. It vests all the parental rights of the deprived parent in the authority, which means that his or her custody is vested in the authority. But he is not relieved of liability to contribute to the child's maintenance. One parental right unaffected by the resolution is the right to determine the religious persuasion in which the child is to be brought up.[37] But in general, once a resolution under section 2 is passed, the local authority has a wide discretion in deciding on what is the best course to be followed to further the child's welfare. So if anyone, even a parent, intervenes by attempting to have the child made a ward of court and thereby put under the jurisdiction of the High Court rather than the local authority, the move will fail. In re M.[38] the Court of Appeal made it clear that the Act conferred a discretion upon the local authority to take decisions about the welfare of the child and it would be wrong for the courts to interfere unless the authority was acting in disregard of its statutory duties. The result is that there can be no external interference in the decision of an authority with respect to a child over which it has assumed parental rights unless it has abused or disregarded its statutory duties, or possibly has made decisions about the child which no reasonable authority could have reached.

Where there has been no resolution passed under section 2 the position is more difficult. So long as the child remains in care, the principle in re M. applies so that if, for example, the authority deem it to be in accordance with their duties to remove a child from foster parents, a court should not interfere with that decision, so long as the authority is not acting improperly or unreasonably, even if the court might have taken a different view of the best course for the

37. Children Act 1948, s. 3.    38. [1961] Ch. 328.

child.[39] But once a parent requests the return of the child into his care under section 1(3), the authority loses its statutory right to keep the child. It has been said that the request does not put the authority under a mandatory duty to hand the child over[40] and this is sensible because the authority may judge that an immediate return would be harmful to the child. But it must look elsewhere than to the Act for authority to keep the child, and the issue therefore becomes one of disputed custody between the parent and the local authority (or foster parents). This can be resolved by either side making application to the High Court for the child to be made a ward of court, or, more exceptionally and possibly only if the child is very young, by the parent applying for issue of the writ of habeas corpus. The court will make an order deciding who is to have custody of the child and in deciding the matter will do so in accordance with the normal principles upon which it exercises its general jurisdiction over all minors to ensure their well-being.[41] This ancient power was traditionally exercised by the Chancery Division of the High Court, but now it is exercised by judges of the Family Division (see p. 278).

The major principle upon which the court will decide the custody dispute is that the welfare of the child is to be given paramount consideration. A striking example of the application of this principle occurred in *J.* v. *C.*, a case which was decided in the House of Lords in 1969.[42] The son of Spanish parents was placed with foster parents when he was only four days old and he was subsequently received into care by a local authority as his mother was unable to look after him, owing to ill health. Although she was still extremely delicate, the boy was returned to his parents after ten months and accordingly discharged from care. The parents then returned to Spain, but the boy became unwell and unhappy and when he was just over three years old his parents returned him to the foster parents. He was again received into care under section 1 of the Children Act 1948. Two years later the mother requested the return of the child. The foster parents now said they wished to adopt him and the local

39. *Re A.B.* [1954] 2 All E.R. 287.
40. *Re R.(K.)* [1963] 3 All E.R. 337; *Krishnan* v. *London Borough of Sutton* [1969] 3 All E.R. 1367.
41. *Re G.* [1963] 3 All E.R. 370.
42. [1969] 1 All E.R. 788.

authority commenced proceedings to make the child a ward of court. These were subject to many delays, but eventually, when the child was seven, the High Court ordered that the child remain in the care of the foster parents, but left it open for the parents, who had not been represented before the court, to make further application. This they eventually did after the lapse of a further two years. By this time the boy was nine years old and had settled down happily in the foster home. The judge, after a meticulous consideration of the evidence, refused to order the return of the child because he felt that in all the circumstances, and especially in view of his long absence from Spain, there would be too many risks in ordering him to return. This decision was finally upheld by the House of Lords but only after a further two years had elapsed.

This case illustrates that even where an authority has not passed a resolution assuming parental rights over a child in its care, the very act of placing a child into care puts the parents at some risk of losing the custody of the child. The facts in *J*. v. *C*. were indeed highly unusual involving, as they did, the absence of the parents abroad and inordinate legal delays arising, at least partly, as a result of that fact. But it also lays bare a dilemma of principle in child care practice. When a child is in care, every effort is made to provide the child with the most beneficial surroundings, especially in a home atmosphere into which he can be happily assimilated. If this succeeds, the greater will be the danger to his welfare if he is removed and returned to his parents, especially in the case of a young child, or one who has been in that atmosphere for a long period. Earlier judicial attitudes accepted that, as between parents and strangers, the parents had a *prima facie* right to the child which would be lost only if they were manifestly unfit to care for the child. Now the courts will pay attention primarily to the child's welfare. This does not necessarily mean that parents are to be treated in the same way as strangers but only that the issue is more finely balanced. In *Re F*.[43] Mr Justice Megarry, discussing the application of the dominant 'welfare' principle in disputed custody cases on divorce, remarked that, though the welfare of the child might be paramount, this did not exclude other considerations. If the welfare of the child were to be served equally well whichever side obtained its custody, these secondary matters would determine the

43. [1969] 2 All E.R. 766.

issue, but, he warned, such a decision cannot be calculated arithmetically. Bearing in mind the general policy expressed in the Children Act that the authority is to endeavour to restore children to their own families, and the danger of weakening the confidence of parents who entrust their children into care if they fear they may lose custody, it seems legitimate to consider the claims of parents as a strong 'secondary' element. If an immediate transfer to the parents would create an unjustifiable hazard to the stability of the child, the child will stay where its welfare will be better served and the parents will be refused custody for the time being. But this does not deprive the parents of the child permanently. In *J*. v. *C*. the court paid considerable attention to the fact that the child was kept aware of his Spanish background and expressed the hope that, when he was older, he would resume his ties with his family. Therefore in cases where immediate transfer of the child is undesirable, his re-integration with his original family could be encouraged by requiring contacts to be retained or resumed with it until such time as the transfer is safe.

Although the courts will decide disputed custody cases between parents and foster parents on the basis that the welfare of the child must be given paramount consideration, it has often been said that the foster parents are not given sufficient security. This lack of security arises partly from the inherent nature of the foster relationship, which is generally understood to be a merely temporary one, and partly from the fact that the claims of the parents, though secondary in law to the welfare of the child, are naturally and, it is thought, rightly, given much weight. Nevertheless, an interim working paper published in October 1970 by the Home Office Committee on the Adoption of Children (Houghton Committee) has suggested that consideration be given to strengthening the position of foster parents. The method suggested is that foster parents should be able to apply to magistrates for the legal custody of the child to be granted to them under the Guardianship of Minors Act 1971. At present foster parents generally take no steps to obtain legal custody of the child unless a dispute arises, in which case they may seek custody by instituting wardship proceedings in the High Court. The suggestion is advantageous to foster parents in so far as an application for custody under the 1971 Act is comparatively simple and, if it succeeds, puts them at a procedural advantage over the parents, for, if the parents wish the child returned to them, they will have to apply for a variation of the custody order to be made in their favour. The Committee also refers to the custody order as granting 'guardianship' to the foster parents, and to be designated the child's legal guardians may increase the foster parents' sense of security.

On the other hand, these gains may not be very solid. First, the Committee itself suggests that an application for 'guardianship' by foster parents should not be permitted until they have looked after the child for at least a year, and even then, only with the consent of the local authority, unless they have had the child for five years or more. Second, the application will be determined on the same principles as at present, which presumably means that the claims of parents will continue to be given great weight. The order would be open to review at any time if the parents seek return of the child. Finally, it is not entirely clear what the expression 'guardianship' means. It probably means no more than 'custody', which refers to the right to supervise the more important aspects of the child's upbringing. It may be useful for a foster parent to regularize his relationship with the child in this way, but it is not entirely certain whether applications by foster parents to a court to do this when no dispute has arisen should be encouraged. Such a step may well alarm the parents, who might oppose the legal formalizing of a situation they were happy to allow to exist in fact. It may be better to enable the position of foster parents to be regularized by some less formal method, while always leaving it open for the parents to seek the return of the child by instituting custody proceedings if the return is opposed by the foster parents.

The reception of children into care in the manner described is a voluntary facility should the need arise. When families have broken down to such a degree that it is harmful for children to remain in their home environment it becomes necessary to use compulsory powers of intervention. These are set out in section 1 of the Children and Young Persons Act 1969, which came into operation on 1 January 1971. This section applies to all persons under seventeen and gives to a juvenile court power to make certain compulsory orders if it is satisfied of certain conditions with respect to the person, namely that

(a) His proper development is being avoidably prevented or neglected or his health is being avoidably impaired or neglected or he is being ill-treated; or

(b) It is probable that the condition set out in the preceding paragraph will be satisfied in his case, having regard to the fact that the court or another court, has found that that condition is or was satisfied in the case of another child or young person who is or was a member of the household to which he belongs; or

(c) He is exposed to moral danger; or

(d) He is beyond the control of his parent or guardian; or

(e) He is of compulsory school age . . . and is not receiving efficient full-time education suitable to his age, ability and aptitude; or

(f) He is guilty of an offence, excluding homicide;
*and also* that he is in need of care or control which he is unlikely to receive unless the court makes an order.

The court may order the young person's parents or guardian to be bound over to take proper care and control of him, or it may make a 'supervision' order, a 'care' order or a hospital or guardianship order if the child or young person suffers from mental illness. The two major forms of order are the 'supervision' and the 'care' order. Where the child concerned is under fourteen the supervision must be done by the local authority, and this will be performed by an officer of the children's department. The only exception is where there already is a probation officer in contact with another member of the child's household.[44] But if the person is over fourteen but under seventeen supervision may be either by the local authority or by a probation officer, so that if the reason for the order is neglect of the child, the children's department may be involved. If it is an offence the matter may be better dealt with by the probation service. Section 14 states that 'while a supervision order is in force it shall be the duty of the supervisor to advise, assist and befriend the supervised person'. Supervision is essentially compulsory 'care' without removing the child from his home surroundings. However it is possible for the supervisor to require the supervised person to live at a specified place for a continuous period not exceeding, in all, ninety days, or to attend before a certain person or participate in certain activities at specified days; but these cannot be for more than thirty days a year

44. s. 13.

for the maximum period of three years for which supervision orders may run. The degree of flexibility conferred is considerable and may vary from short-term detention under a rigorous disciplinary regime, or attendance at training or recreation centres to compulsory treatment by a medical practitioner or as a resident or non-resident patient in a hospital.

The 'care' order results in the person being *committed* to the care of the local authority. These orders may last until the person concerned reaches eighteen, unless he was over sixteen when committed, or there are other special circumstances, in which case they may continue until he is nineteen. Committal to care under the Act automatically confers upon the local authority parental rights over the person committed and, in addition, the right to 'restrict his liberty to such an extent as the authority consider appropriate'.[45] The authority is put under the same general duties with respect to the children committed in this way as they are regarding all children in their care,[46] except that their duty under section 12(1) of the Children Act 1948 to further the child's best interests is qualified in so far as this is necessary to protect members of the public.[47] These children will generally be accommodated in community homes of the same type as the previous 'approved schools'. If a child accommodated in one of these homes proves particularly destructive, the local authority may, if he is over fifteen, bring him before a juvenile court which may order his removal to a borstal institution.[48]

A notable feature of the Act is the considerable degree of discretion conferred on the local authority, either as the 'supervisor' of the child or as the authority into whose care a child or young person has been committed for the purpose of treatment or punishment. But the involvement of the authority's social workers will commence at an even earlier stage. If proceedings under section 1 are brought by a person other than officer of the local authority (e.g. by a police constable or an officer of the NSPCC), that person is obliged to inform the local authority of the proceedings.[49] The local authority must then investigate the matter for itself and provide the court with

45. C.Y.P.A. 1969, s. 24(2).
46. Children Act 1948, s. 11 as amended by C.Y.P.A. 1969, s. 27(1).
47. C.Y.P.A. 1969, s. 27(2).   48. *ibid.*, s. 31.
49. *ibid.*, s. 2(3).

the relevant background information.[50] This will be necessary even where the person concerned has committed a criminal offence, because a care order with respect to him can be made only if it is also proved that he is in need of care or control *which he is unlikely to receive unless the court makes an order*. It was the intention of the Labour government, which sponsored the Act, that this protection should eventually apply to all young offenders under fourteen. At present it covers only young offenders under the age of ten, for over that age they may be subject to criminal prosecution. The Conservative government, however, proposes to extend its protection to children under twelve, but not further. The present government has also decided not to proceed with another aspect of the Act. This is section 5, the purpose of which was to restrict the occasions upon which persons under seventeen who *were* liable to prosecution would actually be prosecuted. It was proposed to limit their prosecution to certain *types* of offences and to allow prosecution even of those offences only if the prosecutor was of the opinion that 'it would not be adequate for the case to be dealt with by a parent, teacher or other person or by means of a caution from a constable or through the exercise of the powers of a local authority'. It would have been necessary to have informed the local authority about any prosecution and normally to have sought its opinion before bringing a prosecution.

The philosophy behind these controversial proposals regarding young offenders originated in the Labour government White Paper, *The Child, the Family and the Young Offender* (1965). There it is stated that 'it is at least clear that much delinquency – and indeed many other social problems – can be traced back to inadequacy or breakdown in the family. The right place to begin, therefore, is with the family.' The purpose of involving local authority social workers at early stages of criminal delinquency cases was to see whether a better solution could not be found by discovering what had gone wrong with the family and, perhaps, by bringing family pressure to bear on the delinquent and trying to re-integrate him into his family. It represented a significant expression of belief that the family is an effective social force to prevent deviance and, had the policy been fully implemented, would have been a major step along the path

50. s. 9.

taken by family policy in 1948. But serious doubts were felt about the procedure. In particular, the necessity to make social inquiries would, it was suggested, unduly hamper the police in their work. This does not appear to be a strong objection if it is in fact true that the procedure provides a better way to cure delinquency than straightforward criminal prosecution. More important is the doubt expressed by Cavanagh (1966) whether, in many of these cases, much can be achieved by social work with the family. The rift between it and the delinquent may already be unbridgeable. In many cases the parents will themselves be 'muddled, inadequate, beaten, pathetic or truculent'. But if this is the situation in many cases of delinquency, it only serves to underline the importance of preventive social casework with inadequate families.

# Chapter 5
# During Marriage:
# Emotional Security

To assist a family's economic circumstances or its resources in the upbringing of its children is to lessen specific strains that might be imposed upon it. But these aids provide only ancillary support for the main core of the marriage, which is the relationship between the husband and the wife. No one suggests that the success of this relationship in emotional terms can be controlled by legal means, but it would be wrong to conclude that legal factors cannot *influence* it. Some examples of this will be discussed here, but it must be emphasized that the degree of influence of the legal provisions must remain a matter of speculation in each case.

## Three-year bar to divorce

The general prohibition barring divorce within the first three years of marriage, unless the circumstances are exceptional, has been discussed earlier in relation to its possible deterrence against hasty marriage (see p. 72). Its second purpose, relevant here, is to encourage spouses encountering the initial adjustment difficulties of married life to try to resolve them, rather than to seek a solution in immediate divorce. Whether or not this objective is achieved cannot be said with any degree of certainty. Two extensive American studies, one by Kephart (1954) and the other by Monahan (1962) showed that, of marriages resulting in divorce, a higher percentage of *separations* occurred within the first year of marriage than in later years. In Kephart's Philadelphia sample, as many as 40 per cent of those who were eventually to divorce had parted by the end of the third year. There is no evidence about this in England, and all that can be claimed for the American evidence is that it suggests that, where a marriage is destined to break down, there is nearly a 50 per cent chance that it will do so within the first three years. Therefore it seems that the relationship is particularly vulnerable during that period, and a provision which restricts resort to *divorce* during this period may be a wise safeguard, so that when difficulties do arise the couple cannot seek that remedy as a quick solution. It may be hoped that the problems will be sorted out before the period has elapsed. Of course in those cases where the relationship remains broken, the effect of the bar is simply to postpone the legal recognition of the breakdown. It this were common, one might expect that the percentage of divorces granted in the fourth and perhaps fifth years after marriage would be significantly higher than those of, say, the seventh or eighth year as they would include the delayed divorces of marriages in fact broken within the first three years. But the figures in Table 2 (see p. 38) show that this is not the case, for it is not until the eighth year that a tendency to level out appears, and this is only very slight. This might possibly suggest that, in England, the degree of permanent breakdowns of marriage within the first three years is not so high as in the American samples; but whether this, even if true, is partially due to the presence in England of the three-year bar cannot be said to be proved.

### Childlessness and impotence

It was stated earlier that there is no proof that childlessness in itself is a contributory factor to marriage breakdown (see p. 44). However, the strain it may impose upon even happily married couples is clear enough. Impotence is a separate, though related, problem. It is possible for a child to be conceived through external fecundation or by artificial means, despite the fact that full sexual intercourse between the parties is not possible. But failure to achieve satisfactory intercourse will in most cases itself cause difficulties in the marital relationship. It is therefore necessary to consider the legal responses to both of these sources of potential discord. One possible response is to permit a quick remedy by annulling the marriage as soon as the condition becomes apparent. Another is to assist the parties fully or partly to overcome the disability. These will be examined in turn.

Annulment of marriage was possible by the canon law applied in the ecclesiastical courts if at the time of the marriage one or both of the spouses were physically incapable of consummating it, and if this condition was incurable. This rule of the canon law still applied on 1 January 1971, and in almost every case a marriage annulled on this ground is, and would have remained, childless. But a marriage may be childless despite the ability of the spouses to have intercourse with each other, and so it became necessary to decide whether the canon law remedy was restricted to impotence or whether it could be applied also in cases of sterility. The question was settled finally only in 1947 when, in *Baxter* v. *Baxter*[1] the House of Lords held that a marriage was consummated even though conception was prevented. The law of nullity, therefore, provides no remedy where a marriage is threatened by sterility alone. It is relevant only where sexual consummation is impossible or, by a statutory extension of the canon law ground in 1938, where it is wilfully refused by one of the spouses.

Is it right to refuse to annul a marriage on the ground of sterility? To answer this question requires consideration of the present use and purpose of the law of nullity. Until it was changed by the Nullity of Marriage Act 1971, a nullity decree was conceptually quite distinct from a divorce decree. It had the effect of nullifying the marriage retrospectively. Before it was granted the marriage remained in full force and acts performed in reliance on its validity were effective. But after it issued the marriage was thenceforth treated as if it had never existed.[2] The advantage of this doctrine is that, where divorce is disallowed, or is severely restricted, the courts can legally terminate a marriage which has broken down without purporting to *dissolve* it. The court simply declares that the marriage never existed. But this aspect of nullity ceased to be of importance since the law governing divorce as from January 1971 seeks to give a remedy in almost all cases where the marriage has in fact broken down. (This will be discussed in detail in Part 2.) The justification for nullity proceedings must be sought elsewhere. It may be found in fact that nullity petitions, unlike divorce petitions, are not subject to a three-year bar. Indeed, the emphasis is quite the reverse because delay in bringing the petition may prejudice the petitioner's case. Where the non-consummation is due to the incurable incapacity of one of the parties, this exception to the three-year rule is amply justified, for to require parties to wait three years in these circumstances is not only to impose on them hardship, but also it cannot possibly serve any

1. [1948] A.C. 274.   2. *Re Rodwell* [1969] 3 All E.R. 1363.

purpose in deterring such marriages. Nor, since the condition is incurable, can it encourage the parties to overcome the situation. In the absence of any other reason for treating a marriage that has broken down for this reason any differently from a marriage which has broken down for any other reason, there seems to be a strong case for including impotence or wilful refusal among the conditions the presence of which, coupled with evidence that the other party (or either party) found the situation intolerable, will satisfy a court, on petition for divorce under the new divorce law, that the marriage has broken down irretrievably.[3] The Nigerian Matrimonial Causes Decree 1970, which follows the English Divorce Reform Act 1969 closely, contains a provision specifying persistent and wilful refusal to consummate a marriage as a condition upon which irretrievable breakdown may be found. An objection to extending the substance of the Nigerian provision to cases of impotence would be that an impotent spouse would always be at risk that this condition might be made the basis of a divorce petition against him, no matter how long the marriage had lasted. But this objection lacks force. It may be conceded that the legal risk would exist, but this would only be so because there is always a strong *actual* risk that the relationship would break down. If this therefore happens, a divorce law based on breakdown should be prepared to accept it. If it was thought that a petitioner, after a long marriage, was using the impotence of his partner as an *excuse* for divorce and that the breakdown resulted from other causes, it would always be open to the court to disbelieve that he really found the lack of sexual relations intolerable. In any case, strong safeguards to the economic position of a spouse divorced for this reason could be imported. (See ch. 9 for the present financial safeguards on divorce.)

Is there a good reason for restricting these considerations to non-consummation and refusing to extend them to sterility? If it can be established that one party to the marriage is incurably infertile and thereby the marriage breaks down, will this provide adequate justification for allowing a swift termination of the marriage without the necessity of waiting until three years have passed from the wedding and then resorting to the ordinary law of divorce? The relevant

3. The conditions entitling divorce under the new law will be discussed in chapter 9.

factors are so close to those in the case of impotence that to draw a distinction between the two is difficult to defend. To maintain the three-year bar is unlikely to encourage reconciliation where the condition is incurable. There can again be no question of deterring others.

This view of impotence and sterility, which treats them solely as problems of marriage breakdown, was not that taken by the Law Commission (1970). Although the Commission recommended that nullity decrees should no longer invalidate marriages retrospectively, so that in future their effect would be identical to that of divorce decrees, it recommended against assimilating impotence (and the related ground of wilful refusal to consummate a marriage) into the law of divorce. Both of these recommendations were implemented in the Nullity of Marriage Act 1971. These grounds for nullity differed, it was said, from conditions entitling divorce in that, unlike the divorce situation, the defects existed at the time of the ceremony, a point of importance in Christian jurisprudence. The Commission also thought it would be wrong to identify nullity with divorce because divorce gave rise to a 'stigma' which nullity should not do, because the three-year bar, appropriate for divorce, would be inappropriate for nullity and the Church would oppose it. This reasoning can be strongly criticized. Temperamental defects which may lead to divorce (e.g. an inclination to drunkenness) may exist at the time of the ceremony just as much as a person's sexual make-up; in both cases their *effects* are felt afterwards. It is extraordinary that the body which recommended the reform designed to remove as far as possible the stigma from divorce should make a proposal which perpetuates the distinction between divorce and nullity largely on the ground of the stigma of the former. The difficulty regarding the three-year bar could easily be overcome by enacting an exception to it in these cases. Nor did the Commission adequately justify the lack of a legal remedy where sterility causes breakdown of a marriage. The objection that it would put every childless marriage at risk has been dealt with in connection with a similar objection to assimilating impotence into the divorce law (see p. 176).[4]

4. The Departmental Committee on Human Artificial Insemination (1960) (Feversham Committee) also recommended against introducing sterility as a ground of nullity. But they did so because of the difficulties it would create for the conceptual framework of the law of nullity as it then stood.

The advantage of a quick termination of the marriage in these cases is that it may put an end to an intolerable situation the continuation of which can serve no good purpose. But not all marriages break down if these events happen, and in so far as the parties attempt to overcome their difficulties they should be assisted. If the parties are childless, artificial means of conception may be attempted. Alternatively, they may adopt a child. The legal implications of artificial insemination were the subject of the Report of the Feversham Committee. Where the donor is the husband, there is little difficulty because, whether or not the other spouse consented, the child born would be legitimate. If the donor is not the husband, special problems arise. In Scotland it has been held that, even if the husband does not consent to the insemination, the act does not constitute adultery[5] and this view would probably be taken in England. But the child born from a donor would be illegitimate, irrespective of the husband's consent. The Committee recommended that AID without the husband's consent and a donation by a husband without his wife's consent should be made new grounds for divorce. The new divorce law introduced by the Divorce Reform Act 1969 is silent on this point. The Committee refused to recommend that an AID child should be treated in all respects as a legitimate child, but did suggest that the child should be allowed succession rights against the estate of his mother's deceased husband. This recommendation has not been implemented. An illegitimate AID child would therefore have rights of succession against his mother and father (the donor) because illegitimate children now have such rights against their parents (see p. 212). But he would have none against his mother's husband, a person almost inevitably more important for him than the donor. With respect to maintenance, an AID child does not suffer by reason of his illegitimacy because he will generally be a 'child of the family' and have been accepted into it within the relevant maintenance statutes. The position of that child is, therefore, not completely secure, and there seems little reason why a child so conceived with the consent of the husband should not be treated in all respects as the legitimate child of the husband and wife.

If a childless couple do not attempt artificial insemination, they may wish to adopt a child. The primary purpose of adoption is not,

5. *Maclennan* v. *Maclennan* 1958 S.L.T. 7.

however, to provide children for childless couples. It is to find suitable homes for homeless children. Nevertheless, the home of a childless couple may well be quite suitable for such a child, in which case adoption serves a double function in providing for the emotional and social needs of both the child and the couple. Adoption by a childless couple, even if successful, will not always remove the strains of childlessness and gives rise to special problems of its own. But while there is no direct evidence to confirm how far adoption can increase the happiness of an otherwise childless marriage, that it often does so is certain. There is even evidence that the adoption of a child might be a causative factor in the subsequent conception by the wife of her own child. It would, therefore, be relevant to consider the law of adoption in this context, but it is thought more appropriate to consider it is a remedial institution assisting defective families and it will be treated fully in Part Two.

One final aspect of the problems raised by attempts to use artificial insemination or adoption to escape from a situation which might otherwise result in a decree of nullity should be considered. This concerns the effect which steps taken to obtain a child by these methods have on the spouses' entitlement to a nullity decree. The general principle applicable was stated by Lord Selborne in *G.* v. *M.*:[6]

. . . There may be conduct on the part of the person seeking this remedy which ought to estop that person from having it; as, for example, any act from which the inference ought to be drawn that during the antecedent time the party has, with a knowledge of the facts and of the law, approbated the marriage . . . or has taken advantages and derived benefits from the matrimonial relation which it would be unfair and inequitable to permit him or her, after having received them, to treat as if no such relation had existed.

Seen in the context of nullity this doctrine is unassailable. Nevertheless extraordinarily difficult decisions have to be made as to whether a petitioner should be denied a remedy as a result of having tried to extract from the relationship some of the advantages which normally accrue to married persons. If a spouse consents to the adoption of a child[7] or sues the other for maintenance[8] we seem to

6. (1885) 10 App. Cas. 171.   7. *W.* v. *W.* [1952] P. 152.
8. *Tindall* v. *Tindall* [1953] P. 63.

have clear cases of 'approbation'. But what if a spouse makes attempts at artificial insemination? Even if these fail, cannot it be said that there was an attempt to 'affirm' the marriage? Yet in *L.* v. *L.*[9] Mr Justice Pearce held that a wife who had repeatedly attempted to conceive a child by this method (and had eventually succeeded) was nevertheless entitled to a decree. It was said that she had not intended to affirm a marriage which would remain essentially abnormal for she had always hoped that her husband might be cured. The way in which this case can be reconciled with *W.* v. *W.* is to draw a distinction between those acts done with the purpose or hope that they will lead to a cure (which are not approbative) and those which show willingness to accept the marriage despite the affliction (which are approbative). But while sound in theory, the distinction breaks down when an attempt is made to apply it to the tangled web of hopes, fears and motives of parties in a situation of this kind. Every day that a spouse entitled to the decree delays seeking his remedy he does, to some extent, affirm the marriage. On the other hand, even an apparently clear affirmatory action such as adoption may well be undertaken with the secret hope that this will save the marriage on the emotional and sexual side, and may not really indicate a clear intention to persist with the relationship if the desired improvement does not take place. There is the additional point that it would surely be unfortunate if a spouse were to be deterred from resorting to a step such as adoption for fear that it might deprive him of a remedy should the strains resulting from the impotence of the other spouse continue, despite this attempt to save the marriage.

The Law Commission (1970) has recommended that the concept of approbation should be retained and redefined in a statutory clause which would deny a nullity decree to a spouse who, knowing a remedy was available, so behaved as to lead the other to believe he would not seek it.[10] But if one looks to the realities and treats the problem as one of marriage breakdown, the purpose of this bar becomes obscure. The hardship suffered by a respondent spouse lies not in the granting of a decree against him but in the fact that, despite the attempt to save it, the relationship has broken down. Under the new divorce law, the breakdown of a marriage is deemed

9. [1949] 1 All E.R. 141.   10. See Nullity of Marriage Act 1971, s. 3.

to be irretrievable if (amongst other things) the respondent has committed adultery or has behaved in such a way that the petitioner cannot reasonably be expected to live with him. Is there any reason why a breakdown caused by impotence or sterility should not equally be considered irretrievable? Why should a spouse defeated by the approbation clause be required to resort to the separation grounds of two or five years before the marriage can be dissolved (see ch. 9)? If incurable impotence or sterility found intolerable by the petitioner were added to the conditions establishing irretrievable breakdown, the complexities of nullity would be avoided and the interests of the parties and the children (if any) would be protected in the same way as they are in divorce proceedings.

## Marriage under mistake or duress

Besides the grounds mentioned above, nullity of marriage can be obtained, within limits, if one of the parties to the ceremony did not truly consent to marriage. Here it is obviously sensible to terminate the legal status as soon as possible, and the law of nullity is appropriate because it is the state of affairs at the time of the ceremony which is the essence of the complaint, in contrast to non-consummation cases, where the real reason for the complaint is the situation pertaining at the time of the hearing. Cases of imperfect, or total, lack of consent to the ceremony do not arise very often, but are certainly not unknown. In a very rare case a party might 'marry' the wrong person. This will, however, entitle a nullity decree only if the petitioner actually married a different person from the one expected. It is not enough to complain that one has been misled, even fraudulently, over something *about* the other person – e.g. his family connections. Where a party is under a misapprehension as to the nature of the ceremony, this too, will entitle him to a decree. More common, however, are cases where a party has entered a marriage under duress. Indeed, at least four such cases (one taking place in Malta, but nullified in England) were reported in England between 1967 and 1969. In one case the girl's parents, mistakenly believing she was pregnant, threatened to send her to a convent unless she married the boy.[11] The extent of pressure which must be present to override

11. *McLarnon* v. *McLarnon* (1968) 112 Sol. Jo. 419.

free consent is a question of fact and degree in each case. There must be some element of fear. It is not enough for one spouse to allege after the marriage that he or she entered it for some ulterior motive. Such a marriage cannot be nullified and this is clearly sound policy, otherwise the law of nullity would become the vehicle for an indefinable assortment of allegations. One point, however, was unsatisfactory. It was unclear whether these marriages were void or voidable. If they were void, either party, or even third parties, might at any time treat the marriage as if it never had existed no matter how long it may have lasted in fact. If they were voidable, the remedy of nullity was open only to an aggrieved party and even that might be lost by affirmation. The Nullity of Marriage Act 1971 settles the matter in favour of voidability. This is welcome since it would be undesirable if, after many years of communal life, one party were able to repudiate the marriage because of a defect relating solely to a ceremony which had taken place many years earlier.

### Reconciliation

Only one official service deals with marriage counselling and this is the probation service. In view of its other functions, this might at first sight appear strange but it is a result of the wide matrimonial jurisdiction conferred since 1895 on magistrates' courts. A wife whose husband was failing to support her would normally have recourse to these courts and it would be quite possible that the first person she would see would be a probation officer who, taking a broad view of his functions, might try to bring about a reconciliation and so avoid the necessity of court proceedings. At one stage a fear grew that this practice might be to the prejudice of the wife because the probation officer might be more assiduous in seeking reconciliation than in relentlessly pursuing her legal rights (as a lawyer might do), and so it was enacted that these officers were to act as conciliators if requested to do so by magistrates.[12] Fortunately common sense prevailed over this legalistic viewpoint and probation officers continue to see most of their clients for conciliation before the case comes to court. Eventually section 7 was repealed by the Magistrates' Courts Act 1952. However, nothing was put in its place so that there

12. Summary Proceedings (Domestic Jurisdiction) Act 1937, s. 7.

appears to be no statutory *duty* upon the probation service to undertake this work. The probation service considers this work to be relevant to its wider functions of reducing delinquency and this is certainly true in so far as family breakdown is a cause of deviance. But the association in the public mind of the service with 'criminals' is unfortunate in relation to their conciliation work. The preventive work by local authority children's departments under section 1 of the Children and Young Person's Act 1963 is wide enough to comprise marriage counselling, and indeed all the social services directed at preventing family breakdown which have been mentioned earlier can play a role here.

The major voluntary services especially concerned with marriage guidance are the National Marriage Guidance Council, the Catholic Marriage Advisory Council and the Family Discussion Bureau which is part of the Tavistock Institute of Human Relations. These receive financial support from the central government. In a field such as this one cannot expect statistical evidence *proving* the success of marriage conciliation work. But certainly many couples can be helped by these services, even if it is only by obtaining a clearer picture of the problems which face them. Even taking into account the difficulties in making this assessment, however, the sample of cases dealt with by the National Marriage Guidance Council which Wallis and Booker (1958) have studied indicate that in about a third of the cases the problem was either overcome or the relationship was reported to be improved. A rather higher success rate in Australia is reported by Harvey (1969). The extent of help given to married couples by general practitioners, mental health clinics, clergymen, lawyers and so on cannot be calculated. But even the most optimistic view of conciliation work concedes that, to be effective, it must take place relatively early in the deterioration of the relationship. Once divorce proceedings have started the experience of countries with a compulsory conciliation procedure at this stage shows that this is virtually worthless. The task is therefore to promote and give publicity to the conciliation services so they may be used at an early stage. The Divorce Reform Act 1969 contains a provision which attempts to make lawyers 'conciliation minded', for it requires rules of court to be made 'for requiring the solicitor acting for a petitioner for divorce to certify whether he has discussed with the petitioner the possibility of reconciliation and given him the names and addresses of persons qualified to help effect a reconciliation'.[13] A similar provision exists in the Australian divorce legislation, and it is estimated that some 7 per cent of all cases dealt with by the approved marriage guidance organizations in that country are referred to them by lawyers.

If reconciliation is to be encouraged, legal rules should not deter parties from it. The law of condonation did so. The attempt to remedy this in 1963, and its subsequent apparent failure, has already been discussed (see p. 121). It is to be hoped that the similar attempt to safeguard overtures for reconciliation which has been made in the Divorce Reform Act 1969 will meet with greater success. The reason for the presence of these safeguards in the 1969 Act lies in the fact that three of the situations which the Act specifies as giving rise to the presumption of marital breakdown involve the parties having lived apart continuously for a specified time. For desertion or divorce by consent this period must be two years; for divorce against the will of an 'innocent' spouse, the period must be five years. (These conditions will be discussed fully in Part Two.) It is therefore enacted that, in computing those periods, 'no account shall be taken of any one period (not exceeding six months) or of any two or more periods (not exceeding six months in all) during which the parties resumed living with each other'.[14] Such occasions are not to be counted as part of the period of separation either. This wording is much wider than the corresponding provision concerning condonation which was discussed earlier, and there seems to be no room for speculation as to the motives why the parties resumed cohabitation. This is a great improvement and should prove a satisfactory compromise between the policy of promoting conciliation and making living apart for stipulated periods a condition for the granting of divorce.

### Discouraging divorce

The use of the divorce law to deter from marital breakdown can involve either or both of two propositions. One is that if divorce were made impossible, or virtually so, this would compel spouses, even if not blissfully happy, to minimize their differences and to repress any motivations to seek another partner. The other is that

13. s. 3(1).  14. s. 3(5).

the law of divorce should be seen as having a quasi-criminal character designed to punish a 'guilty' party with a view to deterring others from matrimonial misconduct. These assumptions have formed the foundation of the whole structure of the divorce law of this country until the passing of the Divorce Reform Act 1969. The first was admirably expressed by Sir William Scott, later Lord Stowell, in an ecclesiastical court in 1790:

When people understand that they must live together, except for the very few reasons known to the law, they learn to soften by mutual accommodation that yoke which they know they cannot shake off; they become good husbands and good wives, from the necessity of remaining good husbands and wives; for necessity is a powerful master in teaching the duties which it imposes. If it were once understood, that upon mutual disgust married persons might be legally separated, many couples, who now pass through the world with mutual comfort, with attention to their common offspring and the moral order of civil society, might have been at this moment living in a state of mutual unkindness – in a state of estrangement from their common offspring – and in a state of most licentious and unreserved immorality. In this case, as in many others, the happiness of some individuals must be sacrificed to the more general good.[15]

The second assumption underlines the intricate complex of legal rules which surrounded the doctrine of the matrimonial offence. With the solitary exception of unsoundness of mind, which was introduced by statute in 1938,[16] divorce could be granted only against a spouse who was morally blameworthy. The law of collusion, connivance, conduct conducing and condonation grew up to attempt to ensure that it was only against a morally blameworthy spouse that a decree would be granted. In the years following the introduction of judicial divorce in 1858, guilty spouses were penalized when it came to deciding who would have custody of the children and whether maintenance should be ordered. It was, for example, a general rule, departed from in only very exceptional circumstances, that a wife divorced for her adultery should be denied custody and even *access* to her children[17] (this at a time when the husband could not be divorced on the ground of his adultery unless it was accompanied by some other

15. *Evans* v. *Evans* (1790) 1 Hagg. Const. 35.
16. Matrimonial Causes Act 1937.
17. See *Handley* v. *Handley* [1891] P. 124.

offence), and it was not until 1883[18] that it was recognized as not improper to order some kind of allowance for a guilty wife, though this was no more than to prevent her starvation. These severe doctrines have now disappeared. This does not mean that considerations of conduct are irrelevant to determine maintenance or custody applications, but the dominant purpose of the court will no longer be to punish the erring spouse.

With regard to the first assumption, it has been observed already (see p. 42) that the expectations of spouses entering marriage have risen and that it would generally be regarded as unjust for the unhappiness of a few to be perpetuated in the hope that this in some way promotes the general good. The injustice is particularly emphasized by the consideration that it cannot be proved that refusal of a divorce in cases of incompatibility has any effect on the causes or extent of marital breakdown. Some of the factors which are related with the increase in the divorce rate have already been mentioned (see pp. 36-44) and it is clear from these that many more forces than the mere legal code of divorce are at work in influencing the divorce rate and, even more so, the breakdown rate. This has been clearly shown by a German study by Wolf, Lüke and Hax (1959). The authors examine the divorce rate in Germany over a period in which the legal grounds for divorce underwent extreme fluctuation, from the liberal Prussian law before 1900, through the stricter period of the civil code to the return to liberalization under the Nazis. In all areas of the country, even those which experienced the most abrupt legal changes, the divorce rate rose consistently, and no appreciable influence attributable to the legal changes could be detected.

In Australia, the divorce laws of the various states were codified into a uniform Act in 1959 which came into effect on 1 February 1961. A new ground of divorce was introduced which allowed a petitioner to seek divorce if the spouses had separated and had lived separately and apart for five years and were unlikely to become reconciled. A decree would be granted, even if the petitioner was responsible for the separation, unless this would in some special way be harsh and oppressive to the respondent or contrary to the public interest. It is perhaps still too early to discover whether this provision has led to a weakening of the marriage bond. The graph in

18. *Robinson* v. *Robinson* (1883) 8 P.D. 94.

Figure 3, however, shows that in the years immediately following its introduction there has been no dramatic impact on the divorce rate. The provision would have been known to most married couples when it was enacted in 1959, and its use by couples not then separated would be possible as from 1964. But the years 1964–1967 show no abnormal increase in the number of petitions filed or, except in the case of New South Wales, in the numbers of decrees granted. New South Wales does show a significant increase in the total number of divorces granted between the years 1964 and 1966. This, however, does not indicate any increase in marriage breakdown rate, for the number of petitions presented increased only slightly. The reason for the difference between the statistics of that state and the others is that in 1964 the judges in that state were taking a very restrictive view of the scope of the 'separation' ground. In that year, in New South Wales, only 60 per cent of petitions based on the separation ground, or separation combined with desertion, succeeded, in contrast to success rate of 77 per cent in Victoria, 70 per cent in Queensland, 95 per cent in South Australia, 86 per cent in Western Australia and 79 per cent in Tasmania. However, in 1966 the judicial attitude in New South Wales had changed,[19] and 77 per cent of petitions on those grounds succeeded.

These facts are of significance for a number of reasons. It can be seen that the proximity to which the divorce rate approximates the actual breakdown rate, even under a relatively 'liberal' system of divorce will depend on the prevalent judicial attitude. This can vary even in the application of the same statutory provision. This is a factor to be borne in mind when considering the new divorce code applicable in England and Wales from 1971. It is also indicative of the fact that though judicial attitudes will clearly be reflected in the divorce rate, they have little or no effect on the rate of marriage breakdown as indicated by the number of petitions filed. One final comment must be made. The increase in the total number of divorces granted in New South Wales and Victoria over the period was 44 per cent and 64 per cent respectively. In England and Wales, where there was no alteration to the grounds for divorce, the increase over the same period was 69 per cent.

19. See *Macrae* v. *Macrae* 9 F.L.R. 441.

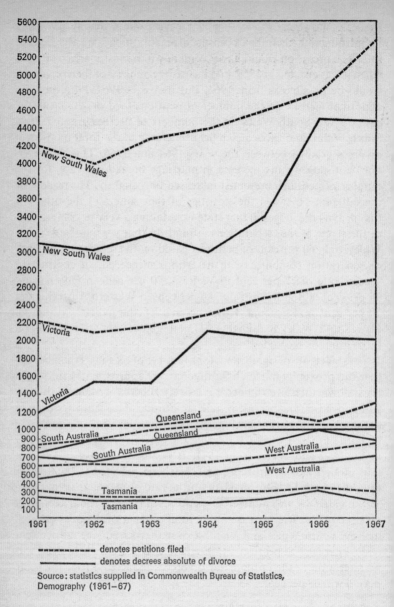

Figure 3 Divorce petitions filed and decrees absolute (selected states of Australia)

# Part Two
# Family Breakdown

# Chapter 6
# Illegitimate Children

We now turn to consideration of those aspects of legal policy which seek to provide some form of remedy when a family situation goes wrong. The family might, as has been seen, fail to mature, as where it consists only of an unmarried mother and her child. It may also disintegrate after marriage by death, separation or divorce. The reaction of the law to these situations is the subject of this Part.

## Adoption

If an unmarried, pregnant woman decides to have her baby, she must decide whether she wishes to keep it or to arrange for its adoption. At first only a very small percentage of illegitimate children were adopted, although, since the Adoption Act 1926 first permitted legal adoption in England and Wales, the use of this means of providing homes for illegitimate children has greatly increased. In 1965 the Registrar-General published information of the subsequent history of illegitimate children as regards their status and this is reproduced in Figure 4.

In 1967 there were 69,928 live illegitimate births. In the same year 18,313 children were adopted. This is 26 per cent of the total figure of illegitimate births, though of course not all the children adopted that year were born that year. Of those adopted, 14,144 were adopted jointly by couples neither of whom was a parent of the child. This means that about a quarter of all illegitimate children are now being adopted, mostly by strangers. It may be that there has very recently been an increase in the proportion of unmarried mothers who decide to keep their babies, but this is very slight (Home Office Committee on the Adoption of Children, 1970, para. 14). Since adoption is so greatly used one may ask what factors lead unmarried mothers to

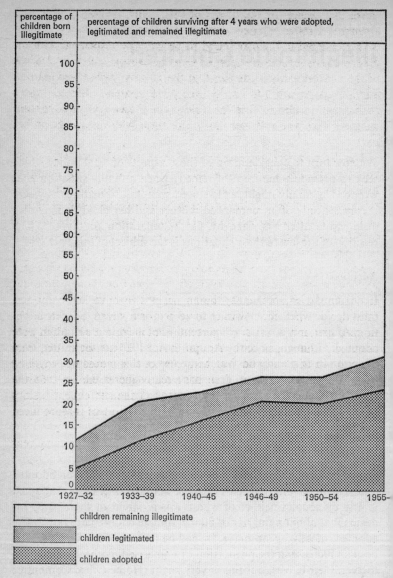

| percentage of children born illegitimate | percentage of children surviving after 4 years who were adopted, legitimated and remained illegitimate |
|---|---|

100 –
95 –
90 –
85 –
80 –
75 –
70 –
65 –
60 –
55 –
50 –
45 –
40 –
35 –
30 –
25 –
20 –
15 –
10 –
5 –
0 –

1927–32    1933–39    1940–45    1946–49    1950–54    1955–

children remaining illegitimate

children legitimated

children adopted

*Adapted from Commentary on the Statistical Review of England and Wales* 1965

Figure 4  Illegitimate children adopted, legimated and remaining illegitimate 1927–59

make this choice for the future of their child. Yelloly (1965) took a sample of 160 unmarried mothers of whom 88 kept their child and 72 surrendered it. Factors found to be strongly associated with the decision to have the baby adopted were the presence of other children of the natural mother, the fact that the putative father was married and a negative attitude on the part of her parents. Indeed, where the mother decided to keep the child in the presence of these circumstances, there was a 40 per cent correlation with instability on her part.

The decision whether to keep the child or surrender it is of the greatest difficulty and delicacy and one which the law of adoption must treat with the utmost care. Of Yelloly's group, one-third of the mothers had not taken a final decision by the time the child was born, and one-third of those had thought they had made a definite decision by then but changed their mind afterwards, almost always reversing a previous decision to have the child adopted. It is, therefore, not uncommon for the birth of a child to cause the mother to reverse a previous decision in favour of adoption. Therefore the law does not recognize the consent of the mother given before the child is born. Indeed, the child must already have been six weeks old before the mother can give a form of consent admissable for adoption proceedings.[1] One might have thought that, with that safeguard, once the consent of the mother had been obtained, it would no longer be open for her to retract it. It is, after all, required that the consent must be witnessed by a justice of the peace, magistrates' clerk or county court officer. However, this is not so, for the consent may be withdrawn at any time before the making of the order and an order cannot be made until three months after the prospective adopters have given notice of their intention to adopt.

The result is that as the law stood in January 1971 prospective adopters are at constant risk of the mother reversing her decision and reclaiming the child. If this happens a very unpleasant situation can develop. The first point to consider is the welfare of the child. Reference has already been made to findings showing damage inflicted upon children as a result of failure to develop a relationship with a maternal figure within the early months of life. The development of this relationship can be seriously impeded by the disruption of

1 Adoption Act 1958, s. 6(2).

growth of attachment to a particular figure. Evidence by Yarrow (1963) and others shows that, while infants up to about twelve weeks old may be moved with little risk, the dangers of disturbance increase steadily after that age, so that they are high by the time the child is six or seven months old. The degree and permanence of the disturbance will depend on surrounding circumstances, but adoption agencies nevertheless recognize that a child should be placed with prospective adopters as early as possible. It is therefore encouraging to note that of the 14,144 illegitimate children adopted by strangers in 1967, 10,195 were under nine months when the adoption order was made, by which time they will already have been with their new parents for at least three months.

The effects made to minimize the risks of uprooting a child can be destroyed if a child who has been with prospective adopters for three months is required to be returned to his mother when she changes her mind and withholds her consent. The prospective adopters may also suffer emotionally by losing the child. Their remedy is to seek to have the mother's consent dispensed with by the court. Under the Adoption Act 1958 this can be done if the court is satisfied that she 'has abandoned, neglected or persistently ill-treated the infant; or cannot be found or is incapable of giving her consent or is withholding (her) consent unreasonably'. Even if none of those conditions is satisfied, the court may still dispense with the consent of a parent who 'has persistently failed without reasonable cause to discharge the obligations of a parent or guardian of the infant'.[2] The most difficult allegation is that consent is being withheld unreasonably. Earlier cases[3] emphasize that the mere fact of refusal to consent by a parent is not in itself to be considered unreasonable because it is only natural for a parent to oppose a complete severance of the parental tie. Nor, they asserted, was the governing criterion to be the best interests of the child, otherwise there would be a danger that a parent might lose his child simply because the prospective adopters could offer the child a more affluent life.

In what circumstances, then, might a court decide that consent has been withheld unreasonably? In re C.L.[4] the Court of Appeal

2. Adoption Act 1958, s. 5(2).
3. *Hitchcock* v. *W.B.* [1952] 2 All E.R. 119; *re K* [1952] 2 All E.R. 877.
4. [1965] 2 Q.B. 449.

appeared to rule that a mother would be held to be refusing her consent unreasonably only if her conduct was culpable, displaying a 'callous or self-indulgent indifference to the welfare of the child'. A later Court of Appeal decision[5] strongly endorsed that view, but it had no sooner done so when the same court, differently constituted, took a contrary view.[6] It was now said that it was not necessary for the mother to be behaving reprehensibly for her consent to be dispensed with. Provided that the evidence showed that adoption was in the child's best interests, a mother would be acting unreasonably if she refused to allow it. And in deciding what was best for the child, Lord Justice Davies said that one should consider 'the prospects and outlook for the child if adopted as compared with those if unadopted; these prospects would include material and financial prospects, education, general surroundings, happiness, stability of home and the like'. The judge thought it worth mentioning, in favour of allowing the adoption, that the adopters had put the child's name down for Eton.

The House of Lords finally resolved the conflict by holding that blame was, indeed, irrelevant in determining whether consent was being withheld unreasonably.[7] The true test was whether, taking into account all the circumstances, including the child's welfare, the mother was being unreasonable in refusing to consent. Unfortunately it is not very helpful for magistrates and county court judges to be told that they must assess what a reasonable mother would do in the circumstances. Surely the law must provide firmer guidelines than that on such a vital matter. Is it, for example, unreasonable to refuse consent when the child, if adopted, is offered better material prospects in a conventional middle-class setting as opposed to upbringing in near poverty by a loving mother who has been unfortunate in her relationships with men? It seems, however, that the House of Lords did not approve of the adoption in re W simply because adoption would have been *better* for the child, but because there would be grave risks to his welfare if he was not adopted.

In 1968, the Standing Conference of Societies Registered for Adoption urged that disputes of this kind should be decided by

5. *re W*. [1970] 3 All E.R. 990.
6. *re B*. [1970] 3 All E.R. 1008.
7. [1971] 2 All E.R. 49.

putting the child's welfare first. This call was repeated by the Association of Child Care Officers (1969) and the working paper expressing the tentative ideas of the Houghton Committee (1970) accepts this. However an earlier Home Office Committee on the Adoption of Children (Hurst Committee) (1954) recommended *against* making the welfare of the child 'paramount'. That might be the right test when *custody* was in issue, because a custody order does not irrevocably destroy the relationship between child and parent. But an adoption order does that and for that reason the Hurst Committee thought that a parent should have his consent overridden only if he could be held to have forfeited his rights respecting the child. It is suggested that this view is correct. It is sometimes said that to speak of 'parental rights' over a child is to treat a child as if he was the property of the parent. This is false. In a family situation the law is concerned with *relationships*, whether between husband and wife, child and mother-substitute or parent and child. They must all be given adequate protection. It is difficult to see how the parent–child relationship can be said to be adequately protected if it may be destroyed simply because a child's prospects are better in an adoptive home.

Unless a parent has clearly demonstrated his unfitness to be entrusted with the upbringing of his child, or has shown so little interest in him that no true relationship can be said to exist, the forcible transfer of the child from him to someone whom the court, or a social worker, believes can look after the child *better* is not justified. But in a situation where a mother has revoked her consent respecting a child placed out for adoption, it may be that at that particular point in time to return the child to her would create unacceptable risks for the child. Even this, it is suggested, does not justify the *permanent* severance of the parental tie. In such a case the custody of the child should remain with the would-be adopters, as happened in *J.* v. *C.* (see p. 165). The mother would not permanently lose her child and, provided that it would not be actually harmful to the child to permit it, she should be allowed access to him with a view to establishing a fully reciprocal relationship with him.

Of course that outcome would not be satisfactory from the point of view of the would-be adopters, who will have taken the child in the expectation of adopting him. It might be observed, however, that their relationship with the child should provide its own satisfaction as a personal relationship and, if successful, should not be threatened by the child's mother. But this is not a complete answer and two measures can mitigate the problem. One is that the security of would-be adopters caught in this situation might be strengthened by granting them 'guardianship' of the kind suggested by the Houghton Committee (see p. 167). A second is to minimize the occasions when these conflicts can arise. As they happen only where a mother changes her mind after the child has been placed out, the chances of them arising will be narrowed if her consent becomes irrevocable at an earlier stage than at present. The Houghton Committee (1970) has put forward for consideration ideas which seek to achieve this object. The system envisaged is one where recognized adoption agencies alone would be permitted to place children out for adoption with non-relatives. When releasing her child to an agency for placement, the mother would give a general consent to the child's adoption. This would be irrevocable. To ensure that it was genuine, this consent would be given before a court (preferably of magistrates) at an informal hearing at which the mother would be accompanied by an officer of the adoption agency. The effect of the consent would be to confer full parental rights on the agency, which would then place the child in a suitable adoptive home.

It is open to debate whether it is desirable that a mother should be required to attend at a magistrates' court for this purpose, especially at a time which is likely to be very soon after the birth of the child (the Committee considers that four weeks may be a sufficient time to allow for recovery from childbirth). Nevertheless it is thought that it is clearly desirable that at some precisely stated moment the consent becomes irrevocable. In Australia this happens thirty days after the consent has been signified, unless the adoption order is made within that period, in which case it is irrevocable when the order is made. This enhances the security of the child and the adoptive parents and removes from the mother the agony of knowing that all she need do is change her mind and the child will probably be returned to her. If consent were to become irrevocable either before placement or very shortly thereafter, the risks of moving the child on the change of mind of the mother are largely avoided.

But in one respect the tentative proposals of the Houghton Committee are more contentious. Although the Committee's scheme would prohibit children being placed out with non-relatives *for the purpose of adoption* unless this was done by an agency, it would still be open for non-relatives who had accepted a child initially on a fostering basis to apply to adopt the child. They would only be permitted to do this if they had the child for a year, and then only with the consent of the local authority, though if they had fostered the child for five years or more, local authority consent would not be necessary. If a parent opposed an adoption order in those circumstances, the Committee takes the view that the opposition should be disregarded if adoption would be for the long-term welfare of the child. Acceptance of this suggestion would mean that, in situations such as *J. v. C.* (see p. 165), where Spanish parents were refused custody of their son because to remove him from his environment would have been inimical to his welfare, foster parents might well be able to adopt a child against the wishes of the natural parents. This could work great injustice on parents and it is suggested that, unless the circumstances are exceptional, their refusal to consent to the adoption of their child should prevent the making of an adoption order. However, it would always be open for a court to grant *custody* (or 'guardianship') to the foster parents if they considered that it would be too risky to uproot the child. This would not be unfair to the foster parents, who would have initially received the child on a temporary basis in any case.

The above discussion treats consent in general terms and does not draw a distinction between legitimate and illegitimate children. The distinction, however, is of importance because the consent of both parents is required for the adoption of a legitimate child, but that of the mother only is required for the adoption of an illegitimate child. A natural father's consent is not required for the adoption of his child, though if he is liable to maintain the child under any order or agreement he must be informed of the application so that he may make his views known. If he is not so liable, there is no duty on the court making the order to seek him out to ascertain his wishes (though some courts in fact do this). The reasons for treating a natural father differently are clear enough. His identity may be in doubt; even if this is known, it may have become difficult or impossible to trace him. Furthermore, some unmarried mothers are unwilling to reveal his identity even if they know it, and to require his identity to be disclosed for adoption proceedings could be a strong deterrent against the use of adoption by unmarried mothers. Nevertheless, some natural fathers become extremely attached to their children. A man may genuinely have intended to marry the mother, but the couple may subsequently (and wisely) have decided against this. He may be supporting the child and visiting him regularly. Indeed, it is now thought highly desirable to try to encourage the relationship between natural fathers and their children (see p. 211). When such a relationship has developed, is there any reason to treat it differently from a father–child relationship where the father married the mother before the child's birth but divorced her (or was divorced by her) shortly thereafter? It is difficult to see why any such distinction should be made. Two recent cases illustrate this point admirably.

In *re E. (P.)*[8] the mother had refused to marry the father of her illegitimate child, but a magistrates' court order allowed him to visit him every Sunday morning. This the father had been doing for two years, and he showed devotion to the child. The mother now married another man, and wished to adopt the child into her new family. This would have deprived the father of his access to the child, and he therefore attempted to prevent the order by obtaining the custody of the child himself. The Court of Appeal held that his application must be dismissed. Lord Justice Harman pointed out that the adoption would remove the 'stigma of illegitimacy' from the child, and added that he thought that 'so solid an advantage certainly ought not to be thrown away in order that the father may have the pleasure of seeing the child and dandling him on his knee two hours a week on Sunday morning before he goes off to play football'. The Family Law Reform Act 1969 has now removed many of the disadvantages of illegitimacy (see p. 212). The stigma may nevertheless remain, of course, though it is doubtful how far an adoption order removes this if, as should happen, the truth about the child's parentage is not concealed. But more important, if the parents had married before the birth of the child and subsequently had divorced, it is extremely unlikely that the father's consent would have been dispensed with. Indeed, the Houghton Committee has taken the tentative view that adoption of a *legitimate* child by a parent and a step-parent should be prohibited because this would sever the link of the child with one half of his

8. [1969] 1 All E.R. 323.

legitimate family. But surely it is the relationship, not its legitimacy or otherwise which is important. And although the Committee gives as the reason for its suggested prohibition the fact that such an adoption might be damaging to the child, it is surely equally important that the extinction of the relationship with his child of a faultless parent who has had the misfortune of a broken marriage would be an intolerable injustice. It is suggested that it may in some cases be equally as unjust to extinguish the parent–child relationship where the father has suffered the misfortune that the mother subsequently refused to marry him.

The second case is *re C. (M.A.)*.[9] Again, the mother refused to marry the father of her illegitimate child and, without his knowledge, handed the child over to an adoption society for placement. He discovered this, however, before the order was made and brought custody proceedings to forestall it. This had the effect of delaying the adoption hearing because the custody issue must be disposed of first. The Court of Appeal confirmed an order giving the father custody. The basis for the decision was that it would in the long term be in the best interests of the child to maintain the 'blood-tie' between himself and his natural father. A number of points about this case are unsatisfactory. It is unsatisfactory that the only way in which a natural father can intervene is by bringing custody proceedings which are *separate from* the adoption hearing itself. Furthermore, as already remarked, the test in custody proceedings is that the welfare of the child determines the matter, whereas in a consent dispute in adoption proceedings this may not be the case. But most important, the success of the father led to the removal of the child from a home in which he had been reared from the age of one month to eighteen months. As so often, the court appeared to fail to appreciate the dangers of doing this. A better solution, it is thought, would be to permit a natural father to *object* to the adoption of his child if he so wishes, and to override this only in the same circumstances as the refusal of consent of the mother may be overridden. In this way he may prevent the adoption of the child. But it would not follow that the custody should be transferred to him, because the welfare of the child may very well dictate that its custody should remain with the adopters to whom guardianship could be entrusted if the suggestions

9. [1966] 1 All E.R. 838.

of the Houghton Committee about guardianship were to be accepted. As in the case where a mother retracts her consent (see p. 196) this arrangement may appear 'second best' to the would-be adopters. But if a natural father were to be allowed to object to the adoption of his child, he should not be permitted to do so after a definite stage in the proceedings had been reached, which should be as soon as possible after the child had been placed with the prospective adopters.

One of the major suggestions for consideration made by the Houghton Committee is that all placements with non-relatives should be made only by recognized adoption agencies. Under the Adoption Act 1958 private persons (such as a doctor) may act as intermediaries in arranging such placements, and when they do this they are obliged to notify the local authority of the proposed arrangement not less than two weeks before the child is placed. When the child is received by the prospective adopters he becomes a 'protected child' within the Act.[10] While the child is a 'protected child', local authorities are under a statutory duty to secure visits to him by the officers of its children's department and they must ensure the well-being of the child and 'give such advice as to (his) care and maintenance as may appear to be needed'. The local authority is to be kept informed about the child and may obtain a juvenile court order to remove him if his environment is detrimental to him. But these provisions have not been working very well. They do not apply in any case where the placement is *direct* (i.e. the child is placed by the parent or parents without resort to an intermediary) until the prospective adopters give notice of their intention to apply for an order, by which time an unsatisfactory situation may have developed from which it might be difficult to extract the child. Third parties may fail to give the required notice, in which case similar difficulties may be encountered when the local authority is eventually informed. As the selection of persons suitable to adopt children is a highly skilled process, there are good grounds for the suggestion that non-agency placements with non-relatives should be prohibited.

Where a parent prefers his or her child to be adopted by relatives rather than by non-relatives, special problems arise because adoption creates, in law, a new parent–child relationship. If the adoptive parents

10. Adoption Act 1958, ss. 37(1) and 40(3).

are already relatives of the child strange consequences might follow. If, for example, they are the child's maternal grandparents, the result in law will be that the child's mother will be his sister. Adoptions of this kind are invariably arranged by direct placement and the evidence suggests that there is a distinct tendency for the results to be unsatisfactory. The Houghton Committee, however, does not feel that they should be prohibited, although it considers that guardianship would generally be more appropriate than adoption in circumstances such as these. Adoption may also be sought by a parent of his own child. This may be done by a parent alone or jointly with another person, usually someone whom he or she has married (as in *re E. (P.)* (see p. 199). In 1967, of 18,313 adoptions of illegitimate children, 3963 were by couples one of whom was a parent. This practice was strongly criticized by the Association of Child Care Officers (1969) on the ground that, if adoption is sought in order to strengthen the relationship of the child with his step-parent and to integrate him completely into the new family, the legal formality in itself cannot ensure this. This, of course, is true, but, provided the cloak of falsity is not thrown over the child's true origins, and provided also that the other natural parent does not raise reasonable objection to the severance of his relationship with the child, it is difficult to see how adoption can harm the new relationships. There is positive advantage to be gained for the child if he is treated by the law in every respect as the legitimate child of the step-parent instead of remaining a legal stranger to him. Where the adoption of an illegitimate child is sought by one parent alone very little is gained and there are indeed dangers. It may be used as an attempt to hide from the child his illegitimate origin, a practice which is always inadvisable. Further, it severs the relationship with the other parent and, in so far as such a relationship exists, it should in normal circumstances be encouraged rather than broken. The fact that it is an illegitimate relationship is of no consequence in this context. The Houghton Committee is therefore inclined to the view that adoptions by a single natural parent of his or her own child should be disallowed.

When a child is adopted, the final order must be made by a court which is satisfied that the order would, if made, be 'for the welfare' of the child[11] The court will not, therefore, make an order if it would

11. Adoption Act 1958, s. 7(1)(b).

be detrimental to the interests of the child. This judgment may be a difficult one requiring sympathy with and appreciation of an emotional situation which may be complex and delicate. The court may be one of magistrates, but the county court and the High Court may also be used. Indeed, as Table 4 shows, county courts are becoming increasingly popular and are generally preferred by adoption agencies. The reason is that they are thought to be more confidential than magistrates (who may be closely integrated in the local community), they accept affidavit evidence and in general are believed to have a greater discretionary power in difficult cases (though this is not strictly true). But county court judges sit alone and, whatever the values of a legal education, it is not always calculated to further

Table 4
Courts making Adoption Orders 1927–68

| Year | High Court | County court | Magistrates' court | Total |
| --- | --- | --- | --- | --- |
| 1927–30 | 403 | 961 | 12,662 | 14,026 |
| 1956 | 44 | 5,118 | 8,036 | 13,198 |
| 1962 | 53 | 9,572 | 7,269 | 16,894 |
| 1968 | 39 | 16,499 | 8,293 | 24,831 |

Source: *Statistical Review of England and Wales* (*1968*)

the qualities necessary to make the kinds of decisions involved in adoption situations. There are a sufficient number of reported instances of highly idiosyncratic decisions by county court judges in adoption cases to throw some doubt on the suitability of the county court as the proper forum for this type of family case. There have been instances where there was unwillingness to permit white applicants to adopt coloured children, or Americans to adopt English children or to allow atheists to adopt at all, and some judges have required the consent of the mother's parents to be obtained, although this is not a legal requirement. Magistrates' courts have the advantage that they consist of laymen and, in adoption cases, they must include a woman. The Standing Conference of Societies Registered for Adoption (1968) has strongly supported a suggestion that adoption cases should be heard by a panel of people with experience in social work, psychiatry and marriage guidance as well as law. However, it should not be forgotten that the court would remain a court of law charged not only with the task of applying statute and case law but, as has been seen, of weighing the conflicting evidence of witnesses and, above all, the claims of parties in dispute against the measuring rod of justice. For this reason a trained lawyer should either preside or be available to guide the bench on points of law, as is at present done by the clerk in a magistrates' court.

The Houghton Committee considered that it would be desirable if a unified scheme in which all family matters were heard in the same group of courts could be established, but is prepared to accept that jurisdiction could continue to be exercised either by a judge sitting alone or by a bench of laymen. However, the Committee suggests that the court might be given a discretionary power to appoint an expert to inquire into a particularly difficult case and report back to the court, and even, if it wished, the power to appoint an additional expert assessor to sit with it if it required his assistance. All these suggestions have merit, but they do not meet the case where the court has failed to appreciate that a particularly complex situation does exist. Furthermore, more important than the difficult case where a 'non-legal' approach might throw useful light on a problem, is the frame of mind developed by a judge in deciding a long series of 'run-of-the-mill' cases. For this reason it is thought that the combination of legal and lay elements in courts deciding family matters would be particularly valuable. The 'lay' element need not be 'expert', but it would be very important that the tribunal would be composed of adjudicators of both sexes for, in family disputes above all others, it is dangerously easy for the adjudicator's judgment to be coloured by his or her own family experience and sexual role in society.

Under the law prevailing in January 1971, courts hearing adoption applications appoint a special officer to represent the interests of the child in the proceedings. He is known as the guardian *ad litem*, and, although an officer of the court, he may in fact be an officer of the local children's department and indeed may be the same person who has been supervising the child under the authority's duties towards 'protected' children (see p. 201). Guardians usually pay only one visit to the applicants and, although rules made under the

Adoption Act 1958 set out in detail the type of inquiry that must be made (concerning such matters as the means, accommodation, mental and physical health of the applicants) it is difficult for them, without more background knowledge, to form a balanced judgment about the true interests of the child. Furthermore, his appearance on the scene at a late stage often confuses the prospective adopters, who may be undergoing some strain in the period immediately before the court hearing. There is clearly room for clarification of the functions of the guardian. The Houghton Committee suggests that guardians should not automatically be appointed, but that a court should be able to appoint one in special cases. The problem lies in the fact that the court is required to be satisfied that the order would be in the child's interests. Is it automatically to accept the agency's assertion that it is so? In practice this is what regularly happens because the guardian usually endorses the agency's application. This is inevitable and in no way reprehensible since control and supervision over the agencies by central or local government should ensure their reliability. Nevertheless, there may be something to be said for the presence of a guardian in *all* cases to make sure that the case is properly put before the court and to detect any possible irregularity 'behind the scenes' which might be hidden from the Bench.

If an adoption order is made, the child stands in relation to the adopters with respect to all matters concerning its custody, maintenance and education as if it were a child of their own born in lawful wedlock.[12] They are brought within the prohibited degrees for the purposes of the law of marriage, but this does not extend to other persons in the adopters' family. The adopted person is treated as the legitimate child of the adopters for the purposes of the law of intestate succession provided only that the adoption order has already been made when the death of the intestate occurs. If property is disposed of by will or other instrument made after the order has been made, any reference to the child of the adopter is to be taken as referring to the adopted child unless the contrary is actually proved. A disposition in a will is considered to be 'made' when the testator dies. Conversely, the adopted person is excluded from all property rights in his natural family, and they not only also lose property rights against him but also any right to custody or access.

12. Adoption Act 1958, s. 13(1).

In this way an illegitimate child can be completely assimilated into a new family unit, either completing it (if the adoptive parents were previously childless) or adding to it. Nevertheless, the fact remains that an adopted child can never be in exactly the same position as a natural child. He will almost certainly eventually discover the truth about his origins. This may be when he sees his birth certificate, which is an extract from the Adopted Children Register. However, this may be avoided by obtaining the shortened form of the certificate which will mention nothing of the adoption unless the child was born abroad. But in any case, adopted children discover the truth in many unforeseen ways and can be considerably disturbed by the discovery. This raises the question as to how far adoption should raise an 'iron curtain' between the child and his ancestry. The view now widely held amongst adoption experts is that the truth should not be evaded, far less should it be fraudulently concealed. Such a course may be fraught with danger. It is more desirable for adoptive parents to make a success of the relationship *as an adoptive relationship* rather than a fictitious natural one, and they should be required to tell the child at an early age.

It is difficult to assess how far adoption by strangers is successful in providing those elements important in the upbringing of children who would otherwise be deprived of them. However, the evidence that is available suggests that adoption is more often successful than not and that, as may be expected, greater risks of failure are attendant upon informally arranged adoptions, especially where there are family relationships between the natural and adoptive parents. The literature on the subject is reviewed by Kellmer Pringle (1967). There are also special difficulties which adoptive parents must be prepared to meet. One is that of telling the child about his adoption and coping with the attendant difficulties this might cause the child. It seems clear that many adopted children experience acute anxiety over not knowing about their genealogical origin. As the law now stands in England and Wales, an adopted child has no right to examine his original birth certificate and so discover his biological parentage. He can only do so if he obtains a court order permitting this. It is otherwise in Scotland. There seems to be no good reason for putting obstacles against a person discovering information of this kind and it is a little surprising that the Houghton Committee (1970) has not felt disposed to recommend a change in the English practice on this point. Adopted children may suffer quite unjustified fears about their origins which can be set at rest, or at any rate lessened, by giving them this information. It is the adoptive parents who may feel threatened by this procedure. But it appears that where adopted children do take steps to discover their parentage, or even of visiting their mother, this serves only to allay their curiosity and does not lead to them establishing personal relationships outside their adoptive home. This will more especially be the case if the adoptive home is a happy one.

## Legitimation

If the parents of an illegitimate child marry each other after its birth, the child will be legitimated by the operation of section 1 of the Legitimacy Act 1926 which for the first time introduced into English law the doctrine, long known in European law, of legitimation by subsequent marriage. At first the benefit of the Act did not extend to a child who was born while one of his parents was married to a third person (i.e. an adulterine child), but this restriction was lifted by section 1 of the Legitimacy Act 1959. As shown in Figure 4 (see p. 192) the provisions affect only a small minority of illegitimate children, but they serve their purpose in legally regularizing operative family units which have come into being in a slightly abnormal way. There is, however, reason to believe that the usefulness of this particular remedy to illegitimacy will be enhanced under the new divorce law which commenced in 1971. It has been noted earlier (see p. 30) that about 40 per cent of illegitimate children are born to couples living in a stable illicit union where one of the parents is married to a third person. If persons in this position make use of the new divorce provisions and then marry their new partners, the Law Commission (1966) estimated that about 180,000 living illegitimate children could be legitimated and that in each future year some 19,000 children who would otherwise be condemned to permanent illegitimacy might either be born in wedlock or subsequently legitimated. If this were to be achieved and the percentage of illegitimate children who are adopted maintained at its present level or increased, the extent of illegitimacy could be considerably reduced in our society.

## Affiliation

A mother who decides to keep her illegitimate child will always face special problems both before and after its birth. The obvious source to which she may look for support is the natural father. This is provided for in the Affiliation Proceedings Act 1957. A 'single' woman may lay a complaint in a magistrates' court against a man within twelve months from the child's birth (or later if the man has paid maintenance towards him within that period) and if the court is satisfied on her evidence, which must be corroborated, that the defendant is the father of the child, it may order him to pay a weekly sum for the child's maintenance, a sum necessary to cover expenses incidental to the birth and, if the child has died, to his funeral.[13] A married woman may be considered 'single' for the purpose of the Act if she is living apart from her husband and is not entitled to support from him. It is notable that, though a complaint may be made while the woman is still with child, the court cannot order the putative father to maintain the woman during her pregnancy. The nearest it can go to doing this is to order him to pay the expenses incidental to the pregnancy, which would not seem to cover actual maintenance of the woman during that period.

But even in the area in which it can operate, the outstanding characteristic of this legal measure is its lack of effectiveness. First of all very few women make use of it. Only about 13 per cent of unmarried mothers seek affiliation orders. This figure looks less meagre when it is recalled that some 30 per cent of illegitimate children are adopted or legitimated and about another 40 are born into stable unions. It nevertheless remains small, especially when it is considered, as McGregor (1968) shows, that about one quarter of affiliation orders are sought by women whose stable illicit unions have broken down. There are a number of reasons why this is so. Many women feel aversion to taking legal proceedings against their erstwhile lover and many may even continue to love him and hope for a reconciliation. This aversion to resorting to law will be accentuated by the fact that affiliation proceedings are brought in courts which are commonly associated with crime. Another reason is that, even if the proceedings

13. Affiliation Proceedings Act 1957, ss. 1, 2 and 4 as amended by the Maintenance Orders Act 1968. The order may remain in force until the child is sixteen, but may be extended until he is twenty-one.

are taken, they are so often ineffective. A research project undertaken by Bedford College, London, found that of all affiliation orders in their sample which were live on 1 January 1966, one-third were in arrears for amounts exceeding £20. The sums ordered tend to be very low. The Bedford project found that, in 1966, the average amount ordered was 33s a week. The maximum limit of 50s has since been removed[14] but this will make little difference as only 8 per cent of the orders made were at the maximum. Finally, when arrears are due, the onus is upon the woman to apply for a summons to be issued against the man. To have to take this step, sometimes at regular intervals, is a process for which many women will feel reluctance. Apart from anything else, it is a continuing reminder of their rejection by the man. But even if the step is taken, the means for enforcement open to the court are unsatisfactory. One of these is to make an attachment of earnings order under the Attachment of Earnings Act 1971. This Act, as has been described earlier (see p. 129) sought to strengthen the effectiveness of attachment of earnings as a means of enforcing debts. Whether it will have the desired effect in the case of maintenance and affiliation orders remains to be seen.

The practical result of the weakness of this procedure is that unmarried mothers must rely on social insurance or social security benefits. An unmarried mother will qualify, on her own record, for maternity benefits and, if she already has at least one child, for family allowances. She may also receive sickness benefit with a supplement for each dependent child of hers, but this only covers absences due to her own sickness, not that of the child. Most of the unmarried mothers in need, therefore, have to resort to supplementary benefit. In 1965 there were 36,000 of these women who were in receipt of supplementary benefit. Of these, 25 per cent did in fact have an affiliation order in their favour and in two-thirds of these cases the order was regularly complied with but was insufficient to raise the mother above subsistence level. In 14 per cent of the cases the mother had an out-of-court arrangement with the father (most of which were kept) but in 56 per cent of the cases there was no such order or arrangement, mostly because the father's address was, or was said to be, unknown, or because he had no means to pay (Home Office Committee on Statutory Maintenance Limits, 1968). It is therefore pro-

14. Maintenance Orders Act 1968.

vided that where the Supplementary Benefits Commission makes payments with respect to illegitimate children, the Commission itself may, if it wishes, apply for an affiliation order to be made against the father, or if there already is one in existence, it may apply for its variation so that the father pays directly to the Commission.[15] Where payments under an affiliation order are so small that they fail to bring the mother above subsistence level, it is of advantage for the mother to use this procedure as she is then saved the trouble of going to the magistrates' court personally to collect the money (which may or may not have been paid by the father that week), and removes from her the problem of taking enforcement proceedings if he defaults. It is better for her to collect her flat-rate supplementary allowance from the Commission and to leave to the authorities the task of reclaiming from the father.

These arrangements for persons who qualify for supplementary allowances have prompted suggestions that a similar process might be used over a much wider field. The suggestion is that a sum greater than supplementary benefit be paid by the state to unmarried mothers, and that the authorities should reclaim from the father through the machinery used for tax collection under PAYE. The father's liability would affect his PAYE coding, the reasons for which are confidential, and this would apply wherever he was employed. A system of this kind, advocated by Wynn (1964) is attractive and has already been mentioned in relation to the maintenance of families of deserted wives and husbands (see p. 132). At the beginning of 1971 the matter was under review by the Finer Committee.

Certain less radical suggestions might be made. One is that affiliation proceedings should be removed from magistrates' courts into tribunals especially set up to deal with family matters. It is possible to go further and try to avoid court proceedings altogether, or at any rate remove the onus for their initiation from the mother. Under the 'Castberg laws' enacted in Norway in 1915 it was provided that an order would be made against a man whom the mother registered as being the father when she notified the authorities of the birth of the child. It was open for the man named to appeal and, if he did so within a stated time, the authorities would, on his behalf,

15. Ministry of Social Security Act 1966, ss. 22(1) and 24.

commence proceedings which would require proof of his paternity by the mother (see Castberg, 1916). The objective of the law should be to remove as far as possible any trace of sordidness from the proceedings and, if possible, to attempt to bring the couple to an amicable arrangement about finances and the care of the child. The statistics quoted earlier confirm what common sense would expect – that a man is far more likely to honour an agreement which he has entered into voluntarily than an order obtained against him in court. The recently enacted Maintenance and Recovery Act of Alberta[16] provides a good example of an attempt to apply this policy. Under the Act a Director of Maintenance and Recovery is appointed to give aid and advice to unmarried mothers. He may be consulted during the pregnancy, and he is encouraged to involve the natural father in the situation at an early stage because he is empowered to enter into an agreement with the father about payment for the expenses of the birth and the maintenance of the child. Should this course fail, the Act permits the Director as well as the mother to take legal proceedings against the father, and it is the Director who will take the necessary steps to enforce an order on which the father has defaulted. The introduction of a service of this kind, together, possibly, with a state unmarried mother's allowance where this is reclaimable from the father, would go far in assisting these women to keep their defective family unit viable and to provide the best possible home environment for the children which the circumstances allow.

## Status

Status can arise from social attitudes or legal rules or both. The status of illegitimacy arises from each of them. If all the legal disabilities on illegitimate children were to be removed, it is probable that a social stigma would still remain. But a legal change of this kind could in the long term influence social attitudes. It is now widely thought that discrimination against illegitimate children is unfair, and indeed to impose on them an inferior social or legal status can only add to the difficulties they will usually in any case face by being reared in an incomplete family. For these reasons legal discrimination against illegitimate children can only be justified if it

16. Chapter 67 of 1969.

serves some more general, greater good. The view that the status of illegitimacy was a necessary adjunct to the institution of marriage was cited earlier (see p. 15) but was criticized as resting on too narrow a view of marriage. Marriage is no longer primarily concerned with determining a legitimate lineage or ensuring the proper direction in which property is to devolve on death. As these matters are no longer of significant social importance, there is no reason why an illegitimate relationship should not be recognized alongside legitimate ones, nor why property should not be shared amongst illegitimate as well as legitimate successors.

The Family Law Reform Act 1969 went very far in recognizing the changed social facts mentioned above. Under sections 14–19 of that Act the property rights of illegitimate children (or their issue) against their parents are very closely similar to those of legitimate children. They are given succession rights against either of their parents who dies intestate equal to those of legitimate children, and the parents are given reciprocal rights against them. References to 'children' in wills and other dispositions made after 1 January 1970 must be construed as including references to illegitimate children unless the contrary appears to have been the intention of the person making the will or disposition. Illegitimate children are to be considered as dependants entitled to claim against the estate of a deceased parent who has not made reasonable provision for them in his will, a benefit formerly confined to legitimate dependants (see p. 219). In short, for succession purposes illegitimate children are almost in the same position as legitimate children. In one respect discrimination remains. They are given no succession rights under the law of intestacy against other kin (e.g. brothers or sisters) apart from their parents.

Despite that slight restriction, the Act brings about a considerable alleviation of the hardships of illegitimacy. Nevertheless, the status persists. Suitably worded wills and other instruments will still be able to exclude illegitimate children from benefiting under them; the distinction remains important, as has been seen, (see p. 198) in the law relating to the custody and adoption of children; the status may be evident in official documents. It is therefore instructive to contrast with the Family Law Reform Act 1969 the New Zealand Status of Children Act 1969. This enacts that:

For all purposes of the law of New Zealand the relationship between every person and his father and mother shall be determined irrespective of whether the father and mother are or have been married to each other, and all other relationships shall be determined accordingly.

This provision abolishes the status of illegitimacy from the law of New Zealand. The Act goes as far as to provide that, in construing documents, the use of the expressions 'lawful' or 'legitimate' will not be sufficient to exclude illegitimate relationships. It is of interest to note (see Cameron, 1969) that the abolition of illegitimacy by this Act brings the whole community in New Zealand into line with the absence of this status amongst the Maori people. However, the impact of this legislation on the social attitudes of the community cannot be expected to be immediate.

The abolition of illegitimacy, and even its mitigation as in the Family Law Reform Act 1969, brings incidental problems in its wake. One is that the appearance of a man's pre-marital child or children to claim against his estate on his death might come as a considerable surprise and shock to his widow and legitimate children. Perhaps, as Castberg hoped when similar reforms were introduced in Norway in 1915, this will encourage husbands to inform their wives about any illegitimate children they know they have. But more important is the problem of proof. How is paternity to be established many years after the birth of the claimant, perhaps even after the death of the alleged father? There is no English procedure designed solely to establish paternity. Questions of paternity do, of course, arise incidentally in a number of contexts (e.g. a disputed will, or in settling maintenance on divorce) and it will be relevant to discover whether the man has had an affiliation order made against him with respect to the child, or whether he has registered himself as the father. But neither the affiliation procedure nor that of registration creates a legally recognized relationship between the man and the child. A putative father may pay contributions to the child's maintenance; he may apply for its custody under section 3 of the Legitimacy Act 1959; he may put his views forward if the child is sought to be adopted. But in other respects he lives in a legal twilight. Most European countries allow a man to *recognize* a child as his own, either formally or by implication (as, for example, by failure to repudiate an allegation of paternity by the mother). This, subject to safeguards, creates a legally recognized relationship between the man and the child; he will obtain rights against the child equal to those of the mother and, in return, will owe to it the duties of parenthood. These duties are not imposed upon him as a result of court proceedings, as in England, but as a result of his act of recognition. The case for voluntary recognition by a natural father has been supported by the Church of England (1966a) and the Association of Child Care Officers (1969). It has been introduced into New Zealand by the Status of Children Act 1969 under which either a joint instrument signed by both parents before a solicitor or the registration, with his consent, of the father's name in the Register of Births will establish the paternity of the man, although if he is to benefit by his paternity, this must be done in the child's lifetime.

In the absence of such recognition, proof of paternity must be sought by other means. When this issue arises in affiliation or other proceedings, this allegation must be proved in the same way as any other allegation in civil proceedings. Statements and circumstantial evidence may be admitted (though in affiliation cases the evidence of the mother must be corroborated by some other evidence). If the alleged father is still alive when the issue arises, use may be made of modern developments in blood grouping. By these techniques it is possible to get a result which will prove virtually conclusively whether the person tested is not the father of a child. If, therefore, the test shows that the man could not have been the father, this can safely be accepted as conclusive that he was not the father. It does not follow that failure to obtain this result indicates that the man was the father, though, if he was *not* the father, there is about a 70 per cent chance that this will be conclusively demonstrated. Indeed, the test is such that it can never safely indicate whether a particular person is the father. It can only exclude people. Nevertheless, the relatively high possibility of obtaining an exclusion result makes it advisable to take the test, especially if the man alleged to be the father (or one of the men who may be the father) denies paternity. However, the test requires the blood of the man to be compared with that of the child, and the latter could not be obtained unless the child's guardian, or its guardian *ad litem* consented. After some hesitation, it was decided that the High Court had power to override the objections of a guardian to the child's blood being used for a test so long as the test was in the child's best interests.[17] Suppose, however, that the only conceivable result of the test would be to eliminate as the possible father of a child the only man in a position to maintain it, as would happen if, for example, a husband denied paternity of a child long after its birth and the alleged adulterer had disappeared. It might be argued that the interests of the child are best served by maintaining the *status quo*. On the other hand, justice demands that the husband be allowed the best evidence available to prove his allegation. In *S.* v. *S.*[18] the House of Lords resolved the dispute in favour of justice. The High Court, it was asserted, has an inherent power to order parties, even adult parties, to undergo these tests as part of its general duty to require litigation to be determined in accordance with the best evidence. This does not, however, mean that an adult who refuses to undergo a test can be physically compelled to submit to it,[19] nor that an order would be made which would be damaging to a child.

The Family Law Reform Act 1969 contains, in section 20-25, provisions which will supplement the powers of the High Court to give direction about blood tests. In any civil proceedings in which the paternity of any person fails to be determined, the court may, on application by any party to those proceedings, order blood to be taken from that person, his mother and any party alleged to be his father. Such a person may, of course, refuse to submit to the test (unless he is under sixteen, when it will be sufficient if the person with care and control of him consents on his behalf), but if he does this, the court 'may draw such inference, if any, from that fact as appear proper in the circumstances'. The powers formerly confined to the High Court will when the provisions come into operation be exercisable by county courts and magistrates' courts. But they were not yet operative on 1 January 1971. The ruling of the House of Lords in *S.* v. *S.* will be important when courts decide whether to order a blood test under the Act. It would not, it now seems, be sufficient to oppose the making of the order on the ground only that the result of the test might deprive the child of a person to whom he would otherwise look for support.

17. *B.R.B.* v. *J.B.* [1968] 2 All E.R. 1023.
18. [1970] 3 All E.R. 107.
19. *W.* v. *W.* (*No. 4*) [1963] 2 All E.R. 841, as explained in *S.* v. *S.*

# Chapter 7
# Provision on Death

## Succession

Where a family has come fully into being, the most common event which destroys it is the eventual death of one of the partners. The law of succession comes into operation to determine the devolution of the property of the deceased, and the development of this area of law provides another illustration of how the concept of the family as a lineage has slowly given way to that of an autonomous unit in its own right. It has already been seen how, in early English law, a husband acquired wide powers of enjoyment of his wife's freehold property during the marriage and complete ownership of her personal (movable) property (see p. 99). When the husband died, his real property would descend to his heir at law, who would generally be his eldest son. But even at this stage the interests of the wife were not ignored. She would retain her own land when he died. She was given a life interest in any land he left on his death. This was called her dower. Her leaseholds, which belonged to her husband during the marriage, would revert to her on his death, provided he had not disposed of them during his lifetime. As to movable property, this became her husband's absolutely during the marriage, but when he died she was entitled to half of what remained of all his movable property (including the portion which was formerly hers) once debts had been paid. If, however, there was a child, the wife would only take one third, a second third being reserved for the offspring. In the twelfth and thirteenth centuries the law went as far as to confine the husband's power to dispose of his movable property by will to his half (or one-third) share. This ensured that the widow and children would succeed to their 'legitimate portions' and is a technique widely adopted in continental countries and, indeed, in Scots law. However, by the fourteenth century these restraints had ceased to form part of the general law of England, though they continued as local customs in some parts. In London, for example, they continued until 1724. The reasons for the decline of the rules are obscure, but are probably associated with the division between the common law courts, which were concerned with the rights of the spouses during the marriage, and the ecclesiastical courts, which were applying rules incompatible to those of the common law when one of the parties had died. The result was that the relative security created for the family unit by the restraints upon testation could be defeated by a will of the husband, a position which was not to be remedied until the twentieth century.

The decline of these restraints threw the law of intestate succession into such confusion that clarification by statute became necessary. The principal legislation was contained in the Statute of Distributions of 1670 which governed intestate succession to personal property. A widow would get one-third or one-half of the residuary personalty (i.e. movable property and leaseholds) depending upon whether there were issue. So if there were no issue she could not get more than one-half, the other half going to the husband's next of kin. Since much of his personalty may have come from his wife in the first place, the justice of this rule may not always have been evident. As to real property, the position of the widow was weakened when the Dower Act 1833 enabled a husband during his lifetime to defeat his wife's right to dower. The end of the nineteenth century therefore saw, in addition to the reform of the property rights between spouses during marriage, a re-examination of the position between them on death.

The Intestates' Estates Act of 1890 radically altered the position if the net estate of the deceased did not exceed £500. In that case, if there were no children, the widow took the whole of the real and personal property of the husband. If the value of the estate was above £500, she would be assured of receiving at least that sum from it. Radical alteration of the whole system came in 1925 with the Administration of Estates Act, and it is the scheme established by that Act, as amended by the Intestates Estates Act 1952 and the Family Provision Act 1966 which is at present operative. The rights accorded to a surviving spouse apply whether the survivor is a widow or widower.

That person is entitled to the personal chattels (meaning, in effect, goods of a personal nature not connected with business) of the deceased. The rights of the surviving spouse to the main body of the estate will depend upon whether there is issue, and whether the deceased has left any parent or brother or sister or their issue. If none of these is left, the surviving spouse is entitled to the whole estate. If there are also children (or their issue) then the survivor is entitled to £8,750 out of the estate and a *life interest* in half that is left after that. The children take the rest. If, however, there are no children (or their issue), but a parent, brother or sister survives the deceased, the surviving spouse can take £30,000 from the estate and one-half of whatever is left *absolutely*. The security of the surviving spouse, especially if a widow, is further enhanced by the provision that, subject to special exceptions, if the estate includes a dwelling house in which the survivor was residing at the time of the death, the survivor may opt for the house towards satisfaction of the share to which he or she is entitled; if the house is worth more than that share, it can still be acquired if the excess is paid. If there is no surviving spouse, the estate will be divided amongst the children (or their issue). In this context it must be remembered that, from 1970, illegitimate children (or their issue) are given the same rights against their parents, and their parents against them, as legitimate children.

This increasing protection of the interests of the immediate family dependants of a spouse would be frustrated if the deceased spouse could defeat the whole scheme by the provisions of his will. Six centuries of freedom of testation therefore came to an end with the enactment of the Inheritance (Family Provision) Act of 1938. Rather than revert to the rigid 'legitimate portions' reserved for dependants in the early medieval law, the Act adopts a flexible approach by allowing a dependant of the deceased to apply to the court to make an order in his favour out of the estate if the deceased's will was not 'such as to make reasonable provision for the maintenance' of the applicant. It was not to be expected that an alteration as fundamental as this would receive liberal interpretation from the courts, and indeed Mr Justice Wynn-Parry once stated that the Act was 'an invasion of that unqualified right' (of freedom of testation) and it was, therefore, 'natural that in exercising the jurisdiction conferred on them the courts have on numerous occasions been careful to point out that the jurisdiction is one which should be exercised only with great circumspection and to a limited extent'.[1] In dealing with applications under the Act, then, the courts asked themselves the question whether the deceased had acted unreasonably in making the provision he did, or in making no provision, as the case may be. If they could not say that he had done so, they would refuse the application even though the provision, or lack of it, in the event had turned out unreasonable.[2] Although this approach has recently been repudiated by Mr Justice Megarry[3] it cannot yet be said to have been finally dispelled.

Dependants who may claim under the Act are the widow or widower, an unmarried daughter (of any age) of the deceased or a son of his who has not reached twenty-one, or any son or daughter of his who cannot support himself or herself as a result of some disability. Adopted and illegitimate children are included. The order which the court makes will usually be for maintenance of the survivor or other dependant by way of periodical payments. But an interim order may be made if the dependant is in need of urgent support, and the court also has power to order payment by way of lump sum, no matter how large or small the estate.[4] This technique of entrusting the distribution of the estate, at least to some extent, to the court was carried a stage further in the Intestates' Estates Act 1952 which allows dependants to apply for reasonable provision out of the estate of someone dying *intestate*. The rules of intestacy are broadly drawn, but any system of rigid rules cannot provide for every contingency, and their strict application in all circumstances would sometimes lead to injustice. The 1952 Act allows the court to sanction departure from those rules when this would be reasonable.

The dissolution of a marriage by death raises broadly similar problems to its dissolution on divorce. In each case the family assets should be redistributed equitably, though, in the case of death, there may be the additional factor that the deceased has disposed of some or all of his property by will. Subject to this last factor, therefore,

1. *Re Andrews* [1955] 3 All E.R. 248.
2. *Re Howell* [1953] 2 All E.R. 604.
3. *Re Goodwin* [1968] 3 All E.R. 12.
4. Family Provision Act 1966, ss. 4 and 6.

there is much to be said for creating uniformity in the powers and practice of courts dealing with family assets in each case. The redistribution of property on divorce will be discussed fully at a later point (see p. 250). Here it is relevant only to observe certain discrepancies between the legal provisions applicable in the two situations. In the first place, the class of dependants under the family provision legislation does not include a 'child of the family' as does the divorce legislation. Thus a child fully dependent on the family will have no claim against the deceased if he is not the child of the deceased. Under the divorce legislation, maintenance payments normally terminate when a child reaches eighteen; under the family provision legislation they may continue until a son reaches twenty-one, while there is no age limit at all for an unmarried daughter. The reasons for these distinctions are obscure. In a family provision context there is, however, good reason to include at least one additional class of dependants who would not qualify for consideration on divorce. These are the parents and parents-in-law of the deceased. They should not qualify on divorce because a divorcee will retain his moral obligation to his own parents and cannot reasonably, on divorce, be expected to continue to support the extended family of his divorced spouse. But on death of a child the need of elderly parents formerly dependent on him might become acute and, there being no estrangement between the two family groups, there is no reason why parents-in-law in the same position should not equally be protected.

The second major distinction between the powers exercisable by courts on death and on divorce is that in the latter situation the court has wide powers to order the transfer or settlement of the property of one spouse to or on the other. No comparable powers are exercisable in family provision applications. This limitation could put a spouse (especially a wife) whose marriage is terminated by the death of the other in a considerably inferior position to a divorced spouse. In particular, if her husband has disposed of the matrimonial home by his will, she may lose accommodation for herself and her children. The courts already have the power to interfere with freedom of testation in order to ensure reasonable maintenance for a surviving spouse. There is no reason why they should not equally do so to protect the roof over the survivor's head; this is a reform which should be made as a matter of urgency.

It must be observed that any reforms in the law of matrimonial property would have profound effects on the property distribution when a marriage is terminated on death. If spouses acquired concurrent interests in the matrimonial home by the operation of law, the position of a survivor in the home would be much stronger than it would be if the survivor had no property interest in it. If a 'deferred community' of the Scandinavian kind were to be introduced, a survivor would *prima facie* be entitled to half of the family property on death once the debts of the deceased had been paid. It would not be open for the deceased to dispose of more than half the net assets in his will, so that the survivor would be normally entitled to her half share as of right. She would not be obliged to rely on the discretion of a court, though there is no reason why the courts should not retain a discretionary power to make an award to the survivor from the deceased's half share if this should be appropriate. And there would be an additional, valuable, advantage. This would lie in the ability of a spouse who suspected that the other was disposing of his assets in an irresponsible or deceitful way (so that the property available to her on dissolution by death would be greatly diminished) to apply to a court for an order immediately terminating the community and fixing the shares at that moment.

### Claims against third parties

The provisions which have been discussed are aimed at the distribution of the deceased's estate in such a way as to do justice to those who had a claim upon him for his support while he lived. But the death might also have the effect of bringing a dependant into direct relation with a third party. A widow, living in a flat of which her husband was a statutory tenant will, on his death, have to deal with his landlord. If her husband has been killed by the wrongful act of some third party, she may have a claim against him. Finally, her husband's death may entitle her to payment under an insurance policy, or to payments by way of widow's benefits or increased retirement pension. As to the first of these situations, a widow who was residing with her husband when he died is given special protection under the Rent Act as her husband's statutory tenancy will automatically be transmitted to her. If he leaves no widow, similar protection is given to a member of his family who has been residing with him for not less than six months immediately preceding his death.[5]

Where a spouse's death has been caused by the wrongful act of a third party, dependants of that person are given an action against the wrongdoer, provided the deceased could himself have brought an action against him. This is to obtain compensation for the financial loss which the death has brought upon them. The legislation which creates these rights, the Fatal Accidents Acts 1846–1959, is strictly limited to financial loss. There can be no claim for mental suffering or grief. Dependants include the other spouse, children (including illegitimate children), parents, grandparents, brothers, sisters, aunts, uncles and their issue. If the claimant has become entitled to a pension as a result of the death, this will be disregarded in calculating the financial loss suffered.[6] The enactment stipulating this also states that a 'gratuity' is similarly to be disregarded, and, although it is not yet clear how this term is to be interpreted, it is likely to be given a wide meaning because, in Lord Reid's words, 'it would be revolting to the ordinary man's sense of justice, and therefore contrary to public policy, that the sufferer should have his damages reduced so that he would gain nothing from the benevolence of his friends or relations or of the public at large, and that the only gainer would be the wrongdoer.'[7] But apart from these instances, the principle of compensation is strictly applied so that if, for example, a widow re-marries a comparatively wealthy man who receives the children into the family, and thereby incurs a legal liability to maintain them (see p. 270), the claims of those children will be reduced.[8] If the claimant has not remarried, it is necessary for the court to try to assess her chances of doing so in order to arrive at a fair sum for compensation of her probable economic loss. It is hardly necessary to say that this is a distasteful task for a court. The Committee on Personal Injuries Litigation (1968) (Winn Committee) agreed that this was so, but regarded that a recommendation on the subject was outside its terms of reference. Since defendants to these actions are almost invariably covered by insurance, a solution whereby the wrongdoer

5. Rent Act 1968, s. 3 and sched. I.
6. Fatal Accidents Act 1959, s. 2(1).
7. *Parry* v. *Cleaver* [1969] 1 All E.R. 555.
8. *Reincke* v. *Gray* [1964] 2 All E.R. 687

would pay the claimant periodical (e.g. monthly) payments, adjustable on change of circumstances, does not seem impracticable.[9]

## Pensions and other benefits

The occasions where compensation under the Fatal Accidents Acts can be obtained are limited. They are restricted to instances of death caused by a wrongful act, whether deliberate or negligent. If the defendant is not liable for his act, the claim will fail; if the victim was himself to blame, the damages will be reduced in proportion to that blameworthiness. All the Acts do, in effect, is to enlarge the range of persons whom a wrongdoer must compensate to include other people his act has harmed beyond the immediate victim. But comparatively few deaths are caused by legally actionable conduct. The victims may be struck down by disease or by accident. In such cases a spouse who seeks compensation beyond the immediate family resources must rely upon private or state insurance schemes. The many different kinds of private schemes available cannot be discussed here, but note should be taken of the legal framework in which they operate. A husband or a wife may effect an insurance policy on the life of the other spouse, so that if that other dies, he or she will receive the sum due on the death. But more commonly a husband will effect a policy on his *own* life. He alone will pay the premiums, but the policy will be expressed to be for the benefit of his wife and/or his children. If this is done the beneficiaries will be able to claim the sum due in the event of his death even though they have not themselves entered into any legal relationship with the insurance company. They are enabled to do this because the Married Women's Property Act 1882, section 11, treats them as beneficiaries under a trust. This technique has the further result that the money due will be safe from the husband's creditors, unless he took out the policy specifically in order to defraud them. Income tax relief is claimable on the premiums.[10]

Private schemes do not always provide adequately for a widow's

9. The Law Reform (Miscellaneous Provisions) Act 1971 has now removed consideration of a widow's remarriage prospects when her loss is assessed. This is unjustified sentimentality. While damages are paid in a once-and-for-all lump sum, speculation about relevant future events is both inevitable and necessary.

10. I.C.T.A. 1970, s. 19.

pension. Some provide none at all. While many people might be sufficiently covered by a private occupational scheme, many more are not. The principles of the state flat-rate retirement pensions, supplemented by an earnings-related addition have already been discussed (see p. 139) and in this context it is necessary to observe the provisions for widows' benefits. First, the widow herself may have been above pensionable age (sixty) when her husband dies. If he was already in receipt of a pension, she will be entitled to the pension payable to a single person by virtue of her deceased husband's entitlement. If her husband had not reached retirement age (sixty-five) when he died and she is over sixty, she will have qualified for a retirement pension on reaching sixty and her entitlement to this will continue, though if she is under sixty-five she may prefer to choose the widows' pension, for which there is no earnings rule reducing the pension by the amount of her earnings until she reached sixty-five, as happens in the case of a retirement pension. If she is under sixty and her husband had not yet retired when he died, the benefits payable will depend on her age and circumstances. She will be entitled to a *widow's allowance* of £8·40 a week for the first twenty-six weeks after his death, the sum payable being adjustable according to the number of children she is caring for. The sum will also be increased by a supplementary allowance based on her husband's contributions graduated according to his earnings. These payments will continue after twenty-six weeks if the widow still has to look after one or more children, in which case they are styled a *widowed mother's allowance*. They used also to continue after the end of that period if the woman was over fifty when widowed and had been married at least three years to her deceased husband. This is the *widow's pension*. This pension is now payable where the woman was over *forty* when widowed. The three-year marriage condition has been removed. But the amount of the pension payable to a woman under forty will be reduced by 7 per cent for every year she is less than fifty. On attaining the age of fifty she is entitled to the full rate of £6.[11] The result is that a woman of any age will receive state assistance for the first twenty-six weeks after her husband's death. After that she is left to fend for herself, unless she has a young

11. National Insurance (Old Persons' and Widows' Pensions and Attendance Allowance) Act 1970, ss. 2 and 3.

family about her or, alternatively, unless she herself is passing middle age. The benefits cease on remarriage and are not payable if the woman is living with a man. The state also provides small lump sums payable on the death of a person to assist towards covering the immediate expenses of that event.

Between the standard social insurance benefits available to all insured persons and the limited claims for damages for wrongful death under the Fatal Accidents Acts lies an intermediate system of compensation for persons and their families where injury or death is caused out of and in the course of employment. Only employees are therefore covered by this system, which was introduced in 1946 to replace an earlier system of workmen's compensation legislation. The governing Act is now the National Insurance (Industrial Injuries) Act 1965. The benefits are of three main kinds. *Injury benefit* is an allowance at a flat rate higher than normal sickness benefit payable during absence from work due to industrial accident or disease. *Disablement benefit* is payable to the victim of such an accident or disease whose faculties are impaired by it. *Death benefits* are payments by way of gratuities or pensions to the relatives of persons killed by industrial accidents or diseases. These too are higher than the ordinary widows' benefits, but a claim can be made under only one of the schemes. Unlike national insurance, there are no contribution conditions to be satisfied in order to qualify for industrial injury benefit. Sickness and death at work, then, are compensated to a greater degree than if these misfortunes were to befall the breadwinner at home or on the roads. The reason is not hard to discover. The community as a whole benefits from the productive activities of its industrial workers. The risks undertaken by those workers and their families should therefore be borne by the community as a whole. But sound though this principle appears, its application is becoming increasingly open to question. Employers benefit in a particularly direct way from the activities of their employees, yet, as we have seen, their liability towards them (and to their families under the Fatal Accidents Acts) rests upon the establishment of civil liability against them, which often requires proof of fault. They are not treated as *insurers* of their employees upon whom the risk of bearing the cost of accidents must fall. And are there not activities other than those associated with industry by which the community benefits but which inevitably put many people at risk? The growth of motor transport is an example. Yet the community does not take it upon itself to compensate the growing thousands of victims of this beneficial activity. It may also be questioned whether the prospect of larger state benefits in the event of accident or disease provides the real compensation to a worker in a hazardous occupation. It is more probably to be found in the higher wages payable. Consideration of these questions falls outside the scope of this book, but as they involve matters which can be very important to a family struck by disaster, it is necessary that they should at least be brought into view.

# Chapter 8
# Separation

Estimates of the number of families broken by separation have been referred to on earlier pages and the protection given to spouses threatened by separation, or undergoing it in the short term or in the long term has been discussed in Part One. The legal remedies available to spouses during the subsistence of a marriage disrupted by separation have therefore been dealt with in the context of preventive law, for they apply in situations which may only be of temporary hardship, though, regrettably, the disruption is often permanent. One remedy, however, was omitted in that context because its use is indicative that the separation is considered by both parties as being permanent. This is the maintenance agreement between estranged spouses. Maintenance agreements are extremely widely used and, as may be expected, are comparatively well honoured. Relatively few separated wives who have an out-of-court arrangement apply for supplementary benefit. In 1965 they formed only 11 per cent of the separated wives who applied, as compared to 41 per cent who had a court order and 48 per cent who were without either.

The agreement may be in any form. But if it is in writing there are distinct advantages. It is more likely to be seen to be intended to create legal relations between the parties and its terms will naturally be easier to prove than in an oral agreement. Furthermore, if it is written, it falls within sections 13 and 14 of the Matrimonial Proceedings and Property Act 1970. These sections provide that if an agreement contains a promise by one party not to seek a court order for maintenance, that stipulation will be void, but this will not prejudice the enforceability of any other financial provisions in the agreement. They also provide machinery for variation of the agreement by either party on application to a court, and variation may be ordered if the court is satisfied that 'by reason of a change in circumstances in the light of which any financial arrangements . . . were made . . . or . . . omitted' the agreement should be altered. The court may also vary an agreement which fails to make proper financial arrangements respecting a child of the marriage. Variation may even take place after a party to the agreement has died. Enforcement of these agreements is by an ordinary civil action for damages for breach of contract, but this is of little importance alongside the fact that an agreed settlement has a high likelihood of being kept. It is therefore strongly in the interests of parties intent on separating to come to an amicable agreement about maintenance. Before 1971, however, there might have been some reluctance to do this, for the very amicability of the arrangement might suggest that the separation was consensual and thus operate as a bar to a party subsequently wishing to bring divorce proceedings on the ground of desertion. However, the post-1971 divorce law, to be examined shortly, does not contain this embarrassment.

Support is not, of course, the only matter that should be considered when parties separate. Some arrangement has to be made about the matrimonial property, in particular, the home. The position of property rights during marriage has already been discussed (see ch. 2), and, unless the parties obtain a decree of judicial separation, the fact of separation does not alter those rights. That decree, however, can be obtained only if conditions are present which would, had the marriage completely broken down, have justified the grant of a decree of divorce.[1] The economic arrangements available on judicial separation are, therefore, the same as those available on divorce. Short of obtaining divorce, or decree of judicial separation, then, a spouse wishing to ascertain his matrimonial property situation on separation should take out a summons in the High Court or county court under section 17 of the Married Women's Property Act 1882 and, if he or she wishes to obtain increased security in the occupation of the home, a registration or caution should be entered under the Matrimonial Homes Act 1967, as amended. And while the parties remain separated, but are not divorced, they remain spouses and are entitled to benefits as a 'husband' or 'wife' accordingly. The most important of these are the benefits payable under private or state pension schemes to a man's widow. A separated wife will still be her husband's widow at his death.

1. Divorce Reform Act 1969, s. 8.

Finally, and most importantly, separation raises questions as to the custody of the children of the spouses. Where the High Court or a county court makes a maintenance order under section 6 of the Matrimonial Proceedings and Property Act 1970, section 19 of the same Act gives the Court power to make orders as to the custody of any child of the family who is under eighteen. Magistrates making maintenance orders under the Matrimonial Proceedings (Magistrates' Courts) Act 1960 may make provision for the legal custody of any child of the family who is under sixteen years. They may even, in 'exceptional circumstances making it impracticable or undesirable' to entrust the child to either of the parents, make an order committing him to the local authority. But the powers of the magistrates are limited in this regard. They cannot make an order prohibiting the removal of the child from the country without their consent,[2] and they cannot, under this Act, order custody to one parent and care and control to the other.[3] But this is a mere technicality because, where such an order is desired, magistrates have jurisdiction to make it if proceedings are by way of summons for custody under the Guardianship of Minors Act 1971. The result is untidy, but not serious. In determining custody applications, the courts have first regard to the welfare of the child. The implications of this have already been mentioned in connection with clashes between a parent and strangers. Where the problem concerns separated parents, special issues arise, but as they are also met in divorce cases, their discussion will be postponed to the following section.

2. *T.* v. *T.* [1968] 3 All E.R. 321.
3. *Wild* v. *Wild* [1968] 3 W.L.R. 1148.

# Chapter 9
# Divorce

The problems of remedial law which arise on divorce are little different from those present when spouses separate. The legal effects of divorce, however, go further than those of separation. Firstly, and most importantly, the spouses become free to re-marry. On separation, spouses often reconstitute new *de facto* family units but, except as regards children, these create no new legal obligations. Divorce on the other hand, puts each spouse into a position to contract extensive new family obligations. It is to that extent a licence given by the law that the spouses are entitled to contract anew the legal obligations of marriage. Although widely thought of as 'freeing' the spouses from the previous marriage, it does this to a very limited extent because, while the obligations arising out of the previous marriage are indeed terminated, these obligations are generally replaced by new ones arising out of the divorce. The justification for this is the principle of compensating members of the former family unit for the consequences of its destruction. The powers of the court to achieve this are considerably greater in divorce proceedings than on separation (unless a decree of judicial separation is granted.) Viewed in this way, the divorce process can be seen, not as a means which itself breaks up a family, but as a mechanism providing for the most effective re-adjustment of obligations once the group has already broken. But the fact that the decree also looks forward to the creation of new legal family obligations introduces factors which may conflict with the adjustment process. So, in making its arrangements for compensating the former family, a court must keep in view the fact that new family obligations may be incurred. Conversely, the fact that these new obligations may arise should be kept in mind when assessing the effectiveness of the compensatory provisions. Just as in separation, the most difficult decisions in divorce lie in balancing the claims of two family units.

This analysis of the process of divorce in secular law is not meant to minimize the wider emotional and religious implications of divorce. Divorce is an official and public recognition of the permanent severance of the relationship. On the other hand it would be wrong to associate the legal action with emotional upset. Goode's study (1956) indicates that, where 'trauma' is associated with divorce, this tends to be concentrated in the period before the legal process, especially at the time of the final physical separation. Most divorces are preceded by separation and in those cases the divorce itself adds little to the emotional disturbance which had preceded it. The more that the legal suit is seen as a mechanism for re-adjusting economic consequences of the final separation, the less emotion is likely to be associated with it. There are, of course, many for whom divorce has profound religious significance. Nevertheless the Church of England (1966) recognizes that 'how the doctrine of Christ concerning marriage should be interpreted and applied within the Christian Church is one question: what the Church ought to say and do about secular laws of marriage and divorce is another question altogether'. This has not always been the clerical view. When the Matrimonial Causes Act of 1857 introduced secular divorce in England and Wales, its restriction to cases of adultery reflected the furthest point to which some schools of Christian opinion were prepared to go in permitting divorce at that time. The extension of the offences to include cruelty and desertion by the Matrimonial Causes Act 1937 went beyond traditional Christian teaching. Justification of the doctrine of the matrimonial offence had thenceforth to be put on other than Christian grounds, and the nine members of the Morton Commission (1956) who advocated the retention of the doctrine did so on the ground that it 'makes for security in marriage, because husbands and wives know that they cannot be divorced unless they have committed one of the matrimonial offences which is ground for divorce'. The fallacy of this argument is to equate security of marriage with unavailability of divorce. As has been indicated earlier (see pp. 185–8) it is highly unlikely that there is any connection between marriage breakdown and grounds for divorce. If it is true that the grounds of divorce have little or only marginal effect on marital security, divorce can be viewed primarily as a process of economic re-adjustment and not as a code of punishment intended to influence the behaviour of married couples.

## The new divorce law

It is this latter approach to divorce which won acceptance in the Divorce Reform Act 1969. The Act was preceded by two important reports, one from a group appointed by the Archbishop of Canterbury to review the Church's attitude to the secular law of divorce (1966) and the other from the Law Commission (1966). The Archbishop's group concluded that, if divorce were available on the sole ground that the marriage had irretrievably broken down, this would not be 'an unworthy or improper conception for the law of a secular society to uphold'. The Law Commission agreed that the foundation of the divorce law on the matrimonial offence was unsatisfactory. It tended to discourage reconciliation. 'It does not enable all dead marriages to be buried, and those that it buries are not always interred with the minimum of distress and humiliation. It does not achieve the maximum possible fairness to all concerned, for a spouse may be branded as guilty in law though not more blameworthy in fact.' The Commission, however, was unwilling to propose breakdown of marriage as the sole determinant of divorce because this would involve, in its view, an inquest into the state of the relationship which would be judicially impracticable. The alternative which they favoured was the addition to the existing list of offences a separation ground which would allow divorce after a period of two years if the other spouse consented (or did not object) and after five years, subject to safeguards, even if there should be such objection. The Bill which eventually became the Divorce Reform Act 1969 and took effect on 1 January 1971 embodied a compromise between these two views. Marriage breakdown was to be the sole ground of divorce, but certain situations were set out on proof of which *alone* such breakdown was to be established.

The time has passed to add to the literature condemning the pre-1971 divorce law. Suffice it to say that the requirement that the balance of guilt should be proved to lie against the respondent and the horror of allowing divorce where any element of consent between the parties was present led, in an arbitrary and unpredictable way, to many marriages being held together in law although they had in fact been irretrievably destroyed. The issues upon which divorce cases turned became increasingly detached from the matters relevant to the situation and often from truth itself. There may be some reason for refusing a decree if to grant it might seriously prejudice the financial position of one of the parties, but to do that because both parties were equally innocent or equally guilty of the destruction of their relationship could be defended only by appeal to ideas about the nature of marriage no longer shared by the population as a whole, or by vague speculations as to the consequences that would follow were another path chosen.

Taking the aim of the 1971 divorce law as being to remove the necessity to allocate blame from the decision whether the marriage should be dissolved and to concentrate attention upon a fair economic adjustment between the parties, it remains to be seen whether the terms of the Act of 1969 will achieve this. The fundamental reforms are contained in section 1 and 2(1). These state:

1. After the commencement of this Act the sole ground on which a petition for divorce may be presented to the court by either party to a marriage shall be that the marriage has broken down irretrievably.

2(1). The court hearing the petition for divorce shall not hold the marriage to have broken down irretrievably unless the petitioner satisfies the court of one or more of the following facts, that is to say –

(a) that the respondent has committed adultery and the petitioner finds it intolerable to live with the respondent;

(b) that the respondent has behaved in such a way that the petitioner cannot reasonably be expected to live with the respondent;

(c) that the respondent has deserted the petitioner for a continuous period of at least two years immediately preceding the presentation of the petition;

(d) that the parties to the marriage have lived apart for a continuous period of at least two years immediately preceding the presentation of the petition and the respondent consents to a decree being granted;

(e) that the parties to the marriage have lived apart for a continuous period of at least five years immediately preceding the presentation of the petition.

If the purpose of the legislation was to reduce the decision whether or not to dissolve the marriage to formality, this has only partially been achieved. Simplicity might have been achieved by confining the conditions under which breakdown could be found to stated periods of actual separation between the parties. Proof of this separation would be a simple question of fact and would not involve detailed examination of the matrimonial behaviour of the parties. But a solution along these lines was rejected because it would ignore those cases where prompt relief is necessary as a result of 'outrageous conduct'. Clauses (a) and (b) of section 2(1) were therefore inserted in order to provide speedy relief in these situations.

Although accepted by the Law Commission (1966), it is thought that the argument for the necessity of provision for immediate relief is unconvincing. Where one spouse is threatened by intolerable conduct by the other the remedy does not lie, at least immediately, in the law of divorce. It lies first and foremost in physical separation, supported by a separation order if this should be necessary in order to prevent one spouse from molesting the other. It should not be necessary for the wronged spouse to leave the home, for, as has been seen (ch. 2), the High Court has power to expel the other from the house or regulate his occupation of it. It would, however, be valuable if this power were extended to lower courts. Economic security, the provision of accommodation and the custody of the children during this period should be governed by the law relating to the rights between the parties during marriage. It should not be necessary to take steps for an immediate divorce to safeguard these interests. It must be only in very rare cases that rapid dissolution of the legal tie itself is necessary to prevent intolerable hardship. If this should be the case, however, an exception could be made on the precedent of the exception already in existence to the general bar to divorce during the first three years of marriage. Indeed, if it is thought right to prevent immediate divorces (unless the circumstances are exceptional) for this period, it is not entirely clear why it is so important to provide for immediate divorce where the breakdown occurs after that period.

It is interesting at this point to note that a proposal for divorce reform put before the Dutch Parliament in 1969 sees no necessity, as a general rule, for 'rapid' divorces. The proposal is of special value because it was made after examination of modern European divorce law, including the Bill which was to become the English Divorce Reform Act 1969. The major suggestion is the replacement of the matrimonial offence doctrine by irretrievable breakdown as the sole ground on which either divorce or judicial separation could be granted to a petitioner. If the parties agreed that their relationship had broken down, they could present a joint petition. The court would not grant the divorce immediately, however, unless the circumstances were exceptional. But should the petitioner or the parties jointly re-assert the petition after one year had elapsed from its initial presentation, the marriage would be held to have broken down and the divorce granted. The purpose of the delay, the proposers explained, is threefold: (a) to check 'hasty' divorces; (b) as proof of permanence of the breakdown; and (c) to give a further opportunity for reconciliation. Should one party oppose the petition and allege that the breakdown was due preponderantly to the conduct of the petitioner, this would, initially, provide a good defence to it. However, it would not provide a defence to the grant of a decree of judicial separation and, once this decree has been in force for five years, the petitioner would be entitled to convert it into an order dissolving the marriage irrespective of the opposition of the other spouse. As in the case of section 2(1)(e) of the English Act (to which this provision corresponds), there would be exceptions where the dissolution would cause financial hardship to the defendant.

## Conditions (a) to (c)

It is suggested that this approach has a strong advantage over the new English procedure because, in England, parties who agree that their marriage has broken down but who are unwilling to wait the two years of separate living in order to bring their case within section 2(1)(d) will make use of sections 2(1)(a) or (b). In Australia and New Zealand, which also have 'separation' grounds similar to sections 2(1)(d) and (e), adultery and (to a lesser extent) cruelty are still widely used grounds for obtaining an immediate divorce. But there is every reason to believe that sections 2(1)(a) and (b) will be highly unsatisfactory in their application. In (a), for example, it is not stated that the petitioner must find it intolerable to live with his or her partner by *reason of* the adultery. Indeed, an amendment to insert this causal link was introduced in the House of Lords, but was withdrawn.[1] Presumably a court will want to know the reasons why the petitioner finds it intolerable to live with the respondent, but the Act gives no

1. See [303] H.L. Deb., col. 1249.

indication how far it will be open to a court to evaluate these reasons. If a court does not *believe* them it will be justified in refusing a decree. But could it do so if it *disapproved* of them, for example, if the reason was that the petitioner was in love and committing adultery with someone else? In the debate on this provision in the House of Lords, Lord Goodman thought that if the petitioner had himself committed adultery, 'many judges would be completely justified in refusing to give a divorce'. But Sir Jocelyn Simon (1970) appears to have taken a contrary view and this seems to be more in line with the wording of the Act.

The Act has also abolished the bars of connivance and collusion.[2] Would it be open to a petitioner, perhaps himself an adulterer, to arrange an act of adultery by the respondent and in this way to obtain an immediate divorce under condition (a)? These questions must be answered by the courts. It is thought very likely that they will introduce into this condition the requirement of a degree of culpability on the part of the respondent greater than that shown by the petitioner. If this were not done the provision could be open to great abuse and substantially 'innocent' respondents could be subject to immediate divorce by unscrupulous petitioners. The courts could discover support for taking this view from the context of condition (a) in the Act as a whole. Special safeguards have been inserted to protect 'innocent' spouses divorced under section 2(1)(d) and (e) (see pp. 245–9). These do not apply to a spouse divorced under (a), and the implication that such a spouse will be morally blameworthy and therefore not deserving of such protection seems clear. If this development occurs, the Act would largely have failed to achieve the policy of removing moral judgments from the decision whether to dissolve a marriage.

A minor curiosity in the wording of condition (a) is that the addition that the adultery must have taken place 'since the celebration of the marriage', which appeared in the original draft of the Bill, has disappeared in the final version. The oddity is deepened by reference to section 3(3) which provides that where the parties have lived with each other 'after it became known to the petitioner that the respondent had, *since the celebration of the marriage*, committed adultery' he cannot rely on that adultery for the purposes of condition (a) if this

2. D.R.A. 1969, s. 9.

cohabitation lasted for more than six months. On the face of it, this suggests that a petitioner can allege an act of adultery committed by the respondent *before* the marriage (perhaps even with himself) and that the six month bar does not apply to that adultery, but only to adultery occurring after the wedding. This would lead to absurdity and injustice and it is to be hoped that the words 'since the celebration of the marriage' will be judicially restored to condition (a) by implication.

Very difficult problems are posed by the requirement in condition (b) that the petitioner must not *reasonably* be expected to live with the respondent. Unlike the test of tolerability in condition (a), which is subjective, this imposes an objective evaluation of the matrimonial situation. The justification for making the distinction between the two conditions was stated by the Law Commission to be that, where adultery has been committed 'it must rest with the petitioner to say whether he or she is able to forgive and forget and not with the judge to say whether he or she ought to do so' (Law Commission, 1967a). This is an understandable view, but, it may be asked, why should the fact of adultery alone absolve a petitioner from meeting the court's standard of 'reasonableness' in repudiating his partner? What of the husband who *attempts* adultery, or who has a homosexual relationship, or who occasionally gets abusively drunk or who misbehaves towards the children? Behaviour of this kind can only be brought within condition (b), where the court cannot have regard to the petitioner's own subjective evaluation of these acts but must form its own view as to how the petitioner taking into account his personal attributes, should reasonably have reacted to them.

It is true that the formula of condition (b) corresponds closely to the present test of matrimonial cruelty, with the exclusion of the requirement that injury to health must be proved. The same test is also to be found in the law of constructive desertion. It was pointed out earlier (see p. 116) that judges might take widely diverse views as to what conduct reasonably entitles a spouse to leave home. The attempt made by Lord Justice Diplock to relate the standards to be applied by magistrates to local opinion is helpful, but would be extraordinarily difficult for High Court or county court judges to apply in divorce cases. There is a further complicating factor. Condition (b) mentions nothing of 'fault' by either party. In this respect it appears to accept the majority view in *Williams* v. *Williams*[3] that a petitioner may be subjected to intolerable behaviour even though the respondent is innocent of blame for his conduct. How, then, is a court to judge the reaction of a spouse to a situation of strain brought about by the physical or nervous illness of the other? If inflictions of this kind result in sexual impotence or indifference, can a petitioner 'reasonably' be expected to live with his partner? Late in 1970, Mr Justice Cumming-Bruce said of a husband whose wife suffered from chronic schizophrenia:

(His) sufferings, the stresses and strains and ensuing depression have not been dissimilar from those which a spouse endures when cohabitation means living with a partner who is struck down by physical disease such as disseminated sclerosis, cerebral thrombosis, or the effects of cerebral haemorrhage, illnesses that for years encumber all communication or active cooperation in the home. These situations engulf both spouses in personal tragedy; the one is called on, as a consequence of the matrimonial obligation, to endure the consequences of the incapacity of the other.[4]

In matters of this kind, the court has to make an evaluation, not of the moral conduct of the respondent (as will probably be the case in condition (a)), but of the whole matrimonial situation and then measure it against its own idea of the duties of 'ideal' or 'reasonable' marriage partners.

In certain circumstances, condition (b) may also require the court to evaluate the conduct of the petitioner. Although the bars of condonation, provocation and misconduct conducing have been abolished by the Act it would appear strange if a petitioner could allege against the respondent as behaviour he cannot reasonably be expected to endure conduct which he has provoked, or in which he himself habitually indulges, or to which he has for many years paid no attention. The old law on these matters may, therefore, reappear under this condition. Support for this possibility is to be found in the Act itself. Where the allegation is of intolerable behaviour under condition (b),

3. [1964] A.C. 698, discussed above p. 119.

4. *Priday* v. *Priday* [1970] 3 All E.R. 554. The reference to behaviour in the condition should cover acts or omissions *affecting the quality of the cohabitation*. Mere absence and conditions not influencing behaviour would thus be excluded, but not more, for that would conflict with the instruction of the Law Commission (1967a) that forms of insanity should be covered.

it is enacted[5] that the fact that the parties lived with each other for a period or periods of six months or less 'after the date of the occurrence of the final incident relied on by the petitioner and held by the court to support his allegation' is to be disregarded in determining whether the petitioner can reasonably be expected to live with the respondent. Presumably, therefore, where such cohabitation exceeds six months, that is a factor to be taken into account.

Condition (c) retains the previous law of desertion except that the period of separation necessary has been reduced from three to two years. Desertion is a hybrid condition requiring the breakdown of the marriage to be proved (as evidenced by the prolonged separation) and that the respondent was responsible for it. The first element is concerned more with the state of relationship between the parties than with their geographical location, for 'desertion is not a withdrawal from a place, but from a state of things'.[6] The second element requires proof of guilt by the respondent. Not only must he be shown to have intended to bring the marriage to an end, but that there was no reasonable cause for wanting this. The condition does not expressly state, as did the provision for divorce on the ground of desertion in the old law, that the desertion should be without 'just cause'. This omission may affect the burden of proof so that a petitioner will not be required to *show* that there was no just cause for the respondent's departure. But it is submitted that it must remain open for the respondent to defend himself by proving that there was good reason for him to leave, otherwise a husband who had brutally driven his wife from home would be able to divorce her after two years under this condition instead of having to wait five years in order to make use of condition (e), which is the intention of the Act.[7]

Reviewing conditions (a) to (c), it appears that condition (a) is likely to require judges to exercise moral judgments between the parties in some cases and that conditions (b) and (c) inevitably import a process of evaluation before it can be decided whether they have been established. This, however, is a major weakness and inner contradiction in the Act. These conditions are presented as situations upon the establishment of which it is safe to presume that breakdown

5. D.R.A. 1969, s. 3(4).   6. *Pulford* v. *Pulford* [1923] P. 18.

7. Just cause is not mentioned in relation to the ground of desertion on which a matrimonial order may be made under the M.P. (M.C.) A. 1960, s. 1.

of marriage has irretrievably occurred. But whether or not a marriage has broken down is a *factual* question. It is illogical to specify a process involving *ethical* judgment as a method of deciding a purely factual matter. This can be simply illustrated. Suppose a husband leaves his wife because she has succumbed to a severe and incurable mental illness. He petitions for divorce. The sole ground he can allege is that the marriage has broken down irretrievably (as it may have done) and he relies on condition (b). A judge, however, would not be wrong if he took the view that the husband ought reasonably to have stayed with his wife. By making this judgment he compels himself to dismiss the petition, thus in effect denying that the marriage had, in fact, irretrievably broken down. It must be seriously questioned whether the reasons for retaining provision for immediate divorce are strong enough to justify the complexities and inconsistencies of conditions (a) and (b). If they are considered strong enough to do so, it would have been better to have followed the example of the Canadian Divorce Act1968–69 (see p. 242) which operates a breakdown ground *alongside* the old matrimonial offences and does not attempt to combine them in a single concept.

## Conditions (d) and (e)

Conditions (d) and (e) were the most controversial reforms effected by the Act. The former is not, as may appear at first sight, a provision for divorce by consent. It simply enshrines the not unreasonable assumption that where parties continue to insist that their marriage has broken down after having lived apart for two years, the marriage is to be assumed to have broken down, and it is the breakdown, not the consent, which is the ground for divorce. Where one party, however, still insists upon retaining the marital tie despite factual separation, the Act requires a longer period of time to pass before finally saying that the marriage is to be considered destroyed. Since three major Commonwealth jurisdictions enacted provisions of a similar nature before their acceptance in England, comparison with them will be useful.

Australia's Matrimonial Causes Act 1959 has a long list of offences which give cause for divorce. The most commonly used are desertion, adultery, cruelty and a few cases of drunkenness. Section 28(m) establishes separation as a ground of divorce distinct from the offences. It is a ground of divorce if

. . . the parties to the marriage have separated and have lived separately and apart for a continuous period of not less than five years immediately preceding the date of the petition, and there is no reasonable likelihood of co-habitation being resumed.

A petition on this ground may be brought by both parties, in which case the position is similar to that created by section 2(1)(d) of the English Act, except that in England the period is two years. But a petition may be brought by one party alone and this is possible even if that party was the one who caused the initial separation. Section 36(1) states:

For the purposes of paragraph (m) of section twenty-eight of this Act, the parties to a marriage may be taken to have separated notwithstanding that the cohabitation was brought to an end by the action or conduct of one only of the parties, whether constituting desertion or not.

Section 28(m) may therefore be used in exactly the same way as section 2(1)(e) of the English Act of 1969. The New Zealand divorce law is regulated by the Matrimonial Proceedings Act 1963 as amended in 1968. It is enacted that it is a ground of divorce

21(m) That the petitioner and respondent are parties to an agreement for separation, whether made by deed or other writing or orally, and that the agreement is in full force and has been in full force for not less than two years.

(n) That (i) The petitioner and respondent are parties to a decree of separation or a separation order . . . and (ii) that decree of separation, separation order or other decree is in full force and has been in full force for not less than two years.

(o) That the petitioner and respondent are living apart and are unlikely to be reconciled, and have been living apart for not less than four years.

It is further provided[8] that where paragraphs (m) and (n) are relied upon, the court 'shall dismiss the petition if the respondent opposes the granting of the decree and it is proved that the separation was due

8. s. 29(2).

to the wrongful act or conduct of the petitioner'. Those paragraphs only apply, therefore, where the respondent does not effectively oppose the petition. They correspond closely to the English section 2(1)(d). Paragraph (o) corresponds to the English 2(1)(e) except that the period of separation is four and not five years.

The Canadian Divorce Act of 1968–69 is an even closer precedent for the English Act. Unlike the English Act, which sets up breakdown of marriage as the sole ground of divorce, the Canadian Act operates the matrimonial offence system side by side with the 'breakdown' principle. Section 3 therefore retains adultery and cruelty amongst the matrimonial offences and, with them, the traditional bars of connivance and condonation. Section 4 establishes breakdown of marriage as a separate ground for divorce and sets out the conditions under which it shall be 'deemed' to have occurred. They are stated in greater detail than in the English Act, specifying such situations as the imprisonment or drug addiction of the respondent for stated periods of time. But the section also makes provision for breakdown resulting from indeterminate causes by providing as a situation establishing permanent breakdown that

4(1)(e) the spouses have been living separate and apart  (i) for any reason other than that described in sub-paragraph (ii), for a period of not less than three years, or

(ii) by reason of the petitioner's desertion of the respondent, for a period of not less than five years, immediately preceding the presentation of the petition.

The English Act is, therefore, no pioneer in admitting the simple fact of separation as a condition for divorce. The experience of these countries will be useful in anticipating the kind of problems which can be expected in applying it. It is of prime importance, for example, to have a clear understanding of what is meant by the words 'have lived apart for a continuous period' in conditions (d) and (e). The requirement of continuity is modified by section 3(5) which provides that 'no account shall be taken of any one period (not exceeding six months) or of any two or more periods (not exceeding six months in all) during which the parties resumed living with each other', but the time when the parties were together within the six months limit will not count towards the separation period. The provision is the familiar one designed to encourage attempts at reconciliation. Section 2(5), however, is more controversial. It states baldly that 'for the purposes of this Act a husband and wife shall be treated as living apart unless they are living with each other in the same household'.

It is not clear how 'household' is to be interpreted, but it may be safely assumed, on analogy with the law of desertion, that parties living in the same house are not necessarily living in the same household. More important, however, is the fact that the section compels courts to hold that, whenever spouses are *not* living in the same 'household', they are 'living apart' for the purposes of the Act. In many respects this is an extraordinary provision. A commonsense first impression of conditions (d) and (e) suggests that they are referring to spouses who have been *estranged* for two or five years respectively. If a husband goes abroad for six months on business, or to study, or in the army, or if he is admitted to hospital for that period, it would be very unusual for people to say that the couple are 'living apart'. The expression undoubtedly has implications beyond a mere statement of geographical fact. This has precisely been the way in which courts in Australia, New Zealand and Canada have interpreted their separation provisions. Parties will not be held to be living apart for the purposes of the separation grounds of those countries unless they are in a state of marital estrangement.

The Commonwealth interpretation appears to be closed to the English courts because of section 2(5). Indeed, an amendment moved in the House of Lords to import that interpretation into the Bill met formidable opposition and was withdrawn.[9] It is suggested that the Commonwealth approach is correct. This is not simply because it is closer to the accepted meaning of the expression 'living apart'. It is because the English interpretation can in some cases completely undermine the whole purpose of stipulating time periods for conditions (d) and (e). The purpose is not simply to provide evidence that the marriage has broken down. That will be obvious enough from the fact that a divorce petition has been filed. It is to provide the best evidence that the breakdown is *irretrievable*. The only way an adjudicator can be made reasonably sure that this is so is by evidence that the *breakdown* has persisted for a reasonably long time. It will not always be enough to show that the parties have simply lived in

9. [304] H.L. Deb. cols. 1082 *et seq*.

separate establishments for some time. Two examples will make the point. Suppose a husband spends two years abroad. There is no question of marital disharmony. Just before his return, he meets another woman and wishes to marry her. His wife agrees to the divorce. The estrangement has been brief, yet a petition under condition (d) must succeed (subject to financial safeguards). The only additional obstacle lies in section 2(3) which will allow the court to dismiss the petition if it is satisfied on all the evidence that the marriage has *not* broken down irretrievably. It is almost impossible to see how a court could be *satisfied* that the breakdown was not irretrievable. It amounts to requiring virtual certainty that the parties will be reconciled. If this subsection was worded so as to allow a court to refuse the petition if it was *not* satisfied that the breakdown *was* irretrievable, the criticism advanced here would to some extent be met, but this is not the case. Suppose, secondly, that a husband is confined to hospital (or prison) for a long period. During this time he is regularly visited by his wife. Some months before five years have elapsed she meets another man and wishes to marry him. As soon as the period is complete she can divorce her husband against his will, subject only to the safeguards, to be discussed below, contained in sections 4 and 6. It must be asked whether it really is safe to presume irretrievable breakdown *conclusively* when the period of actual estrangement may be only a matter of months.

## Special safeguards

In all jurisdictions where a 'separation ground' of divorce is admitted, safeguards are enacted to prevent its application in circumstances which would lead to injustice. In Australia, the safeguards take the form of *requiring* the Court to refuse a decree on that ground if

37(1) . . . the court is satisfied that, by reason of the conduct of the petitioner, whether before or after the separation commenced, or for any other reason, it would, in the particular circumstances of the case, be harsh and oppressive to the respondent, or contrary to the public interest, to grant a decree on that ground on the petition of the petitioner.

(2) . . . the court is of the opinion that it is just and proper in the circumstances of the case that the petitioner should make provision for

the maintenance of the respondent or should make any other provision for the benefit of the respondent, whether by way of settlement of property or otherwise . . . until the petitioner has made arrangements to the satisfaction of the court to provide the maintenance or other benefits on the decree becoming absolute.

(4) Where petitions by both parties to a marriage for the dissolution of the marriage are before a court . . . it is able properly to make a decree upon the other petition on any other ground.

In New Zealand, by contrast, the safeguards are not explicitly set out. The method employed is to give the court a *discretion* whether or not to grant a decree on the separation grounds.[10] Canada, however, follows the example of Australia more closely and imposes on the courts a duty to refuse a decree in any of the circumstances proving breakdown if granting it would 'prejudicially affect the making of reasonable arrangements' for the maintenance of children of the marriage and, in particular, it is to refuse a decree under section 4(1)(e)

9(1)(f) . . . if the granting of the decree would be unduly harsh or unjust to either spouse or would prejudicially affect the making of reasonable arrangements for the maintenance of either spouse as are necessary in the circumstances.

English courts are under a general duty not to make absolute any decree of divorce or nullity unless they declare themselves satisfied either that there are no children of the family or that, if there are, any arrangements which it has been practicable to arrange for the care and upbringing of the children 'are satisfactory or are the best that can be devised in the circumstances'.[11] Where the petition is under condition (e), the 1969 Act lays down special provisions to safeguard the respondent. If the respondent alleges that the granting of a decree against him would result in 'grave financial or other hardship to him and that it would in all the circumstances be wrong to dissolve the marriage', the court is put under an obligation to

4(2) . . . consider all the circumstances, *including the conduct of the parties* to the marriage and the interests of those parties and of any children

10. Matrimonial Proceedings Act 1963, s. 30.
11. M.P.P.A. 1970, s. 17(1).

or other persons concerned, and if the court is of opinion that the dissolution of the marriage will result in *grave financial or other hardship* to the respondent *and* that it would in all the circumstances be wrong to dissolve the marriage it *shall* dismiss the petition.

(3) For the purposes of this section hardship shall include the loss of the chance of acquiring any benefit which the respondent might acquire if the marriage were not dissolved.

The most crucial words have been italicized. It will be evident that even where divorce is sought under condition (e), cases may arise where the granting of a decree will depend on a moral assessment of the conduct of the parties. The Law Commission has stated that it was not its intention that this provision should make the granting of a divorce under condition (e) discretionary, but to provide a 'long stop' where the 'overall justice of the case' required that divorce should be refused. Wide divergences of judicial practice may be expected in the application of the provision and it is thought particularly unfortunate that assessment of conduct should have been introduced as a relevant consideration to a condition whose primary purpose is to allow divorce where there has been irretrievable breakdown *irrespective* of the conduct of the parties.

The Australian safeguard contains a similar weakness, but it has been very strictly interpreted. It cannot be invoked by proving merely that it was the petitioner who was responsible for the breakdown of the marriage.[12] Nor will it be considered 'harsh and oppressive' to a respondent to suffer a degree of social prejudice as a result of the divorce[13] or to be divorced when she has religious objections to it.[14] It is necessary to show a degree of hardship flowing from the fact of legal dissolution which is over and above the hardship that is in any case suffered as a result of the factual separation. The same is true in Canada. There the decree must be refused if to grant it would be *unduly* harsh or unjust. This has been interpreted as requiring 'a real and substantial detriment to the respondent beyond (the) normal consequences of the granting of a decree'[15] and it would seem

12. *Macdonald* v. *Macdonald* (1964) 64 S.R. (N.S.W.) 435.
13. *ibid.*; similarly held in New Zealand, *Fraser* v. *Fraser* [1967] N.Z.L.R. 856.
14. *Macrae* v. *Macrae* 9 F.L.R. 441.
15. *Johnstone* v. *Johnstone* (1969) 7 D.L.R. (3d) 14.

that the requirement in the English Act that the hardship must be 'grave' could be given a similar interpretation.

Should the allegation of grave hardship fail and a decree be granted under condition (e), the respondent has a further opportunity of having the financial arrangements considered. This is because before becoming effective all divorce decrees normally have to be confirmed ('made absolute') after (usually) three months have passed since they were initially granted. Under section 6, the respondent may apply to the court after a decree has been granted against him to consider his financial position if the decree were made absolute. If he does this, the court must

6(2) . . . consider all the circumstances, including the age, health, conduct, earning capacity, financial resources and financial obligations of each of the parties, and the financial position of the respondent as, having regard to the divorce, it is likely to be after the death of the petitioner should the petitioner die first; and notwithstanding anything in the foregoing provisions of this Act but subject to subsection (3) of this section, the court *shall not make absolute the* decree of divorce unless it is satisfied

(a) that the petitioner should not be required to make any financial provision for the respondent, or

(b) that the financial provision made by the petitioner for the respondent is reasonable and fair *or the best that can be made in the circumstances.*

(3) The court may if it thinks fit proceed without observing the requirements of subsection (2) of this section if

(a) it appears that there are circumstances making it desirable that the decree should be made absolute without delay, and

(b) the court has obtained a satisfactory undertaking from the petitioner that he will make such financial provision for the respondent as the court may approve.

The procedure of section 6 is also open to a respondent who has consented to a decree under condition (d). Both sections 4 and 6 expressly refer to the financial consequences of divorce for the respondent. If the divorce is under condition (e) and these consequences would cause 'grave' hardship to the respondent, the decree must be refused under section 4. But if the hardship would not be 'grave', the decree must still be refused under section 6 unless the financial arrangements were 'reasonable and fair or the best that can be made in the circumstances'. The 'circumstances' referred to are presumably those which will arise when the decree becomes absolute. The point is of importance because the range of legal obligations a person may incur is increased when the decree takes effect. While the spouses are living apart but are not divorced, the husband may well have incurred legal obligations towards the children of his mistress. He may also have incurred moral obligations towards his mistress and, as has been seen (p. 130), these will be taken into account in determining his liability towards his wife. But once divorced, he can transform those moral obligations into legal ones, a matter that is relevant in deciding what the best financial arrangements *vis-à-vis* his divorced wife the changed circumstances will allow.

It may be that to give the husband freedom to enter into new *legal* obligations with respect to another woman would so severely prejudice his divorced wife's position that it would impose on her 'grave' financial hardship. In that case the decree must be refused. This happened in the Australian case of *Penny* v. *Penny* (*No.* 2).[16] The court there refused to free the husband to enter into a third marriage because he was in arrears in his maintenance payments to his first wife of about £2,200 and to his second wife of about £1,200. However, if the hardship resulting would not be grave, an English court may grant the divorce providing that the arrangements are the best that the circumstances allow, even though, apparently, it considers them neither reasonable nor fair. This wording is rather unfortunate and does not appear in any of the Commonwealth Acts, which confine themselves to saying that the court must be satisfied that the financial provision is 'just and proper' (Australia) or 'reasonable' (Canada).

Probably the most serious financial loss a wife would suffer on divorce would be of pension rights, either under a private scheme in which her husband participated or under the state pension scheme, for she would no longer be able to qualify as his 'widow'. The position of a divorced wife on the death of her ex-husband is discussed more fully later (see p. 256) but at this point it is relevant to remark that sections 4 and 6 can go far in ensuring that this risk is

16. [1967] A.L.R. 360.

kept down to a minimum when the divorce is sought under condition (e). They enable the court to refuse to grant the decree unless the petitioner makes a financial arrangement sufficient to compensate the wife for the rights she will have lost. In this way the court can indirectly compel the petitioner to make an arrangement which would be beyond the court's powers to order under its statutory powers of redistributing assets on divorce (see p. 250). This is, of course, of value only if the petitioner has the resources out of which compensation can be made. But if he does not have those resources, and the court considers that the loss of pension rights would amount to 'grave financial hardship', it will refuse the decree. This may well mean that a divorce on this condition is more likely to be refused in the case of the poor than of the rich. This, however, is no defect in the law, which must accept the parties as it finds them. It is not only in the practice of consecutive polygamy that the rich are in a better position than the poor.

The safeguard of section 4 applies only where divorce is sought under condition (e). Section 6 applies to conditions (d) and (e). It is not entirely clear why section 6, which merely requires the financial arrangements to be reasonable and fair or the best possible in the circumstances, having regard to all matters, including conduct, should not apply where divorce is sought under conditions (a) to (c). The Nigerian Matrimonial Causes Decree of 1970, closely modelled on the English Act, allows the court to refuse to grant a decree unless satisfactory financial arrangements are made. The implication of the non-extension of section 6 to divorces granted under conditions (a) to (c) is that the moral guilt of the respondent in those cases removes the necessity of making the grant of the decree conditional upon the presence of satisfactory financial arrangements in favour of the respondent.[17] There is an additional, special safeguard for condition (d). At any time before the decree is made absolute, a party who consented to the divorce may allege that he was misled by the petitioner (whether intentionally or otherwise) about any matter he or she took into account in deciding to give consent. If the court is satisfied that this happened, the decree will be rescinded.[18]

17. But moral guilt may not necessarily be required under condition (b).
18. D.R.A. 1969, s. 5. The 'innocent' spouse, however, may put a high price on his consent and abuse of condition (d) is not unlikely.

**Financial re-adjustment**

It is now necessary to consider in detail the powers available to the courts to order financial re-adjustment on divorce. These powers have been rationalized and extended by the Matrimonial Proceedings and Property Act 1970 and became exercisable by the courts on 1 January 1971, the same moment when the reformed divorce law took effect. In examining the re-adjustment process, it may be useful to treat separately two distinct kinds of compensation to which a spouse whose marriage has terminated may be entitled. One relates to immediate loss suffered, and includes provision for urgently needed support as well as the broader loss immediately occasioned by the breakdown of the family. The other concerns making provision as a substitute for the loss of long-term security which the marriage would have given had it lasted.

Either spouse may be ordered to make cash payments to the other when a petition of divorce, nullity or judicial separation is presented.[19] This is called maintenance 'pending suit' and its purpose is to ensure that neither spouse is deprived of support while the suit is awaiting adjudication. Section 2(2) of the Act makes a new provision. When the decree is granted, the court may order a lump sum to be paid to a party for the purpose of enabling that party 'to discharge any liabilities reasonably incurred by him or her in maintaining himself or herself or any child of the family before the presentation of the petition'. The sum may be paid by instalments. Since the Act also abolishes the wife's agency of necessity (see p. 112), this new provision creates an important means whereby either spouse who has had to contract debts in the immediate aftermath of separation, may obtain money from the other to meet them wholly or partially when payment falls due.

Special remedies were provided by the common law by which a party could seek damages against third parties for the general harm suffered by the loss of a spouse. If compensation is payable to the surviving spouse by third parties who cause the death of a married person, there seemed to be no reason to exclude such compensation when the loss of a spouse came about differently. Either spouse could, therefore, sue a third party for enticement of the other spouse if the

19. M.P.P.A. 1970, s. 1.

third party without justification interfered with the right of cohabitation which each spouse has against the other. The action was quite respectable and did not rest on the servile status which was accorded to a wife in early law. However, it became very rarely used and both the Law Reform Committee and the Law Commission recommended its abolition, and on 1 January 1971 the action ceased to exist.[20] The reasons for its unpopularity were well expressed by Lord Denning:

If a husband is to keep the affection of his wife, he must do it by the kindness and consideration which he himself shows to her. He must put his faith in her, trusting that she will be strong enough to thrust away the possessiveness of her parents and the designs of would-be lovers. If she is weak and false to her trust, the harm cannot be righted by recourse to law; nor is money any compensation. The only thing for the husband to do is to set to work, as best he can, to mend his broken life, a task in which these courts cannot help him.[21]

The same motivation underlies the abolition, also from 1 January 1971, of the action which lay at the disposal of a husband (not a wife) for damages against a man with whom his wife committed adultery.[22] The basis of this action was far less respectable than that for enticement, for it derived from the principle that anyone having sexual intercourse with the wife was violating a property right of the husband. The legislatures in Australia and New Zealand remedied this inequality by giving a corresponding action to the wife against a female co-respondent. The English legislators reacted by abolishing the remedy totally. They did so on the advice of the Law Commission (1969) although two previous Royal Commissions had recommended that it be retained with modification. The strongest argument in favour of the remedy is that it would provide a means whereby the court can order the money or property of a seducer to be applied, to some extent, for the benefit of the members of the broken family. The court, as will be seen, has extensive powers to apply the assets of the *spouses* in this way. Why, it may be asked, should it not be able to 'get at' the assets of an interloper but for whom the breakdown may not have occurred?

20. Law Reform (Miscellaneous Provisions) Act 1970, s. 5(a).
21. *Gottlieb* v. *Gleiser* [1958] 1 Q.B. 267n.
22. L.R. (M.P.) A. 1970, s. 4.

The objections of the Law Commission appear to be twofold. First, it is argued that 'an order whereby the co-respondent, who in many cases will have become the second husband, is required to continue indefinitely to pay damages to the first husband would inevitably tend to keep alive bitterness between the parents which can only be harmful to the children'. A subsidiary point along the same lines is that the possibility of an award against the co-respondent might considerably increase the bitterness of divorce proceedings. The second objection is that third parties fall into such a diverse range of personalities that drawing distinctions between them and assessing their relative moral guilt would be impossible. This first objection seems rather weak. Either spouse may be required to make payments to the other for long periods, indeed, for life, and these are not objected to on the grounds that they prolong bitterness. The fact that some proceedings might be hard fought is no true objection. This possibility already exists with regard to the determination of the proper financial re-adjustment between the spouses. Although the fact has been criticized (see below), the conduct of the parties is relevant in determining the issue between them, and if a third party is involved, a finding as to the conduct of the spouses will inevitably involve consideration of that of the third party. This point also largely meets the second objection. In many cases an order against a third party may not be appropriate, but where a case does arise where a substantial measure of blame can clearly be attributed to the third party, there seems no reason why some reparation should not be sought from that quarter by the members of the broken family. When exercising his powers to order damages against an adulterer, an Australian judge recently said:

While it is no doubt correct that in many cases a wife's future needs will be taken care of by appropriate orders for permanent maintenance, the fact is that in many cases the dissolution of the marriage, resulting in two homes having to be maintained by the husband where one previously housed both parties, leaves insufficient both in capital resources and in income to enable the wife to obtain the financial benefits and enjoy the amenities she would have had the marriage been maintained. If damages, properly payable by a co-respondent, enable such gap to be wholly or partly bridged, I can see no reason why damages should not be sought for this purpose.[23]

23. *Kennerson* v. *Kennerson* [1970] A.L.R. 117.

Though deprived of the power to make an order against third parties, English courts are given power under the Matrimonial Proceedings and Property Act 1970 to order one spouse to compensate the other out of his or her assets for the consequences of breakdown of the marriage. Section 5 of the Act states that, in making an order, the court is to have regard to 'all the circumstances of the case', including the income, earning capacity, property and other financial resources of the couple; their financial needs and responsibilities; the standard of living enjoyed by the family before the marriage; the age of each party and the duration of the marriage; the amount each of them contributed to the marriage, including looking after the home or caring for the family and the loss of any benefits incurred by reason of the divorce. Having paid attention to all those matters, the court must 'so far as it is practicable and, having regard to the conduct of the parties, just to do so' make an order so as to place each party 'in the same financial position as that party would or (where the other party failed to discharge his or her financial obligations to that party) ought to have been in had the marriage not broken down'.

Two of the assumptions found in section 5 have been strongly criticized by Cretney (1970). He questions whether it is right in all cases to endeavour to maintain an 'innocent' divorced wife at the same level of prosperity as that of her divorced husband. It could be psychologically damaging to divorced women to face a life of secured indolence in an age when it is quite reasonable to expect women to seek gainful employment. Cretney condemns even more strongly the retention of the conduct of the parties amongst the matters to be taken into account in determining maintenance disputes. Although the new divorce law to some extent will remove the bitterness involved in the scrutiny of matrimonial conduct by the court deciding whether to grant the decree, this provision will, he suggests, re-introduce that bitterness when the financial arrangements are hammered out before the registrar of the court. In place of these assumptions he proposes that there should be a general rule that a wife should receive, on divorce, a modest but adequate sum to enable her to re-adjust to single living in the same way as a young widow receives no more than twenty-six weeks state pension after her husband's death (unless she has children) (see p. 224). This would be coupled with a sharing of family assets under a reformed matrimonial property law. Only in exceptional cases would this rule be departed from. A larger sum would be awarded if the marriage has lasted so long that it has, in effect, been the wife's career. A smaller sum, or none at all, would be justified if it would very clearly be unjust to make the usual provision for her.

These suggestions have much to commend in them. When the matter in issue is how the long-term security expected on marriage is to be provided for on its dissolution, the age and employability of the wife would appear to be more relevant than the minutiae of marital misconduct dating back over, perhaps, many years. On the other hand, it may be said, even if a divorced wife is employable after a relatively short marriage (during which she may also have been in employment), the destruction of her marriage removes from her the long-term security to which she could have looked forward *after* the cessation of her employment. It was this which may have formed a major expectation when she married and indeed may have provided a strong motivation for marrying the man, rather than cohabiting with him. If the woman does not regain that lost security by re-marriage, and the ex-husband has the means to provide it either wholly or partly, there seems little reason why this should not be done. In such a case it would be proper to award a smaller sum in her favour for the period immediately after the dissolution of the marriage on account of the continuation of her earning capacity, but subsequently to raise the sum should her earning capacity decline at such time that her ex-husband's income reached substantial proportions.

The range of orders which courts granting divorce, nullity or judicial separation may make is extensive and is set out in sections 2 to 4 of the Matrimonial Proceedings and Property Act 1970. The order may be that one party makes to the other periodical payments (usually monthly sums) which may or may not be secured against an item of property of the payor. A lump sum may also be ordered. Additional orders of the same kinds can be made for the benefit of any 'child of the family' (see pp. 150, 262). A lump sum payment involves the transfer of capital from one party to the other, but the payor is free to choose from what asset the money is to come. The courts, however, have power to make directions about particular items of capital. They can order that any specified item of one spouse's assets be transferred to the other party or a child of the family who is under eighteen (provisions concerning children will be discussed separately),[24] or that any such item be *settled* for the benefit of the other party or a child of the family, or, if the property specified is itself a settlement made on the parties to the marriage, they may vary the settlement and extinguish or reduce the rights of either of the parties under such a settlement. The Matrimonial Homes Act 1967[25] has a useful provision allowing a court, in effect, to transfer a tenancy protected by the Rent Act 1968 from one spouse to the other. It is impossible to foresee all the kinds of circumstances which may arise and which orders will be the most suitable in each particular case. Therefore it is of crucial importance that the courts have the maximum flexibility to exercise the powers available to them.[26] And, wide though these powers are, it should not be forgotten that the court can indirectly go even further than these express powers by refusing to make absolute a decree *nisi* sought on conditions (d) and (e) unless financial arrangements are made to its satisfaction (see p. 249).

Whether a lump sum order ought to be made will naturally depend on the degree to which the family wealth is to be found in capital rather than income. The order can be made for a great variety of reasons. In one case[27] the husband, whose conduct had led to the divorce, refused to apply for a Jewish 'divorce' which the wife required before she considered herself free to re-marry. The court put pressure on the husband to obtain the 'divorce' by fixing a very high lump sum order against him, but offering to reduce it if he applied for the 'divorce'. In another case[28] the amount was such that it was used by the wife for the purchase of a house for herself and the children. It can immediately be seen that this very wide power of property redistribution on dissolution of marriage achieves in England to a large extent what community of property systems do in European countries. However, the distribution in England is *discretionary*, and may well depend on a judge's (or registrar's) assessment of matters such as the conduct of the parties, the value of a

24. See pp. 259–65.   25. s. 7(1).

26. This point is stressed by Lord Justice Edmund Davies in *Curtis* v. *Curtis* [1969] 2 All E.R. 207.

27. *Brett* v. *Brett* [1969] 1 All E.R. 1007.

28. *von Mehren* v. *von Mehren* [1970] 1 All E.R. 153.

wife's contribution to the marriage and the earning potential of both spouses. This is very different from distributing property rights which accrue from the status acquired on marriage. It looks more like a sharing out of rewards, and is therefore consistent with the tendency of English law to look at marriage through commercial eyes.

Once an order is made, the courts have power 'to vary or discharge the order or to suspend any provision thereof temporarily and to revive the operation of provision so suspended'. This does not, however, apply to lump sum orders or orders relating to property or settlements made on divorce or nullity.[29] Unsecured orders for periodical payments last only while both parties are alive, or until the payee remarries, whereas secured orders last for the life of the payee (or until remarriage) even though the payee may survive the payor. Indeed, a secured order may even be varied after the death of the payor. Allowing a secured order for periodical payments to last beyond the death of the payor is one attempt to meet the problem that a divorced spouse has no rights against the estate of a deceased ex-spouse because he or she cannot be classed as a widow or widower of the other. Alternative rules have had to be constructed so that the legitimate security that a married person (usually the wife) could expect on the death of the other spouse is not totally defeated by divorce.

The continuation of a secured order after the death of the other ex-spouse may go some way to compensate for those lost rights. But it may be that no secured order was made, or that it yields an income insufficient for adequate compensation. Therefore it is open for a former spouse who has not remarried to apply to the court under section 26 of the Matrimonial Causes Act 1965[30] for provision to be ordered out of the estate of the deceased ex-spouse, if the deceased 'has not made reasonable provision for the survivor's maintenance after the deceased's death'. The court may order such provision to be made if it is satisfied both that it would have been reasonable for the deceased to have made the provision and that no provision, or no reasonable provision, was made.

So if a husband divorces his wife after many years of marriage using condition (e) of section 2 of the Divorce Reform Act 1969 and

29. M.P.P.A. 1970, s. 9.
30. As amended by the Family Provision Act 1966.

then leaves all his property to his mistress, the court may intervene so as to ensure that his former wife gets a fair share, by way either of periodical or lump-sum payments out of the deceased's estate. These questions will naturally involve very delicate decisions in which the moral claims of a former wife must be weighed against those of the other claimants. The problem is similar to that which arises in family provision claims under the Inheritance (Family Provision) Act 1938, as amended. Oddly enough, it may be that the tests to be applied in the two situations are not entirely the same. When a former spouse claims under section 26, the courts have asked themselves whether it would have been reasonable for provision to have been made and, if so, whether one (or a reasonable one) was made.[31] The test in family provision claims of dependants, however, has long been whether it was unreasonable for no provision to have been made, a much stricter test (but see p. 219). However, in a recent case a judge has applied the stricter test to a claim by a former spouse.[32] It may be conceded that it is odd that the test is stricter when a widow or widower applies for provision than when a former spouse applies, but uniformity should not be achieved by applying the strict test in both situations.

The ability to apply under section 26 is subject to some weaknesses. There is nothing to prevent the ex-spouse from disposing of his assets before his death. It is also dependent upon the former spouse maintaining sufficient contact with the other so that he or she is informed of the death. Both these difficulties may be overcome, however, by making a nominal order for periodical payments secured against an important asset of the payor. Should the payor wish to realize the asset during his lifetime, the order could be varied by reference to the circumstances then prevailing, and when he died, not only would the secured order continue, but a claim could be made under section 26.[33] It is quite clear, therefore, that a person does not succeed in 'casting off' his or her ex-spouse by obtaining a divorce. Indeed, it has been said that, while 'there cannot be any general rule that a first wife applying under section 26 should be afforded financial *equality* with a widow (on the other hand) the fact that an accretion

31. *Roberts* v. *Roberts* [1964] 3 All E.R. 503.
32. *Re Harker-Thomas's Application* [1968] 3 All E.R. 17.
33. *Foard* v. *Foard* [1967] 2 All E.R. 660.

of wealth to the estate has accrued since the first marriage has ended should not . . . be treated as disentitling a former wife from benefiting from that accretion'.[34]

The remedy under section 26 is of value only if there are sufficient assets in the estate to make the application worthwhile. But in most cases the value of the estate will be too small. In these cases the most valuable right a widow acquires on her husband's death would be her entitlement to benefit under a private or state insurance scheme in which he participated. If she does not become his widow, when he dies this right will be lost. The Law Commission (1969) examined a number of proposals to avoid this, rejected them, and declared that the problem was 'incapable of direct and complete solution'. In dealing with a man who is insured with a private scheme, or who has the means to become so, the matter can be tackled by the court granting the divorce. If he has an interest under a life or endowment policy, the court has power to order this to be transferred to his wife. But this will not necessarily be very satisfactory. The value of the interest in the fund could be quantified at the time of the divorce and paid over to the wife, but this may not be very great and in any case payment of this sum to the wife at the time of divorce gives her no security for the future. The court might seek to avoid this by ordering that the sum be held for her until her retirement or her ex-husband's death (if earlier). Indeed, this could be buttressed by ordering the husband to continue to make contributions to this policy which would therefore increase the sum eventually payable to his divorced wife. The objections seen by the Law Commission to these suggestions are that wives may well prefer an out-and-out lump payment to be made to them on divorce and that they would regard its compulsory investment in an endowment or life insurance scheme as 'excessive paternalism'. The Commission also saw difficulty in enforcing a requirement that a divorced husband should continue to contribute to a fund which would benefit his divorced wife and observed that any requirement of that kind would have the effect of reducing the amount of direct maintenance payments which could be ordered against the husband. Yet an amicably arranged divorce may well contain an arrangement whereby the husband purchases a life or endowment policy for his wife. If the wife wants this course to be taken and the husband has

34. *Eyre* v. *Eyre* [1968] 1 All E.R. 968.

the means to do it, there seems little reason why the courts should not exercise their extensive powers of making orders on divorce as widely as they can to achieve these ends.

Where the divorced wife has to rely solely on state benefits her position is more difficult to protect. When her ex-husband dies she will not be entitled to any of the widows' benefits available to widows under the state scheme (see p. 224). However, if she is caring for a child to whose maintenance her ex-husband was contributing when he died, she will be entitled to a *child's special allowance*. The rate is £2·95 a week for the first child, with lesser amounts for subsequent children. Family allowances may be received with respect to the subsequent children.

As she will not be living with her ex-husband she will not, of course, be able to benefit indirectly from the pension paid to him on his retirement. If she is sixty or over at the time of the divorce she will usually be entitled to the full pension of £6 a week. But if she is divorced before then she must rely on her own contribution record, which may not be good either during or after the marriage. She is allowed, as a concession, to make use of her husband's contribution record during the period of the marriage, and this may be of assistance to her if her own record falls short of entitling her to the full flat-rate pension. On the other hand, if the period of the marriage was relatively short, the husband's contribution record may be of little help to a divorced woman whose contribution record is otherwise poor. On remarriage a divorced woman will lose her entitlement to rely on her first husband's record and will no longer qualify for the child's special allowance. The difficulty in which a divorced woman may find herself with regard to state pension is inevitable in a scheme based on the insurance principle. To qualify for benefits under such a system, either the beneficiary or someone else on his behalf must have made the required contributions. The state scheme allows a husband to contribute on behalf of his wife. Once the parties divorce, the ex-wife is inevitably thrown back upon her own resources to provide insurance for her retirement. If she cannot do this, or does so insufficiently, she can only look to her former husband's resources to compensate her for the loss. If these are also insufficient, nothing can be done. In such a case a court may be compelled to make a straight choice between the wife and the husband's mistress and refuse to dissolve the marriage on the ground that this would cause her exceptional financial hardship within section 4 of the Divorce Reform Act 1969, if the section is applicable (see p. 245).

In concluding the examination of the powers of English courts to make financial provision on divorce or nullity, reference should be made to the corresponding powers of the Australian courts. These are set out in section 87 of the Australian Matrimonial Causes Act 1959. They include power to make the usual orders of secured or unsecured maintenance either by way of periodical payments or lump sum, but there are included powers to appoint or remove trustees, to impose terms and conditions and 'to make any other order (. . . whether or not it is in accordance with the practice under other laws before the commencement of the Act) which (the court) thinks it is necessary to make to do justice'. These powers are further supplemented by sections 120 and 124 whereby the courts may set aside dispositions made with the intention of defeating an order of court and may grant injunctions 'in any case in which it appears to the court to be just or convenient to do so and either conditionally or upon such terms and conditions as the court thinks just'. Australian courts have used these sweeping powers in many ways, including the following:

1. Where the matrimonial home was destroyed by fire, an insurance company was ordered not to pay monies due under the policy to the husband (who had insured the house) and the husband was then ordered to assign his interest in the money to his wife.[35]

2. A husband was ordered to convey certain stocks to his wife and to transfer the powers conferred on him as governing director to his wife.[36]

3. A husband was ordered to leave the matrimonial home to his wife in his will.[37]

4. A husband was ordered to secure the payment to his wife of a capital sum on his death by charging it against the amount payable on his death under an insurance scheme under which his wife would have benefited but for the divorce.[38]

English courts may set aside dispositions by way of gift if made by

35. *Sanders* v. *Sanders* (1967) 41 A.L.J.R. 140.
36. *Burns* v. *Burns* [1967] V.R. 814.   37. *Sparkes* v. *Sparkes* 11 F.L.R. 211.
38. *Hart* v. *Hart* [1968] 3 N.S.W.R. 43.

a party with the intention of defeating a claim for financial provision (and even if it is not a gift, if the person taking the property knew of the transferor's intention) and they could prevent such a disposition from being made.[39] But it is doubtful whether they could exercise all the powers used by the Australian courts in the examples cited. They could not restrain a *third party* from acting, as in example (1) and it is unlikely that they could require powers of directorship to be transferred as in example (2). Orders similar to those made in (3) and (4) may perhaps be possible under the power to direct the settlement of specified property[40] though it is notable that an English court cannot order the payment of a lump sum to be secured. The Australian courts have been given a wider discretion than the English courts, but much may depend on the degree of imagination used by the English courts in the exercise of the powers which they have.

### Custody and maintenance of children

One of the most frequent objections to divorce is that the experience has adverse effects on the children of the marriage. This accusation fails, however, to distinguish between a number of important factors which can make up a divorce situation. One is the breakdown in the relationship between the parties manifested by hostility between them in the household. Another is the departure of one of the spouses accompanied, perhaps, by the intruding presence of a third party. Then there is the divorce process itself which, depending on the form it takes, may or may not aggravate the tensions inherent in the situation. Any or all of these factors may harm the children. It is not necessarily the legal fact of divorce which is the major cause of the harm, if it is, indeed, a factor at all. If harm does result from the legal process this may even be attributable to the tensions created by the traditional legal requirement of the establishment of matrimonial guilt against one party.

It is clearly established that children from broken homes are at higher risk of exposure to delinquency than those from the average unbroken home. But homes may be broken by many reasons other than divorce, and some American studies reveal that there is a greater tendency to delinquency from homes broken by death than by divorce. (S. and E. Glueck, 1959). Nye (1957) has even produced evidence

39. M.P.P.A. 1970, s. 16.   40. *ibid.*, s. 4(b).

that there is less maladjustment among adolescents from broken homes than from those unbroken homes which are unhappy. This is consistent with the findings of Landis (1966) that a large majority of children of divorced parents whose homes were unhappy before the divorce reported a high degree of relief when the divorce was granted and acceptance that this was the best solution for all. Many of those children had felt that, during the marriage, they were being 'used' by one or both parents in the matrimonial conflict.

That children of broken marriages will suffer is, then, inevitable. The legal process of divorce could, if properly arranged, be seen as a method of ensuring that the children suffer the least harm possible from the breakdown. Indeed, it may be a means of *improving* the position of children who would otherwise be suffering in an intensely unhappy atmosphere or in unsatisfactory circumstances of separation. The Matrimonial Proceedings and Property Act 1970 therefore stipulates, in section 17, that a court shall not make absolute a decree of divorce or nullity or make a decree of judicial separation unless, by order, it declares itself satisfied either that there are no children of the family or, if there are, or may be such children, that they are all named in the order and that, unless it is impracticable for the parties to do so, arrangements for the welfare of each of them have been made which are satisfactory or 'the best that can be devised in the circumstances'. An exception is allowed only if circumstances require the making absolute of the decree before the court can be satisfied of these matters. The importance attached to this proceeding is emphasized by the fact that it is expressly enacted that a decree made absolute where this order has not been made will be void. The children of the family who fall within the protection of this provision are minors who are under sixteen or who are receiving educational or vocational training, but any other child may be included if special circumstances exist which the court thinks make it desirable that the child is given this protection. A 'child of the family', it will be remembered, means a child of both the parties or another child who has been treated by the parties as a child of the family, unless he has been boarded out with them.[41]

A judge hearing the divorce is therefore under a duty to inquire into the future prospects of the children. Usually he will ascertain

41. M.P.P.A. 1970, s. 27(1); see p. 150.

sufficient information about the proposed arrangements from reading the petition and asking questions during the hearing. But if he does not feel satisfied with this information, he may ask for a report from a welfare officer. In the High Court in London there are special welfare officers attached to the courts which deal with divorce. Elsewhere, the probation service is used, although other persons, such as the police, the NSPCC and the child-welfare officers may be asked. An investigation undertaken for the Law Commission by Hal (1966) showed a considerable divergence of practice amongst judges in asking for information of this kind. Judges also took markedly different views as to the usefulness of interviewing the children themselves. The Court of Appeal, however, has recently stressed that it is important for the judge to see each party, even though he may have read a welfare officer's report.[42]

If the agreed arrangements are not satisfactory, the court must resort to making orders. Unlike the case of orders for the benefit of one or other of the spouses of the marriage, a court may make orders for the maintenance, custody and education of the children even if it dismisses the petition. This is important in so far as petitions for divorce may still be dismissed in spite of the breakdown of the marriage even under the new divorce law. The court may order periodical payments to be made to the child or someone on its behalf, and redistribution of property may also be ordered for the child's benefit.[43] The Act lays down that, in making the appropriate order, the court must have regard to all the circumstances of the case, including the financial needs of the child, his income and earning capacity (if any), any physical or mental disability he may have, the standard of living of the family before the breakdown of the marriage and 'the manner in which he was being and in which the parties to the marriage expected him to be educated or trained'.[44] In principle, an order for periodical payments, whether secured or unsecured, should stop when the child reaches the upper limit of compulsory school age, but it can be extended until he reaches eighteen if the court 'thinks it right'.[45] If a child of a divorced couple has already reached the age of eighteen when the divorce takes place, the court may make an order in his favour only if he is receiving education or

42. *H*. v. *H*. [1969] 1 All E.R. 262.   43. M.P.P.A. 1970, ss. 3 and 4.
44. *ibid*., s. 5(2).   45. *ibid*., s. 8.

training (or would do so if the order were to be made) or if there are 'special circumstances' justifying the making of the order. An order for periodical payments may extend after eighteen on the same conditions. Again we see that in English law support obligations between parent and child do not arise solely out of that relationship but are subjected to severe restrictions depending on age and the fact of dependency.

The court is also given power to make such order as it thinks fit for the custody and education of any child of the family who is under the age of eighteen. The court may instead, if it thinks fit, order that proceedings be taken to make the child a ward of court.[46] If divorce is actually granted, the decree may contain a declaration that either party to the marriage is unfit to have custody. Normally custody will be granted to one or other of the parties, or to a third person (e.g. grandparents), but in exceptional circumstances, the court may commit the child into the care of a local authority, or order that the child be placed under its supervision.[47] The report by Hall (1966) shows that supervision orders are rarely used.

In deciding which of two parents is to have the custody of the child, the court will put at the head of its considerations the welfare of the child. It is seldom, however, that this is best served by completely cutting a child off from one of his parents. There is, therefore, considerable flexibility and variety in the type of arrangement which a court may order or approve. Where one parent has custody, the other will invariably be given *access*, which is a right to visit the child, or to have the child visit him. This access may be unlimited, or under very severe restrictions as to length of time, place and frequency. An even more refined distinction can be made by giving custody to one parent and allowing the other to exercise *care and control*.[48] Normally, a parent with custody of a child will also have physical control over him. But where care and control has been expressly given to another, the parent with custody no longer keeps the child with him, but his retention of custody means that he has a right to be consulted over important steps in the child's upbringing. An Australian judge has disapproved of this practice[49] and it is easy to see how it could be

46. *ibid.*, s. 18(1).    47. M.C.A. 1965, ss. 36 and 37.
48. *Wakeham* v. *Wakeham* [1954] 1 W.L.R. 366.
49. *Travnicek* v. *Travnicek* [1966] A.L.R. 964.

disturbing to a child if the parent with whom he permanently resides is constantly liable to interference by the other with respect to decisions and plans about the child's future. This is especially so as there can be no clear dividing line between those decisions which fall within the province of 'day-to-day care' and the important ones which must be referred to the custodian. In fact, in *Wakeham* v. *Wakeham*, where a 'split' order of this kind was approved, it does seem that the court was concerned with protecting the parental rights of a father who had been deserted by his wife. It was recognized that the children's welfare demanded that she should keep them with her but the father's 'innocence', it was said, gave him a right to a say in their future.

What the right solution is in each case cannot be easy. The Court of Appeal has fairly recently stressed that, although in custody cases arising on divorce, the welfare of the child is paramount 'the claim of justice cannot be overlooked'.[50] Is an innocent spouse to be deprived of all influence with respect to the future of his children because he is deserted and it is thought that his 'interference' might prevent them settling peacefully in the new home to which the deserter has taken them? Normally, if the deserter is the wife and the children are very young, they will stay with her, but in *re L.* the Court of Appeal ordered two girls, aged six and four, to stay with their father as his wife had left him for no other reason than her attachment to another man. There seems little doubt that, in depriving the mother of custody and care and control, the court was attempting to punish her for her conduct and to provide a deterrent against an apparently causeless desertion of this kind. Three issues appear to be involved besides the welfare of the child: punishment of one individual, deterrence to others and justice between the parties. It is extremely doubtful whether punishment should be even a subordinate consideration in custody cases. It is surely inappropriate to use arrangements concerning the child as a weapon of revenge against one party. It may be relevant to consider whether the practice of courts in arranging custody affects marital behaviour so that a spouse might be less ready to desert if he or she knew that this would prejudice his or her chances of a favourable custody arrangement. However, as was explained earlier (see p. 186), the effect of punitive divorce pro-

50. *Re L.* [1962] 3 All E.R. 1; see also *L.* v. *L.* [1966] 1 W.L.R. 1097.

visions on marital behaviour cannot be assessed. In addition a doubt must be raised whether, even if the fear of losing custody of the children kept some unhappy marriages together, this might not be more detrimental to the children than to allow the divorce (see p. 262). However, the claims of justice are strong, and the natural expectations of a parent to maintain the relationship with his children born to him during wedlock should be overriden only if its maintenance would actually harm the child. Deprivation of access, therefore, should take place only in extreme cases.[51] It will be a question of balance in each case whether giving effect to the parental interest will adversely affect the welfare of the child to such a degree that to allow it to prevail would be to subordinate the welfare of the child to the parental claim. So also in the case of 'split orders'. Justice to a party might strongly suggest the retention of custody in the hands of a father even though the immediate welfare of the children requires their care and control to be exercised by the mother. Whether and, if so, for how long the father should be given custody will depend on an assessment of these factors.

There is a dearth of information concerning the effects of different custody arrangements on children. Goode's study (1956) concentrates upon the reactions of divorced wives to visits by the father. No very clear picture emerges. Often these visits created tension, but whether these were accentuated or weakened in the course of time depended on a multitude of factors such as the child's attitude to the father, whether the child became easier to handle as a result of the visit, the distance the parties were from the date of the divorce and whether remarriage had occurred. Children do not always enjoy these visits. The times when they can be arranged often conflict with other activities, which they may prefer, and this is especially so as they grow older. A reasonable parent would, of course, appreciate this and some change in visiting practice would occur. If this does not happen, an application may always be made to the court for variation of the order. Here again the court must weigh the deprivation of (often transitory) pleasures to the child (such as a visit to the cinema) with the expectation of a parent to retain contact with him.

In applying the principle that the welfare of the child is the major consideration, a number of subsidiary rules have emerged. Young

51. *S.* v. *S.* [1962] 2 All E.R. 1.

children, especially girls, will in normal circumstances be considered to be better off with their mother than with their father. Where it is thought desirable for a father to have care and control, he will have to produce convincing evidence that he can make satisfactory arrangements for their day-to-day care. Generally, courts will try to avoid separating siblings. Occasionally the courts have produced rather questionable assumptions about what is best for children. There is often a desire to prevent a child from coming into any contact with an 'adulterous environment'. In certain cases it may indeed be very undesirable for a child to make this contact, but in many others the environment will become legitimated on divorce and a new regular family created into which it may be desirable for the child to be integrated. Courts have also sometimes appeared to have placed undue emphasis in assessing a parent's character upon his or her conduct in court.[52] The danger here is that a punitive element may enter into the custody arrangements. After all, is a parent likely to be a worse parent if he or she has lied to the court if the purpose of the deception was a desire to retain the child?

It is in decisions about the custody of children, whether on divorce or during marriage that the subjective nature of the assessment of family cases is particularly apparent (see p. 204). Judges may give different weight to the importance of maintaining a religious background for the child. They have adopted conflicting attitudes to the degree of attention that should be paid to the dangers of moving a child from one parent to the other.[53] Judges have often showed themselves hostile to the evidence which psychiatrists submit in custody cases. Where the evidence comes from a psychiatrist instructed by one party only this suspicion is natural, but whether the psychiatrist has been instructed by one party or by both of them jointly, it is clear that evidence of this kind is of crucial importance in cases concerning young children. Whether a High Court or a county court judge sitting alone (as will be the case in divorce proceedings) is the best person to assess this evidence is open to question. Further consideration of the problem of adjudication in family matters will be given in chapter 11.

52. *B. (M)* v. *B. (R)* [1968] 3 All E.R. 170; *F.* v. F. [1968] 2 All E.R. 946.
53. Compare *H.* v. *H. and C.* [1969] 1 All E.R. 262 with *B. (M)* v. *B. (R)*, above.

# Chapter 10
# Remarriage

Whether a marriage has been terminated by death or divorce, the social and personal disruption is best healed by successful remarriage. Remarriage is growing in popularity. In 1931 widowed and divorced men remarried at the rate of 35·8 per thousand total population over fifteen and widowed and divorced women at a rate of 9·8. In 1964, the figures were 53·5 and 13·7 respectively. But since 1951 there has been, first a slight drop, and then a recovery, of the number of *divorced* people remarrying. This is illustrated in Table 5. Why should there have been this decline in the percentage of divorcees remarrying

Table 5
**Remarriage Rates of Divorced Persons per 1000 Population in each Age Group**

| Men | Year | Women |
| --- | --- | --- |
| 234 | 1951–55 | 137 |
| 191 | 1956 | 116 |
| 175 | 1957 | 107 |
| 161 | 1958 | 99 |
| 160 | 1959 | 97 |
| 158 | 1960 | 95 |
| 162 | 1961 | 96 |
| 162 | 1962 | 98 |
| 170 | 1963 | 100 |
| 172 | 1964 | 104 |
| 176 | 1965 | 107 |
| 183 | 1966 | 108 |
| 184 | 1967 | 109 |
| 187 | 1968 | 112 |

Source: *Statistical Review of England and Wales* (1968)

during the late nineteen-fifties, a trend reversed only in 1961? The answer lies in the divorce rate, which itself declined during the same period, and started to increase only in 1960 (see Figure 2, p. 34). The reason for this, as has been explained (see p. 33), was that legal aid was less readily available in the late nineteen-fifties than in the nineteen-sixties. About one-third of divorcees who remarry do so with another divorced person, and in a period where divorce is difficult, fewer of these people will be free to legitimize their cohabitation by remarriage. With an easier divorce law one can expect that most divorced people will remarry. This is immediately clear when one compares the number of divorce decrees made absolute in 1966 (38,352), 1967 (42,378) and 1968 (45,036) with the number of brides and bridegrooms remarrying in the same years who had previously been divorced: 1966 (25,070 and 26,740), 1967 (26,546 and 28,234) and 1968 (28,899 and 30,438). About two in every three people who divorce (especially if they divorce young) will remarry. Although many marriages nowadays may end in divorce, the institution of marriage itself and the desire to form relatively stable family units are therefore seen to be thriving strongly in contemporary society.[1]

The legal and social difficulties surrounding remarriage all relate to the inevitable conflict between the new family unit and the remainder of the old one. It must therefore be decided how far the obligations to the new family are affected by the pre-existing obligations to the old one and, conversely, how far the acquisition of new rights by remarriage affects the rights substituted by the law of divorce against the divorced spouse.

Little need be said about the legal significance the formation of a legitimate family has on the obligations owed by a divorcee to his former spouse. The divorcee will be subject to the usual obligations to his new spouse, but, as the Divisional Court has pointed out, that spouse 'must on marriage be presumed to take the other subject to all existing encumbrances, whether known or not – for example, a charge on property, or an ailment which impairs earning capacity, or an obligation to support the wife or child of a dissolved marriage'.[2]

1. Evidence from the state of Iowa, reviewed by Monahan (1958) shows that the divorce rate of parties remarrying is far higher than for first marriages, and that it increases with subsequent remarriages. Whether this is true in England is uncertain.
2. *Roberts* v. *Roberts* [1968] 3 All E.R. 479.

This means that the obligations to the first wife, which arose first in time, have priority, but that the courts will be realistic in enforcing them and will take into account the husband's new obligations. A person marrying a divorcee will therefore have to be prepared for the fact that the family income may be diminished by reason of the prior obligation. He should also realize that his rights on intestacy against the divorcee and also that person's freedom of testation are subject to a claim being made against the estate of the divorcee by his or her former spouse.[3] If the divorcee has custody of a child of the former marriage, the new spouse will in the ordinary event become responsible for the maintenance of the child if he treats him as one of the family. However the extent of this liability will be fixed by reference to the obligations which any other person might have to that child (see p. 150). Under the Adoption Act 1958 that child can, if the other parent consents, be adopted into the new family, though if that consent is refused it is unlikely that a court will dispense with it. The Houghton Committee (1970) has, however, tentatively suggested that such adoptions should be prohibited and replaced, if desired, by an order giving the divorcee and step-parent guardianship over the child.

Remarrying has much more important legal consequences on the substituted rights created by divorce against the ex-spouse. According to one view, the purpose of these substituted rights (for example, of maintenance) disappears where the person in whose favour they were created acquires renewed security by remarriage. This view commended itself to the Law Commission (1969) and seemed to have widespread approval. On the other hand it has been urged that remarriage will not always compensate a spouse for the loss of financial expectation when the first marriage was dissolved.[4] It would, it is said, be wrong to create a situation where it might be financially advantageous to cohabit illicitly rather than to get married. Also, the payor's duty to provide for the children would not be affected by the remarriage, and the result might be that the children were in receipt of considerably more income than the parent who had custody of them. Cretney (1970) makes the additional point that to require

3. M.C.A. 1965, s. 26; see p. 256.
4. This has been expressed by an Australian judge in *O'Regan* v. *Douglass* [1969] 1 N.S.W.R. 372.

periodical payments to cease on remarriage conflicts with the motivation behind making lump sum payments on divorce with the view to compensating the spouse once and for all for the lost security, because this payment cannot be varied on subsequent remarriage. In general principle, however, one may accept that an ex-spouse who enters a new marriage must be taken to have decided to look to the new joint venture as his or her means of security and to have accepted the economic level which it offers. It is doubtful whether termination of an order on remarriage will encourage people to live illicitly rather than to remarry, because if a recipient is cohabiting and refraining from marrying for this reason alone the court may very well vary the order to nil.

Despite the validity of the principle that orders for long-term security should terminate on remarriage, there may have been cause to leave an area of discretion to the courts to allow the order to continue in force in special circumstances. A court may, for example, be sceptical about the chances of a particular 'match' being successful. However, the Matrimonial Proceedings and Property Act 1970 provides for the automatic termination of maintenance orders on the remarriage of the recipient. If, however, payments are continued by mistake after remarriage takes place the only action the person making the payments is allowed to take is to apply to the court for an order directing repayment of the amount overpaid. If the court thinks that that would be unjust, it may order the repayment of a lesser sum.[5] The rights of an ex-spouse to claim against the estate of the other when the other dies are also automatically forfeited on entering remarriage. If he had not remarried when the application was made and had obtained an order for his maintenance out of the deceased's estate, that order will terminate if he subsequently remarries.[6]

5. M.P.P.A. 1970, ss. 7 and 22.
6. I. (F.P.) A. 1938, s. 1(2); M.C.A. 1965, s. 26.

# Part Three
# The Administration of Family Law

# Chapter 11
# Court Structure

At the present time the administration of family law in England requires the application of a complex series of legal provisions and a wide measure of judicial discretion. The tendency to replace rigid rules by broad discretion, seen in the general application of the welfare principle to custody cases by the Guardianship of Infants Act 1925 has been carried a long way further since that time by, for example, the family provision legislation of 1938 and 1952 and the Matrimonial Proceedings and Property Act 1970. This has not, however, led to greater simplicity in the legal sources, which are a tangled web of statutory enactment and judge-made case law. Although the enactment of a Family Code, which is a long-term project of the Law Commission, should go far in helping the legal practitioner, the social worker and the general public to understand family law, its application will always involve a strong blend of legal 'know-how' and commonsense. This is important in considering the nature of the tribunals which administer family law. There are other characteristics of this area of law which should strongly influence the family court structure. Family law inevitably and intimately affects every citizen. Its courts should be within the reach of all of them. It concerns aspects of life where immediate relief from an intolerable situation may be urgent; where the postponement of decision might irremediably prejudice the welfare of a child. Its courts must be able to act quickly. It concerns matters on which emotion runs high. Its courts must be properly staffed and supervised.

Under the existing judicial system, family matters are dealt with at three different levels. The majority of cases come before magistrates' courts, which will usually sit as a 'domestic court'. Most proceedings for maintenance and separation orders are brought in these courts; so also are most custody proceedings where the dispute is between the child's parents. The domestic court also deals with affiliation cases and applications for overriding parental refusal of consent to marriage. However, proceedings for the *enforcement* of affiliation and maintenance orders are not domestic proceedings and therefore do not fall within the purview of the domestic court. The domestic court must be composed of not more than three magistrates, including 'so far as practicable', a man and a woman. None of them necessarily has legal training, though they are advised on the law by the clerk. The general public is excluded from the hearing and, although newspaper representatives may be present, they can report only the barest factual details of the proceedings. The business of the domestic court must, as far as possible, be separated from the usual business of magistrates' courts, which is, of course, the application of the criminal law.[1] Appeals are directed to the High Court, which may put the domestic court right on a matter of law or send the matter back for rehearing on questions of fact. By an indefensible anomaly, however, an appeal on a matter of fact in *affiliation* proceedings is heard by a court of Quarter Sessions as part of its criminal jurisdiction,[2] although appeal on a point of law would be taken to the High Court.

When dealing with young offenders and in care proceedings involving children and young persons, the magistrates' court sits as a 'juvenile court'. The composition and procedure of these courts is governed by the Children and Young Persons Acts and, though not identical to the provisions regarding domestic courts, they have the same objectives. By a further indefensible anomaly, adoption applications, when made to magistrates' courts, are assigned to the juvenile court rather than the domestic court. The enforcement process (e.g. service of summonses, committal to prison) of magistrates' courts is performed by the police, but the main form of enforcement process open to magistrates is the attachment of earnings order. The social welfare agency used by magistrates sitting as a domestic or juvenile court is the probation service, but, as has been seen, the Children and Young Persons Act 1969 seeks to involve the children's officers of the local authority far more closely with proceedings concerning young offenders.

The county court is the next level at which family matters are

1. Magistrates' Courts Act 1952, ss. 56–8 (as amended).
2. Affiliation Proceedings Act 1957, s. 8.

adjudicated. Some of the matters with which they deal cover the same area as the jurisdiction of magistrates' courts. For example, claims for maintenance may be made in both courts. However, many instances of differences between the county courts and magistrates' courts in determining these applications have been noted (see p. 113). In particular the power of the county court to order lump-sum payments and to secure orders is to be observed. The county court shares with the magistrates the power to make custody and adoption orders, but the determination of property disputes is confined to county courts and the High Court. Family provision applications may be made in county courts where the estate is relatively small. Important disputes, often requiring the speediest solution, concerning occupation of the matrimonial home and protection against molestation by a spouse can be determined only by the county court or the High Court. The most effective remedy of the county court and High Court in matters of this kind is the injunction, which is an order by the court which must be obeyed on pain of being committed to prison for contempt of court. There are, however, procedures open to those courts to enforce financial obligations which are more elaborate than those available to magistrates, such as appointing a receiver to receive income coming to a defaulter. Orders of the county courts and High Court are enforced by the sheriff's officers and the bailiffs. The welfare service used by county courts is also the probation service.

It is only at county court level that petitions for divorce, nullity or judicial separation may be filed. Indeed, such petitions *must* be filed in county courts which have been designated by the Lord Chancellor as divorce county courts.[3] If, however, the petition is defended, it must be transferred to the High Court, where it will be heard by one of the judges of the Family Division (see p. 276). In fact, over 90 per cent of divorce cases are undefended, so the consequence of these provisions is to put the administration of the bulk of the divorce law into the hands of county court judges. This reform looks more drastic than it in fact is because previous to the conferment of divorce jurisdiction on county court judges, it was largely exercized by the same judges sitting as Divorce Commissioners (i.e. *as if* they were High Court judges). Although solicitors as well as

3. Matrimonial Causes Act 1967, s. 1.

barristers may act as advocates in county courts, the procedure is inevitably more formal and slower than that in magistrates' courts. However many of the more contentious issues in divorce proceedings revolve around the financial arrangements and these will generally be settled before the Registrar of the county court, where the procedure is relatively informal.

The family jurisdiction of the High Court grew up in haphazard fashion. The situation was reached that custody issues arising in divorce cases and family provision claims by ex-spouses were dealt with in one division (the Probate, Divorce and Admiralty Division) whereas custody issues arising in wardship cases and family provision claims by widows, widowers and other dependants were heard in another (the Chancery Division). The Administration of Justice Act 1970, in Part I, goes a long way to unify family matters in a single division of the High Court. The legislation had not come into force at the beginning of 1971, but when it takes effect, the Family Division of the High Court will deal not only with defended divorce and nullity cases but with a host of related family matters such as adoption, wardship, guardianship, declarations of legitimacy, proceedings under the Matrimonial Homes Act 1967 and the like. It is ironic, however, that one of the main anomalies of the former dispersal of family business throughout the divisions of the court, namely, the division in the adjudication of family provision claims referred to above, will remain even when the Act is fully in force. When the provisions of the Courts Act 1971 come into force as part of the government's implementation of the report of the Royal Commission on Assizes and Quarter Sessions (Beeching Commission) (1969) on the reorganization of the courts, the High Court will be able to sit in certain centres outside London. Family matters confined to that court will be able to be heard on those occasions. Appeals from both the county courts and the Family Division of the High Court are heard by the Court of Appeal, and finally by the House of Lords.

The distribution of family law business in the present court structure is chaotic. The demarcation which is most difficult to defend is that between the magistrates' courts and the county court. The overlap of jurisdiction is undesirable in so far as it means that the same provisions can be implemented by tribunals of a very different nature. But a more serious criticism is of the division of powers between them. A family crisis is seldom simple and it is highly desirable that the court dealing with it has a wide range of powers at its disposal. In a given situation orders relating to cash support, occupation of the home, ownership of family assets and custody of children might be necessary in order to deal with the situation as a whole. The orders relate to and supplement each other. It is quite wrong that a spouse for whom all those orders may be appropriate must seek them from different courts, differently constituted, using their own characteristic procedures and sitting according to their own individual time schedules.

The tentative views of the Houghton Committee (1970) concerning bringing greater uniformity into adoption court procedure have already been mentioned (see p. 204). More radical proposals have been made by Graham-Hall (1971). She suggests that there should be a single Local Family Court which would deal with an extensive range of family business including undefended divorces, separation and maintenance orders, custody orders, adoption and affiliation proceedings, property disputes between spouses, disputes concerning the occupation of the matrimonial home and various other related matters. How far criminal and care proceedings involving children and young persons should be included within the jurisdiction of a Family Court is more problematical. Graham-Hall suggests that criminal prosecutions, at any rate of young persons between fourteen and seventeen, might be better continued in the juvenile courts, but that it may be more appropriate if care proceedings involving children under ten were dealt with by the Family Court. She also proposes that the court be given the power to issue an injunction and that the welfare officers of the court should continue to be provided by the probation service.

There is great merit in a scheme for the unification of family business at a local level. It could even be argued that the trial of young offenders should be included within its jurisdiction, especially in view of the approach adopted in the Children and Young Persons Act 1969 which sees juvenile delinquency in the context of general family breakdown. Exceptions should, however, be made for crimes of a very serious nature. It would be important that most cases in a family court were heard by at least three persons, in this way retaining the lay element. There should be at least one man and one woman on the bench. In most cases the chairman should be legally qualified, preferably of the status of a county court judge. However, in some cases this may not be necessary and the lists could be arranged so that certain types of cases (for example, applications for variation of orders or their enforcement) could be heard solely by a lay bench, or even by a single justice. The appeal process should be able to operate quickly as this may be important, as for example, it is in custody cases. For this reason appeal should, at least generally, lie from a local Family Court to the Family Division of the High Court (sitting in a regional centre) rather than to the Court of Appeal in London.

# Conclusion

It can probably be said that 1971 saw family law put on a new course. The special nature of the impact of law on family relationships has become more widely appreciated and the implications of this on the system of the administration of justice is now realized. There nevertheless remain areas of considerable controversy. If the health of our society is to be secured by promoting the well-being of the family, how great is the community's obligation towards it? In her thoroughly documented book, *Family Policy* (1970), Wynn, starting from the assumption that a nation's most crucial resource is its children, argues that in the United Kingdom the investment in terms of social services and financial subsidy in the provision of an adequate home environment for the next generation is inadequate. Correction of the present distribution of wealth to meet her objections would require greater support by the childless of families with children. The importance of this support is greater where the children are being reared by a parent who is living without a partner.

The degree to which society should underwrite the security of families with children is a question of political judgment in each case. Without impeaching the strength, even the paramountcy, of the claims of families with children, we must nevertheless be careful not to forget that other people, too, have a claim on the community's resources. Old people, the sick and families supporting them may have an equal claim to attention. Nor is it always by choice that many people are single or childless. Material wealth may, psychologically, be of importance to them as some kind of substitute for 'a family'.

While the prevalent ideals of family policy have been broadly supported in this book, accepted orthodoxy has not always been supported or gone unquestioned. The Latey Committee (1967) gave expression to the widely held feeling that restrictions over young people which might be stigmatized as 'paternalistic' should be reduced. It is therefore instrumental in the removal of restrictions upon marriage for persons under twenty-one but over eighteen. Yet in view of the irrefutable evidence of the high risk that the marriages of young people in this age group may break down, the wisdom of this move was questioned. We have suggested that consideration might be given to some other form of regulation over these marriages (see pp. 39–40, 59–64). This is not to imply legal supervision over the sexual morals of young people. It rests on the quite different ground that entering marriage involves a commitment of a special nature. We have seen that circumstances arising during and after marriage may be made subject to legal supervision. It is therefore justifiable to employ legal means to control the conditions under which it is entered. But the effectiveness of legal control here, as elsewhere in family law, is often a matter of conjecture and care must be taken not to overestimate it. It is almost certainly true that social factors, such as the extent of educational opportunities open to women, influence the age at which people marry more than legal controls do. Nevertheless, where legal provision expresses a desirable ideal and may lead to actual benefit in individual cases, its use may be justified.

In chapter 3 the law relating to the rights and obligations between the spouses while the marriage lasts received extensive criticism. Many criticize the machinery for protecting the economic security of a spouse and children. The efficiency of the procedure of the magistrates' courts, where most maintenance matters are dealt with, has been severely discredited. It is hard, however, to suggest alternatives The use of social-security or income-tax machinery involves extremely complex matters of administration and is at present under consideration by the Finer Committee. But more fundamental objection was found in the difficulty in ascertaining the general principles laying down the respective duties of the spouses. There is a general duty upon each to allow the other to cohabit with him or her, but how the task of providing a home and running it is to be divided between them cannot be clearly seen. It is true that these are matters which are to a large extent dictated by convention or accepted morality and that this will be reflected in judicial decisions about desertion, wilful neglect to provide reasonable maintenance, and the protection of a spouse against eviction by the other. But too often decisions have turned on technicalities which have obscured and often distorted the application of those principles. Too much depends on the court which hears the action. Overriding importance may be placed on matters having little relevance to the real issue, such as whether an isolated act of adultery has occurred, whether the spouses have separated by agreement or whether they are living together again.

In particular, two significant weaknesses were found in matters which are easily susceptible of legal regulation (see Ch. 2). A spouse's security of occupation of a home during marriage was seen to be protected to a certain extent, but in a manner which is still largely unsatisfactory. In common with other aspects of English matrimonial law, the Matrimonial Homes Act 1967 appears to be designed to offer last-minute protection once a crisis has arisen. The status of a home as a *matrimonial* home does not yet, of itself, confer upon a spouse who has no legal interest in it any protection against third parties. Parallel to this imperfect protection of occupation is the even greater injustice that a spouse may be entitled to no share whatsoever in assets which have accumulated in the family over the years. The principle of separation of property still dominates, though it has been mitigated by a purely commercially based doctrine that a spouse who has made a measurable financial contribution to the purchase of property (or has substantially improved it) may have a compensatory share equivalent to the extent of the effort put in. The uncertainty this creates is unsatisfactory; the method of calculation is objectionable. It ignores both the visible activities undertaken by a wife in running a home and the less tangible forms of advice and support given to each other by married people. The result is that, so long as the marriage lasts, the ownership of family assets may reflect a severe imbalance between them, and that injustice may result if a crisis arises. The courts do not have sufficient power to deal with the situation in maintenance proceedings. Even in proceedings for divorce, nullity or judicial separation, a petitioner has to rely upon a judge's discretionary decision as to what is a fair division in the circumstances. It should be the status of a married person, and not of a potential divorcee, which should give legal protection in such a situation.

We have broadly supported the objectives of the sponsors of the

Divorce Reform Act 1969. It has been shown that to refuse to dissolve a factually broken marriage in the hope that this will deter other marriages from breaking down is to pursue an unprovable and probably illusory ideal (see pp. 32–44, 186–7). Even if it does have marginal effect, other methods of achieving marital stability (such as regulating entry into marriage and assisting families in trouble) may be more effective and certainly avoid the suffering brought about by the former approach. The divorce rate has, in the past, had little relevance to the marriage breakdown rate. Even if the rate of marriage breakdown is now greater than in former years, this may have little to do with the law of divorce, but much to do with social factors such as the increase in youthful marriages, reduction of family size and increased expectations of the parties. Divorce is, therefore, properly to be seen as a mechanism of re-adjustment when a marriage has failed. This appears to have been the principle of the 1969 Act. But the Act was a compromise which incorporated within the single concept of irretrievable breakdown a number of incompatible elements (see pp. 232–44). For the sake of retaining provision for 'swift' divorces, courts will continue to be required to make evaluative judgments as to whether a marriage should or should not have broken down. The necessity for an immediate divorce should be obviated if the law relating to the rights between spouses during marriage was amended to enable sufficient protection to be given by simpler means than divorce, nullity or judicial separation proceedings. Divorce should be available on the establishment of the fact that the two parties are estranged and now live apart (whether in separate establishments or not) probably for a period of no longer than a year. This is subject only to safeguards in cases of special hardship. This would remove the futile burden from the judiciary of pronouncing upon the standards of conduct expected from husbands and wives. It would provide the best evidence of the irretrievability of the breakdown. It would have a further possibly beneficial consequence that a spouse would not be free to marry a third party immediately his first marriage breaks down. The new marriage, entered into in the wake of an emotional crisis, might not have commenced in very desirable circumstances – possibly, this is a factor contributory to the apparently high risk of failure of second and subsequent marriages (see p. 269). There may be much to be said for allowing a period of time to elapse from the initial separation of the spouses to allow the situation to clarify. If the objection is raised that this might encourage a separated spouse to cohabit illicitly with a third party before the divorce goes through, it can be argued that this may be better than that they should enter into an insecure marriage. They are more likely to try to avoid pregnancy and there would therefore be less risk of a child being born into a possibly unstable situation. If a child is, however, born and the relationship succeeds, he can be legitimated by subsequent marriage. If the relationship fails, it is true that the child would be illegitimate, and that this may still involve some social stigma. But the insecurity he may suffer by being reared in a one-parent family may not be very different from his position if his parents had married each other before they parted.

Consistently with the view that an irretrievably broken marriage should be capable of legal dissolution irrespective of the moral responsibility for the estrangement, we have criticized the retention of the distinction between divorce and nullity (other than for mistake or duress) (see pp. 174–81). The division is based on, and therefore perpetuates, the social stigma attached to divorce proceedings and reflects ideas about the nature of marriage which are questionable. So long as the framework of the new divorce law is retained, these grounds of nullity (with the addition of sterility) would be more satisfactorily treated as factors the presence of which could be held to establish irretrievable breakdown.

Where a court makes economic re-adjustment on divorce, nullity or judicial separation, the present policy that some attention must be paid to the conduct of the parties has been supported (see p. 253). The decision should not depend on conduct alone, but conduct may well be relevant to decide the most just distribution of family assets to compensate both for immediate loss and loss of long-term security. In the latter case in particular, however, the whole context should be considered and it may well be wrong to impose a heavy burden on an ex-husband's new family in favour of his ex-wife if she is young and easily able to re-adjust. Since the Law Commission has accepted the relevance of conduct of the spouses in these matters we have questioned its view that any relevant misconduct by a third party should be ignored (see p. 251). Further criticism has been made of the restriction of the clauses erecting financial safeguards on divorce to divorces granted under the separation provisions of the Divorce Reform Act 1969 when it seems that divorce might be granted under conditions (a) and (b), where a respondent has been guilty of little misconduct or indeed none at all (see p. 249).

Where a decree of divorce is granted, the courts are under a duty to pay special heed to the position of children of the family. There is a good deal of confusion of thought about the effect of divorce on children. The evidence that family disruption has adverse affects on children is clear. But to attribute this to the divorce process alone is misleading. The discord in the home and the separation itself are probably far more harmful. The divorce process can, therefore, be used as a mechanism for ensuring that the welfare of children in broken homes is paid proper attention. But while the children's welfare is, and should remain, the predominant concern of the court, attention has been drawn to the importance of not disregarding other interests. The relationship of a parent with his child, or that of a person who has stood in the position of a parent with the child, are realities which should be regarded together with the interests of the child. A custody decision therefore remains an essentially judicial one, concerned with assessing sometimes conflicting interests and reaching a conclusion which is in the closest conformity with justice to all parties (see pp. 261–67).

It has also been necessary to emphasize the significance of the protection of adult–child relationships in connection with the law relating to fostering and adoption. It was out of recognition of these relationships that the Houghton Committee (1970) tentatively suggested that the foster-parent–child relationship might be strengthened by means of a guardianship order. This, it was suggested, is a reasonable objective, though some hesitation was expressed with regard to the formal means proposed for achieving it. However, the conception of the adoption law *solely* in terms of a child-welfare service was strongly criticized (see pp. 194–201). The permanent severance of the parental relationship is a serious matter which no society should undertake lightly. The fact that a judge or a social worker believes that the child's welfare would be better served by a permanent severance of the relationship rather than its retention is not, it was suggested, sufficiently certain or significant to justify that step. What the adjudicator should seek to decide is whether the parental relationship has been abandoned or forfeited. Consistently with this view, we have urged that the parent–child relationship should equally be protected whether it is a legitimate or illegitimate one. Reforms of the law concerning the rights of illegitimate persons suggest that it is now becoming accepted that the protection of relationships with children should not necessarily depend on marriage. This development is consistent with the promotion of the desirable policy that attempts should be made to involve putative fathers more closely with the upbringing of their children.

But where parents have freely decided against bringing up their own child, the adoption system enables these children to be reared in a substitute family in relative security. The Houghton Committee's suggestion that placements with non-relatives should be arranged only through specialist adoption agencies was thought to be well founded. It is also imperative that a more satisfactory way of settling when parental consent is to be considered irrevocable be introduced. That an adopted child is told about his adoption and has the means of discovering about his true parentage should he wish to do so were thought to be important requirements. Some would say they were the natural rights of any individual.

Finally it was observed in Part Three that the present distribution of family business across the court system urgently demands attention. But the need is not only one of unification. Close attention must be paid to court procedure, the type of evidence which may be presented in court and the personnel on the bench. It was suggested that there should be a single family court at first instance, combining within itself the family jurisdiction of magistrates' courts, county courts and the High Court. Normally the bench would consist of a legally trained chairman (a judge) and two laymen (magistrates) with specialist training in family matters. There should be at least one woman and one man. But certain matters should be referable to a judge sitting alone or even a single lay magistrate. A case can be made for bringing care proceedings before this tribunal in view of the current trend in policy to view offences committed by juveniles in the light of the home background as a whole.

These, then, are the main issues discussed in this book, around which many peripheral ones have revolved. On a number of them, contemporary opinion may have settled and legal and policy decisions may already have been taken. On others, opinion is still divided and solutions are awaited. From its very inception, the Law Commission has played a major part in stimulating the rethinking of family law and further valuable contributions from it may be expected. Government Committees, too, are paying attention to these problems. The creation of a single Family Division of the High Court will provide a further impetus to the specialized evolution of family law. The Lord Chancellor has recognized the importance of this development and in this climate of opinion the future holds much promise that the problems of families will receive the special attention of politicians, administrators and lawyers.

# References

Adams, B. N. (1960), 'An inquiry into the nature of the family', in G. Dole and R. L. Carneiro (eds.), *Essays in the Science of Culture*, Crowell.

Ainsworth, M. S. (1965), 'Further research into the adverse effects of maternal deprivation', in J. Bowlby, *Child Care and the Growth of Love*, Penguin, 2nd edn.

Association of Child Care Officers (1969), *Adoption, the Way Ahead*, ACCO.

Bettelheim, B. (1969), *The Children of the Dream*, Thames & Hudson.

Bowlby, J. (1951), *Maternal Care and Mental Health*, World Health Organization.

Bowlby, J. (1969), *Attachment and Loss*, Hogarth.

Burgess, E. W., and Cottrell, L. S. (1939), *Predicting Success and Failure in Marriage*, Prentice-Hall.

Burgess, E. W., and Wallin, P. W. (1953), *Engagement and Marriage*, Lippincott.

Burlingham, D., and Freud, A. (1942), *Young Children in Wartime*, Allen & Unwin.

Burlingham, D., and Freud, A. (1944), *Infants without Families*, Allen & Unwin.

Cameron, B. J. (1969), 'The twilight of illegitimacy', *New Zealand Law Journal*.

Castberg, J. (1916), 'The childrens' rights laws and maternity insurance in Norway', *Journal of the Society of Comparative Legislation*, vol. 36.

Cavanagh, W. E. (1966), 'What kind of court or committee?', *British Journal of Criminology*, vol. 6.

Christensen, H. T. (1960), 'Cultural relativism and pre-marital sex norms', *American Sociological Review*, vol. 25.

Church of England (1966), *Putting Asunder*, SPCK.

Church of England (1966a), *Fatherless by Law?*, Church Information Office.

Committee on the Adoption of Children (1954), *Report of the Departmental Committee on the Adoption of Children* (Chairman: Sir Gerald Hurst) HMSO, Cmnd. 9248.

Committee on the Adoption of Children (1970), *Working Paper of the Departmental Committee on the Adoption of Children* (Chairman: Sir William Houghton) HMSO.

**Committee on the Age of Majority** (1967), *Report of the Committee on the Age of Majority* (Chairman: Mr Justice Latey) HMSO, Cmnd. 3342.

**Committee on Children and Young Persons** (1960), *Report of the Committee on Children and Young Persons* (Chairman: Viscount Ingleby) HMSO, Cmnd. 1191.

**Committee on Human Artificial Insemination** (1960), *Report of the Departmental Committee on Human Artificial Insemination* (Chairman: The Earl of Feversham) HMSO, Cmnd. 1105.

**Committee on Local Authority and Allied Personal Social Services** (1968), *Report of the Committee on Local Authority and Allied Personal Social Services* (Chairman: Sir Frederic Seebohm) HMSO, Cmnd. 3703.

**Committee on the Marriage Law of Scotland** (1969), *Report of the Committee on the Marriage Law of Scotland* (Chairman: Lord Kilbrandon) HMSO, Cmnd. 4011.

**Committee on Personal Injuries Litigation** (1968), *Report of the Committee on Personal Injuries Litigation* (Chairman: Lord Justice Winn) HMSO, Cmnd. 3691.

**Committee on Statutory Maintenance Limits** (1968), *Report of the Committee on Statutory Maintenance Limits* (Chairman: Miss Jean Graham-Hall) HMSO, Cmnd. 3587.

**Cretney, S.** (1970), 'The maintenance quagmire', *Modern Law Review*, vol. 33.

**Davis, K.** (1939), 'Illegitimacy and the social structure', *American Journal of Sociology*, vol. 45.

**Devlin, P. A.** (1965), 'Morals and the law of marriage', in *The Enforcement of Morals*, Oxford University Press.

**Dicey, A. V.** (1914), *Law and Public Opinion in England during the Nineteenth Century*, Macmillan, 1963 edn.

**Dicks, A. V.** (1967), *Marital Tensions*, Routledge & Kegan Paul.

**Dinnage, R.,** and **Kellmer Pringle, M. L.** (1967), *Foster Home Care: Facts and Fallacies*, Longman.

**Dinnage, R.,** and **Kellmer Pringle, M. L.** (1967), *Residential Child Care: Facts and Fallacies*, Longman.

**Dominian, J.** (1968), *Marital Breakdown*, Penguin.

**Dror, Y.** (1959), 'Law and social change', *Tulane Law Review*, vol. 33, reprinted in V. Aubert (ed.), *Sociology of Law*, Penguin, 1969.

**Engels, F.** (1884), *The Origins of the Family*, *Private Property and the State*, Lawrence & Wishart, 1940 edn.

**Fairburn, W. R. D.** (1952), *Psychoanalytic Studies of Personality*, Tavistock/ Routledge & Kegan Paul.

**Fletcher, R.** (1966), *The Family and Marriage in Britain*, Penguin, rev. edn.

**Fox, R.** (1967), *Kinship and Marriage*, Penguin.

**Geiger, H.** (1966), *The Family in Soviet Russia*, Oxford University Press.

Glueck, S., and Glueck, E. (1950), *Unravelling Juvenile Delinquency*, Oxford University Press.

Goding, G. (1969), 'The psychology of marriage breakdown', in H. A. Finlay (ed.), *Divorce, Society and the Law*, Monash University Symposium.

Goode, W. J. (1956), *After Divorce*, Free Press. Republished as *Women in Divorce*, Free Press, 1965.

Goode, W. J. (1963), *World Revolution and Family Patterns*, Free Press.

Gough, K. (1959), 'The Nayars and the definition of marriage', *Journal of the Royal Anthropological Society*, vol. 82.

Graham-Hall, J. (1971), 'An outline of a proposal for a family court', *Family Law*, vol. 1.


Habbakuk, H. J. (1950), 'Marriage settlements in the eighteenth century', *Transactions of the Royal Historical Society*, vol. 32.

Hall, J. C. (1968), *Arrangements for the Care and Upbringing of Children*, Law Commission Working Paper no. 15.

Harvey, L. V. (1969), 'Marriage counselling: a therapeutic approach to marital disorganization', in H. A. Finlay (ed.), *Divorce, Society and the Law*, Monash University Symposium.


Kahn-Freund, O. (1955), 'Matrimonial property law in England', in W. Friedmann (ed.), *Matrimonial Property Law*, Stevens.

Kahn-Freund, O. (1970), 'Recent legislation on matrimonial property', *Modern Law Review*, vol. 33.

Kellmer Pringle, M. L. (1967), *Adoption: Facts and Fallacies*, Longman.

Kephart, W. M. (1954), 'The duration of marriage', *American Sociological Review*, vol. 19.

Kinsey, A. C. (1953), *Sexual Behaviour in the Human Female*, W. B. Saunders.


Landis, J. T. (1966), 'The trauma of children whose parents divorce', *Marriage and Family Living*, vol. 22.

Law Commission (1966), *Reform of the Grounds of Divorce: The Field of Choice*, HMSO, Cmnd. 3123.

Law Commission (1967), *Matrimonial and Related Proceedings – Financial Relief*, Working Paper no. 9.

Law Commission (1967a), Statement of the Law Commission, *New Law Journal*, vol. 117, p. 827.

Law Commission (1969), *Financial Provision in Matrimonial Proceedings*, Law Com. no. 25.

Law Commission (1970), *Report on the Nullity of Marriage*, Law Com. no. 33.

Leach, E. R. (1968), *A Runaway World?*, Reith Lecture, BBC.

Leissner, A. (1967), *Family Advice Services*, Longman.

Leslie, G. R. (1967), *The Family in Social Context*, Oxford University Press.

Levinger, G. (1965), 'Marital cohesiveness and dissolution: an integrative review', *Journal of Marriage and the Family*, vol. 27.

Locke, H. J. (1951), *Predicting Adjustment in Marriage: A Comparison of a Divorced and a Happily Married Group*, Holt, Rinehart & Winston.

MacIver, R. M., and Page, C. H. (1950), *Society: An Introductory Analysis*, Macmillan.

McGregor, O. R. (1957), *Divorce in England*, Heinemann.

McGregor, O. R. (1968), 'Social effects of the matrimonial jurisdiction of magistrates', *New Law Journal*, vol. 118. See also McGregor O. R., Blom-Cooper, L. and Gibson, C., *Separated Spouses*, Duckworth, 1970.

Ministry of Social Security (1967), *Circumstances of Families*, HMSO.

Monahan, T. P. (1958), 'The changing nature and instability of remarriages', *Eugenics Quarterly*, vol. 5.

Monahan, T. P. (1962), 'When married couples part: statistical trends and relationships in divorce', *American Sociological Review*, vol. 27.

Murdock, G. P. (1949), *Social Structure*, Free Press.

Myerscough, P. R. (1967), 'An obstetrician's view', in *Unmarried Mothers, their Medical and Social Needs*, Standing Conference of Societies Registered for Adoption.

Ogburn, W. F. (1938), 'The changing family', *The Family*, vol. 19.

Ontario Law Reform Commission (1967, 1969), *Reports on the Family Law Project*.

Parsons, T., and Bales, R. F. (1956), *Family, Socialization and Interaction Process*, Routledge & Kegan Paul.

Pedersen, I. M. (1965), 'Matrimonial property law in Denmark', *Modern Law Review*, vol. 28.

Petersen, K. (1968), 'Demographic conditions and extended family households: Egyptian data', *Social Forces*, vol. 46.

Philp, A. F. (1963), *Family Failure*, Transatlantic.

Pierce, R. (1963), 'Marriage in the fifties', *Sociological Review*, vol. 11.

Renauld, J. G. (1966), 'Les régimes matrimoniaux', in *Travaux de la Deuxième Journée d'études juridiques Jean Dabin*, Brussels, 1966.

Rosenthal, J. Y. (1966), 'Marriage and the blood feud in "heroic" Europe', *British Journal of Sociology*, vol. 17.

Rowntree, G., and Carrier, N. (1957–8), 'The resort to divorce in England and Wales 1858–1957', *Population Studies*, vol. 11.

Rowntree, G. (1964), 'Some aspects of marriage breakdown in Britain in the last thirty years', *Population Studies*, vol. 18.

Royal Commission on Assizes and Quarter Sessions (1969), *Report of the Royal Commission on Assizes and Quarter Sessions* (Chairman: Lord Beeching) HMSO, Cmnd. 4153.

Royal Commission on Marriage and Divorce (1956), *Report of the Royal Commission on Marriage and Divorce* (Chairman: Lord Morton) HMSO, Cmnd. 9678.

**Royal Commission on the Taxation of Profits and Income** (1955), *Report of the Royal Commission on the Taxation of Profits and Income* (Chairman: Lord Radcliffe) HMSO, Cmnd. 9474.

**Schaffer, H. R.,** and **Schaffer, E. B.** (1968), *Child Care and the Family*, London School of Economics, Occasional Papers in Social Administration, no. 25.
**Simon, Sir J.** (1970), Riddell Lecture.
**Slater, E.,** and **Woodside, M.** (1951), *Patterns of Marriage*, Cassell.
**Spence, J. C.** (1954), *A Thousand Families in Newcastle-upon-Tyne*, Oxford University Press.
**Spiro, M. E.** (1954), 'Is the family universal?', *American Anthropologist*, vol. 56.
**Standing Conference of Societies Registered for Adoption** (1968), *Report to the Home Office on Difficulties arising from the Adoption Act 1958*.
**Stephens, T.** (1946), *Problem Families*, Gollancz.
**Stone, I.** (1961), 'Marriage among the English nobility in the sixteenth and seventeenth centuries', *Comparative Studies in Society and History*, vol. 4.
**Stone, O. M.** (1969), 'Fundamental principles in Soviet family law', *International and Comparative Law Quarterly*, vol. 19.

**Terman, L. M.** (1938), *Psychological Factors in Marital Happiness*, McGraw-Hill.

**Wallis, J. H.,** and **Booker, H. S.** (1958), *Marriage Counselling*, Routledge & Kegan Paul.
**Wimperis, V.** (1960), *The Unmarried Mother and her Child*, Allen & Unwin.
**Winch, R. F.** (1968), 'Some observations on extended familism in the United States', in R. F. Winch and L. W. Goodman (eds.), *Selected Studies in Marriage and the Family*, Holt, Rinehart & Winston.
**Wolf, E., Lüke, G.,** and **Hax, H.** (1959), *Scheidung und Scheidungsrecht: Grundfragen der Ehescheidung in Deutschland*, Tübingen: J. C. B. Mohr (Paul Siebeck). Review by Rheinstein, M. reprinted in C. Foote, R. Levy and F. Sander, *Cases and Materials on Family Law*, Little, Brown, 1966.
**Wynn, M.** (1964), *Fatherless Families*, Michael Joseph.
**Wynn, M.** (1970), *Family Policy*, Michael Joseph.

**Yarrow, L. J.** (1963), 'Research in dimensions of early maternal care', *Merrill Palmer Quarterly*, vol. 9.
**Yelloly, M. A.** (1965), 'Factors relating to an adoption decision by the mothers of illegitimate infants', *The Sociological Review*, vol. 13 (n.s.).
**Young, M.,** and **Willmott, P.** (1957), *Family and Kinship in East London*, Routledge & Kegan Paul.

**Zellick, G.,** (1970), 'A new approach to the control of obscenity', *Modern Law Review*, vol. 33.

# Table of Cases

*Re A.B.* (1954) 165
*Allen* v. *Allen* (1961) 90
*Re Andrews* (1955) 219
*Appleton* v. *Appleton* (1965) 90
*Ashley* v. *Ashley* (1965) 129
*Attwood* v. *Attwood* (1968) 131

*Re B.* (1970) 185
*B.* v. *B. and F.* (1968) 152
*B. (L.)* v. *B. (R.)* (1965) 119
*B. (M.)* v. *B. (R.)* (1968) 267
*B.R.B.* v. *J.B.* (1968) 215
*Balfour* v. *Balfour* (1919) 75
*Baxter* v. *Baxter* (1948) 175
*Bazeley* v. *Forder* (1868) 149
*Bedson* v. *Bedson* (1965) 98
*Bendall* v. *McWhirter* (1952) 79
*Bennett* v. *Bennett* (1969) 70
*Biberfeld* v. *Berens* (1952) 111
*Re Bishop* (1965) 97
*Bowman* v. *Bowman* (1949) 73
*Brett* v. *Brett* (1969) 255
*Brooks* v. *Blount* (1923) 147
*Brown* v. *Brown* (1956) 125
*Brown* v. *Brown* (1967) 121
*Buchler* v. *Buchler* (1947) 43, 116
*Bull* v. *Bull* (1955) 85
*Butler* v. *Gregory* (1902) 148
*Button* v. *Button* (1968) 91

*Re C.L.* (1965) 194
*Caras* v. *Caras* (1955) 113
*Caunce* v. *Caunce* (1969) 86–7
*Re Cole* (1963) 97
*Curtis* v. *Curtis* (1969) 255

*Debenham* v. *Mellon* (1880) 110
*Re a Debtor ex p. the Trustee* v.
  *Solomon* (1966) 84
*Des Salles d'Epinoix* v. *Des Salles
  d'Epinoix* (1967) 82
*Dunn* v. *Dunn* (1948) 77

*Re E. (P.)* (1969) 199, 202
*Evans* v. *Evans* (1790) 185
*Eyre* v. *Eyre* (1968) 258

*Re F.* (1969) 166
*F.* v. *F.* (1968) 267
*Falconer* v. *Falconer* (1970) 90
*Re Figgis* (*dec'd*) (1968) 97
*Fletcher* v. *Fletcher* (1945) 77
*Foard* v. *Foard* (1967) 257
*Fribance* v. *Fribance* (1957) 90

*Re G.* (1963) 165
*G.* v. *M.* (1885) 179
*Gissing* v. *Gissing* (1970) 90, 92–3
*Godfrey* v. *Godfrey* (1965) 123
*Gollins* v. *Gollins* (1964) 109
*Re Goodwin* (1968) 219
*Gorst* v. *Gorst* (1952) 124
*Gottlieb* v. *Gleiser* (1958) 251
*Gurasz* v. *Gurasz* (1969) 78, 82, 87

*H.* v. *H.* (1969) 263, 267
*Hall* v. *Hall* (1962) 116–17
*Handley* v. *Handley* (1891) 185
*Re Harker-Thomas's Application*
  (1968) 257
*Hastings & Thanet Building Society* v.
  *Goddard* (1970) 81
*Hearn* v. *Hearn* (1969) 120
*Herridge* v. *Herridge* (1966) 122
*Hitchcock* v. *W.B.* (1952) 194
*Holmes* v. *Holmes* (1755) 42
*Re Howell* (1953) 219
*Hunt* v. *Luck* (1902) 86

*J.* v. *C.* (1969) 165–6, 196, 198
*Jackson* v. *Jackson* (1970) 84
*Jansen* v. *Jansen* (1965) 91
*Re John's Assignment Trusts, Niven* v.
  *Niven* (1970) 88
*Jones* v. *Challenger* (1961) 83

Jones v. Maynard (1951) 97
Jolly v. Rees (1864) 111

Re K. (1952) 194
Kelly v. Kelly (1870) 43
King v. King (1953) 125
Krishnan v. London Borough of Sutton
  (1969) 165

Re L. (1962) 265
L. v. L. (1949) 180
L. v. L. (1966) 265
Lang v. Lang (1955) 117
Le Brocq v. Le Brocq (1964) 119
Lee v. Lee (1952) 79
Lindwall v. Lindwall (1967) 77
Liverpool SPCC v. Jones (1914) 148

Re M. (1961) 164
Maclennan v. Maclennan (1958) 178
McLarnon v. McLarnon (1968) 181
Maynard v. Maynard (1969) 78
Middleton v. Baldock (1950) 81
Miles v. Bull (1968) 79
Montgomery v. Montgomery (1965) 78
Muetzel v. Muetzel (1970) 93

National Assistance Board v. Parkes
  (1955) 131
National Assistance Board v. Wilkinson
  (1952) 132
National Provincial Bank v. Ainsworth
  (1965) 79, 88
Nixon v. Nixon (1969) 93
Northrop v. Northrop (1967) 118, 153
Nutley v. Nutley (1970) 118

Ogden v. Ogden (1969) 119

Parry v. Cleaver (1969) 222
Pettit v. Pettit (1969) 88, 91, 93–5
Postlethwaite v. Postlethwaite (1957)
  125
Priday v. Priday (1970) 238
Pulford v. Pulford (1923) 239

Quinn v. Quinn (1969) 121

Re R.(K.) (1963) 165
R. v. Chattaway (1922) 146
R. v. Gibbins and Proctor (1918) 146

R. v. Instan (1893) 146
R. v. Senior (1899) 146, 148
R. v. Shepherd (1862) 145
Rawlings v. Rawlings (1964) 83
Reincke v. Gray (1964) 222
Richmond v. Richmond (1952) 124
Rimmer v. Rimmer (1953) 89, 91, 93
Roberts v. Roberts (1964) 257
Roberts v. Roberts (1968) 131, 267
Robinson v. Robinson (1883) 186
Re Rodwell (1969) 175
Re Rogers' Question (1948) 89
Russell v. Russell (1897) 118

S. v. S. (1962) 266
S. v. S. (1970) 215
Safier v. Safier (1964) 126
Sanders v. Sanders (1967) 73
Saunders v. Saunders (1965) 117
Sheldon v. Sheldon (1966) 119
Shipman v. Shipman (1924) 77
Smallwood v. Smallwood (1861) 43
Spence v. Spence (1964) 113
Stick v. Stick (1967) 126

T. v. T. (1968) 229
Tarr v. Tarr (1971) 78
Tickle v. Tickle (1968) 117
Tindall v. Tindall (1953) 179
Tulip v. Tulip (1951) 118

Ulrich v. Ulrich (1968) 94

von Mehren v. von Mehren (1970) 255

Re W. (1970 & 1971) 195
W. v. W. (1952) 179–80
W. v. W. (No. 4) (1963) 215
W. v. W. (1966) 73
Wabe v. Taylor (1952) 82
Wakeham v. Wakeham (1954) 264–5
Waller v. Waller (1967) 85
West v. West (1954) 113
Wild v. Wild (1968) 229
Williams v. Williams (1964) 119, 125,
  238
Williams v. Williams (1966) 72

Young v. Young (1964) 154

**Table of Cases  295**

# Table of Statutes

| | | |
|---|---|---|
| 1533 | Ecclesiastical Licences Act | 66 |
| 1670 | Statute of Distributions | 217 |
| 1753 | Marriage Act | 65–6 |
| 1833 | Dower Act | 217 |
| 1836 | Marriage Act | 66 |
| 1846 | Fatal Accidents Act | 222 |
| 1857 | Matrimonial Causes Act | 231 |
| 1882 | Married Women's Property Act | 100 |
| | s. 11 | 223 |
| | 17 | 228 |
| 1890 | Intestates' Estates Act | 217 |
| 1923 | Matrimonial Causes Act | 33 |
| 1925 | Administration of Estates Act | 217 |
| | Guardianship of Infants Act | 275 |
| | Land Charges Act | 80 |
| | Land Registration Act | 79 |
| | Law of Property Act | 86 |
| 1926 | Adoption Act | 191 |
| | Legitimacy Act | |
| | s. 1 | 207 |
| 1929 | Age of Marriage Act | 59 |
| | Infant Life (Preservation) Act | 58, 144 |
| 1933 | Children and Young Persons Act | |
| | s. 1 | 146, 148 |
| | ss. 3–5 | 148 |
| | s. 11 | 148 |
| | 17 | 147 |
| 1937 | Matrimonial Causes Act | 33, 185, 231 |
| | Summary Proceedings (Domestic Jurisdiction) Act | 182 |
| 1938 | Infanticide Act | 145 |
| | Inheritance (Family Provision) Act | 60, 218, 257, 271 |
| 1945 | Family Allowances Act | 133 |
| 1946 | National Insurance Act | 139 |
| 1948 | Children Act | |
| | s. 1 | 143, 159, 161, 163, 165 |
| | 2 | 163–4 |
| | 3 | 164 |
| | 10 | 163 |

| | | |
|---|---|---|
| s. 11 | | 170 |
| 12 | | 161, 170 |
| 13 | | 161 |
| 22 | | 144 |
| Nurseries and Child Minders Regulation Act | | 157 |
| 1949 | Law Reform (Miscellaneous Provisions) Act | |
| s. 9 | | 52 |
| Legal Aid and Advice | | 33 |
| 1949 | Marriage Act | |
| s. 2 | | 59 |
| 3 | | 61, 62 |
| ss. 15–16 | | 67 |
| s. 25 | | 62 |
| 48 | | 61 |
| Part 3 | | 68 |
| 1952 | Cinematograph Act | 55 |
| Intestates' Estates Act | | 219 |
| Magistrates' Courts Act | | 182 |
| ss. 56–58 | | 276 |
| 1955 | Boarding-out of Children Regulations | 161 |
| Children and Young Persons (Harmful Publications) Act | | 54 |
| 1956 | Sexual Offences Act | |
| ss. 5–6 | | 51 |
| 25–28 | | 51 |
| 1957 | Affiliation Proceedings Act | 208 |
| s. 8 | | 276 |
| 1958 | Adoption Act | 270 |
| s. 5 | | 194 |
| 6 | | 193 |
| 7 | | 202 |
| 13 | | 205 |
| 37 | | 201 |
| 40 | | 201 |
| Children Act | | 158 |
| Maintenance Orders Act | | 129 |
| 1959 | Fatal Accidents Act | 222 |
| Legitimacy Act | | |
| s. 1 | | 207 |
| 2 | | 60 |
| 3 | | 214 |
| 1959 | Mental Health Act | 70 |
| National Insurance Act | | 139 |
| Obscene Publications Act | | 53 |
| 1960 | Legal Aid Act | 35 |
| Matrimonial Proceedings (Magistrates' Courts) Act | | 117 |
| s. 1 | | 109, 111–13, 152, 239 |

|  |  |  |
|---|---|---|
| **s. 2** | | 109, 113, 124, 152 |
| 3 | | 113 |
| 7 | | 109, 153 |
| 8 | | 153 |
| 16 | | 153 |
| 1963 | Betting, Gaming and Lotteries Act | 53 |
| | Children and Young Persons Act | 148 |
| | s. 1 | 144, 154, 183 |
| | 31 | 147 |
| | 48 | 163 |
| | ss. 64–65 | 147 |
| | sch. 3 | 147 |
| | Matrimonial Causes Act | 121 |
| 1964 | Licensing Act | 53 |
| | Married Women's Property Act | 95–7 |
| | Obscene Publications Act | 53 |
| | Television Act | 56 |
| 1965 | Family Allowances Act | |
| | ss. 2–3 | 133 |
| | s. 19 | 133 |
| | Matrimonial Causes Act | |
| | s. 2 | 73 |
| | 9 | 70 |
| | 26 | 256 |
| | ss. 36–37 | 264 |
| | s. 42 | 121 |
| | National Insurance (Industrial Injuries) Act | 225 |
| 1966 | Family Provision Act | 217, 256 |
| | s. 4 | 219 |
| | 6 | 219 |
| | Ministry of Social Security Act | |
| | ss. 22–24 | 131, 210 |
| | National Insurance Act | 139, 141 |
| 1967 | Abortion Act | 57–8, 144–5 |
| | Criminal Justice Act | 148 |
| | Criminal Law Act | 51 |
| | Matrimonial Causes Act | 35, 277 |
| 1967 | Matrimonial Homes Act | 77–80, 82–3, 87, 106, 228 |
| | s. 1 | 80, 82, 85 |
| | 2 | 80 |
| | 7 | 255 |
| | Nationa lHealth Service (Family Planning) Act | 56 |
| 1968 | Family Allowances and National Insurance Act | 134 |
| | Finance Act | |
| | s. 15 | 135–6 |

**298 Table of Statutes**

Health Services and Public Health Act

| | |
|---|---|
| s. 60 | 157 |
| Maintenance Orders Act | 113, 153, 209 |
| Race Relations Act | 46 |
| Registration of Births, Deaths and Marriages Regulations | 68 |
| Rent Act | 81, 221–2, 255 |
| Theatres Act | 54 |

1969 Children and Young Persons Act — 271

| | |
|---|---|
| s. 1 | 51–2, 168–9 |
| 2 | 52, 170 |
| 5 | 171 |
| 9 | 171 |
| ss. 13–14 | 169 |
| s. 24 | 170 |
| 27 | 170 |
| 31 | 170 |
| 49 | 161 |
| 52 | 158 |

1969 Divorce Reform Act — 72, 121, 176, 178, 185, 232

| | |
|---|---|
| s. 1 | 233 |
| 2(1) (a) | 233, 235–7, 239 |
| (b) | 233, 237–40 |
| (c) | 233, 239 |
| (d) | 233, 240, 242–9, 255 |
| (e) | 233, 240, 242–9, 253–6 |
| 2(3) | 244 |
| 2(5) | 243 |
| 3(1) | 183–4 |
| 3(3) | 236 |
| 3(4) | 239 |
| 3(5) | 242 |
| 4 | 245–9, 258 |
| 5 | 249 |
| 6 | 247–9 |
| 8 | 228 |
| 9 | 236 |

Family Law Reform Act — 199, 213

| | |
|---|---|
| s. 1 | 52 |
| 2 | 62 |
| 7 | 52 |
| ss. 14–19 | 212 |
| 20–25 | 215 |

| | | |
|---|---|---|
| 1970 | Administration of Justice Act | |
| | s. 1 | 52, 278 |
| | Family Income Supplement Act | 134–5 |
| | Finance Act | |
| | s. 14 | 136, 138 |
| | Income and Corporation Taxes Act | |
| | s. 8 | 136 |
| | 10 | 138 |
| | 14 | 138 |
| | 16 | 138 |
| | 37 | 135 |
| | 43 | 136 |
| | Law Reform (Miscellaneous Provisions) Act | |
| | ss. 4–5 | 251 |
| | 6 | 60 |
| | Local Authority Social Services Act | 156 |
| | Matrimonial Proceedings and Property Act | |
| | s. 1 | 250 |
| | 2 | 250, 254 |
| | 3 | 254, 263 |
| | 4 | 254, 261, 263 |
| | 5 | 150, 253, 263 |
| | 6 | 112, 149–50 |
| | 7 | 112, 271 |
| | 8 | 149, 263 |
| | 9 | 256 |
| | ss. 13–14 | 227 |
| | s. 16 | 261 |
| | 17 | 245, 262 |
| | 18 | 264 |
| | 22 | 271 |
| | 27 | 150, 262 |
| | 33 | 112, 149 |
| | 37 | 91–2 |
| | 38 | 85, 87 |
| 1970 | National Insurance (Old persons' and widows' pensions and attendance allowance) Act | 140–41 |
| | ss. 2–3 | 223 |
| 1971 | Attachment of Earnings Act | 129–30, 209 |
| | Courts Act | 278 |
| | Guardianship of Minors Act | 167, 229 |
| | s. 9 | 151 |
| | 12 | 151 |
| | 15 | 151 |
| | Law Reform (Miscellaneous Provisions) Act | 223 |
| | Nullity of Marriage Act | 70, 177, 180, 182 |

# Index

Abortion, 19, 57–9
Adoption
 agency placements, 201
 childless, by the, 178–9
 court procedure in, 203–5
 father, consent of, 198–200
 foster parents, by, 198
 illegitimate children, of, 191–207
 legal effects of, 205
 mother, consent of, 193–8
 parents, by, 199, 202
 relatives, by, 201–2
 step-parents, by, 199, 200, 270
 success of, 206
 telling children about, 206
 third-party placements, 201
Adultery
 condition for divorce, 231, 235–7
 damages for, 251–2
 ground for maintenance, 112
 when condoned, 120–24
Affiliation
 ineffectiveness of proceedings,
  208–9
Agency of necessity, 111, 149, 250
Artificial insemination, 178–80
Australia, 41
 adoption, consents in, 197
 courts' powers on divorce, 260
 damages for adultery, 251–2
 divorce law, 235, 240–41, 244–6
 incidence of divorce, 186–8
 reconciliation provision, 183–4

Blood tests, 214–15

Canada
 Alberta, affiliation scheme, 211
 divorce law, 240, 242, 245–6

 'homestead' legislation, 104
 Ontario, matrimonial property
  proposals, 106
Care
 assumption of parental rights over
  children in, 163–4
 committal into, 51–2, 168–72, 264
 cost of keeping child in, 156
 reception into, 159–68
Catholic Marriage Advisory Council,
 183
Censorship, 54–6
Childlessness
 marriage breakdown, and, 44
 nullity of marriage, and, 174–81
Child minders, 157
Children
 broken homes, numbers in, 32
 'child of the family', 150, 152, 220,
  262
 criminal prosecution of, 171–2
 custody of, see Divorce, Foster
  parents, Separation
 divorce, effect of, on, 261–2,
  266
 foster children, see Fostering
 general policy towards, 143–4
 institutionalized, 20, 23–5
 maintenance of, 149–54, 263–4
 neglect of, 146–9
 protection of, 144–9, 154–72
 punishment of, 148
 see also Illegitimate children
China
 family in, 22–3
Church of England
 divorce reform, attitude to, 231–2
 marriages in, 61–2, 66–8

Collusion, 185, 236
Community homes, 163, 170
Community of property
  European systems of, 97–107
Condonation
  see Adultery, Reconciliation
Connivance, 123–4, 185, 236
Consent
  adoption, to, see Adoption
  age of, to sexual intercourse, 51
  divorce, to, 240–44, 249
  marriage, to, 181
  parental, to marriage, 61–4
Contraception
  publicity and advice, 56–7
County courts, 276–8
Courts
  administration of family law in,
    275–80
Cruelty
  matrimonial, 108–9, 118–20, 125,
    237

Day nurseries, 157
Denmark
  divorce and pre-marital pregnancy in,
    37
  matrimonial property system, 102
Desertion, 115–17, 239
Divorce
  children, custody of, on, 164, 185,
    264–7
  children, financial provision for, on,
    262–7
  conditions necessary for decree,
    233–44
  discouragement of, 184–7
  factors associated with, 36–44
  financial re-adjustment on, 250–61
  impotence and sterility, suggested
    conditions for, 176–81
  incidence of, in England and Wales,
    32–6
  psychological effects of, 231, 261–2,
    266
  safeguards against, 244–9

three-year bar to, 72–4, 173–4
  variation of orders after, 256
  see also Remarriage
'Domestic courts', 275–6
Drunkenness, 113, 116

Ecclesiastical courts
  death, jurisdiction on, 99, 217
  moral censure by, 82, 185
  nullity jurisdiction of, 174
Economic security
  marital success, effect on, 40–42
Engagement
  'compulsory', 65
  length of, 64
  marital success, indicator of, 36
Enticement, 250–51

Family
  extended, 15–17, 138
  functions of, 13–25
  types of, 11–13
Family Advice Centres, 155
Family allowances,
  see Social Security
'Family assets', 90, 94–5
'Family courts', 204, 279–80
Family Discussion Bureau, 183
Family Division of High Court,
  277–8
Family provision
  dependants, for, 218–21
  former spouse, for, 256–7, 270–71
Fostering
  local authorities, by, 159, 161–2
  private, supervision over, 158–9
  success of, 162
Foster parents
  adoption by, see Adoption
  custody, rights to, 165–8
France
  maintenance obligations, 126
  matrimonial property system, 103–6
Furniture, household
  ownership of, 94–7

Household
  debts, liability for, 106, 110–12,
    126–7
  duty to contribute to, 109–13
  duty to manage, 108–9

Illegitimate children
  adopted, numbers who are, 191–2
  risks to, 26
  succession rights of, 212
  *see also* Adoption, Affiliation,
    Putative father
Illegitimacy
  incidence in England and Wales,
    26–31, 54, 58
Impotence
  *see* Nullity
Infanticide, 145

Joint bank accounts, 96–7
Judges
  adoption, attitudes to, 204
  custody, attitudes to, 267
  marriage, attitudes to, 42–4, 72
Judicial separation, 107, 228, 230
  court orders on decree, 250–62
Juvenile courts, 276

Kibbutzim, 21–22

Law Commission
  on agency of necessity, 111
  on damages for adultery, 251–2
  on divorce, 73, 232, 234, 246
  on maintenance obligations, 127–8
  on marriages under age, 60
  on matrimonial home, 91–2
  on nullity of marriage, 177, 180
  on pension rights, 258
  on remarriage, 270
  on supervision orders, 263
Legitimacy, 15
Legitimation, 207

Maintenance
  amount of, 130–1

enforcement of, 128–30
husband, of, 109, 117, 126
taxation of payments, 128
wife, of, 112–26
*see also* Children
Marriage
  formalities, 65–71
Marriage breakdown
  factors associated with, 36–44
Marriage counselling, 183
Matrimonial home
  duty to acquire, 76–7
  entry to, right of, 78, 82, 85
  expulsion from, 78, 83
  improvements to, 90–92
  location of, 76–7
  occupation of, right to, 76–87
  protection against creditors, lack of,
    80, 84, 105–7
  protection against disposition to
    third parties, 79–82, 83–7, 105
  share in, 88–94
  tenancy under Rent Act 1968, 81–2,
    255

National Marriage Guidance Council,
  43, 155, 183
National Society for the Prevention of
  Cruelty to Children, 147, 155, 170,
  263
Netherlands
  divorce proposal, 234–5
  maintenance obligations, 126–7
  matrimonial property system, 101–4
New Zealand
  adultery, damages for, 251
  divorce law, 235, 241, 245
  illegitimacy, abolition of, 212–14
  'joint family homes', 105
  maintenance obligations, 127
  marriages under age, 60
Nigeria
  divorce law, 176, 249
Norway
  affiliation procedure, 211
  illegitimate children, rights of, 213

Nullity of marriage
  court orders on decree, 250–62
  effect of decree, 175, 177
  for impotence, 174–81
  for mental disorder, 70–71
  for mistake or duress, 181–83
  for pregnancy *per alium*, 70
  for sterility, 175–81
  for venereal disease, 70

Obscenity, 53–6

Paternity
  proof of, 213–15
Pregnancy
  pre-marital, 36–7, 40, 51
Probation service, 182–3, 263, 276–7
Problem families, 17, 25, 31–2
Provocation, 125
Putative father
  adoption proceedings, position in, 198–201
  'recognition' of child, 213–14
  *see also* Paternity

Reconciliation
  provisions for, 182–4
Remarriage
  court orders, effect on, 269–70
  rate of, 268–9

Savings
  ownership of, 94–7
  *see also* Joint bank accounts
Separation
  custody of children on, 229
  property arrangements on, 228
  *see also* Maintenance
Separation agreements, 227–8
Sex
  pre-marital, 37–8
Social security
  divorced spouses and, 259
  family allowances, 133–5

family income supplement, 134–5
  national insurance benefits, 139–42
  separated spouses and, 130–2, 227
  surviving spouse and, 224–6
  unmarried mothers and, 209–10
Social welfare
  family services, 138–9, 154–7, 183
Soviet Union
  experiment at abolition of family, 19–21
Sterility,
  *see* Childlessness, Nullity
Succession rights, 216–18
  *see also* Family Provision
Supervision order
  on divorce, 264
  of juvenile court, 264, 169
Surviving spouse
  claims against third parties, 222–3
  Rent Act 1968, rights under, 221
  *see also* Family provision, Social security, Succession

Taxation
  income tax reliefs, 135–8
  maintenance payments, of, 128
  married persons, of, 136–7

United States
  blood and health tests for marriage, 71
  'homestead' legislation, 104–6
Unmarried mothers
  *see* Affiliation, Illegitimacy, Social security

Wards of court, 52, 165, 264
West Germany
  maintenance obligations, 126
  matrimonial property system, 103–4

Youthful marriages, 59–64
  risk of breakdown, 39–40